B

OME

SAMEER DUA is committed to transforming lives around the world and believes that everyone in this world is a possibility of happiness, success and extraordinary achievement. He empowers people to know what they really love and supports them in getting that so that they lead a life full of joy, success and fulfilment.

Having spent twenty-five years in the field of management and leadership education, he has discovered the generative power in human beings, and how everyone has a choice in what he or she creates. In his first book, *Declaring Breakdowns: Powerfully Creating a Future That Matters, Through 6 Simple Steps* he talks about how each one of us, in every area of our life, is in a certain flow, and if continued, that flow will take us to a certain future. He invites individuals, teams, and organizations to become aware of this and get skilled in creating a future of design, rather than of drift.

While his first book is titled *Declaring Breakdowns*, for him, this book is about mastering the art and science of generating breakthrough results in every aspect of our lives. *Declaring Breakdowns* has already had four reprints and has been translated into Hindi and Marathi. Talks are on to translate the book in Spanish.

He has set up and run management and leadership institutions in India and the UK, and also set up an extensive network of education centres in the early 1990s, then unheard of in India. He has worked with programme participants from fifty-two countries and worked with top-ranked British, American and European universities.

Sameer is the founder director of the Institute for Generative Leadership, India, established in association with the Institute for Generative Leadership, USA. He has worked with senior management teams of top global organizations and has enabled them to design futures of choice. He is known for enabling his programme participants to take a stand for their, and their organization's success. The same participants generated breakthrough results, which at one time seemed impossible.

Some of his global clients include Mercedes-Benz, Siemens, John Deere, BMC Software, Allscripts, Persistent Systems, NetApp, T-Systems, Amdocs, Tech Mahindra, Dana, Cargill, Endurance Technologies, Hager and Cognizant amongst many others. Sameer has also conducted leadership programmes for the Naval War College and gets constant invitations to speak as a keynote speaker, at business off-sites and industry consortiums. He was also recently invited to a TEDx talk in Mumbai, India, where he spoke about *Declaring Breakdowns*.

Sameer has been an adviser to a top ranked and a leading business school in Asia; was the founding chairman of the Bangalore Chapter of the Higher Education Forum; and vice chairman of the Emerging Presidents' Group.

Inside of his purpose to positively impact millions of people around the world, Sameer set up the Gift Your Organ Foundation. As the founder and the chief catalyst of the Gift Your Organ Foundation, Sameer's vision is that there will be no deaths in India for want of organs. The foundation works with the Karnataka and Maharashtra state governments and is the first organization in the country to have introduced the Green Heart Driver's Licence, which has an organ donation option on the driver's licence. This move has the potential to transform the entire organ donation landscape in India.

To invite Sameer as a speaker, or to organize a programme in your firm, you can email Sameer on sameer@sameerdua.com, or visit his website www.sameerdua.com or www. generativeleadership.in

Advance praise for *Become*

'Sameer's passion to help us see our conversational blind-spots is evident in his in-the-face writing style – which I loved. One of the most important and powerful takeaways that I got from the book is: Coaching is not a profession; it is a set of conversational practices. Putting these practices into action is life changing. I would highly recommend leaders and managers in every organization to read this book and invest time in experimenting with the recommended practices.'

Judith E. Glaser, author of the bestselling book *Conversational Intelligence: How Great Leaders Build Trust and Get Extraordinary Results*; CEO of Benchmark Communications, Inc.; and chairman of The Creating WE Institute

'Sameer Dua's book *Become* grabbed me by the eyeballs. The CEO of a company is really the head coach of a team of teams. Leaders at all levels need to put on the coach's hat to bring out the best in their teams. If you aren't getting the results you want, it's probably because your people aren't getting enough coaching.'

Robert Hargrove, CEO Whisperer; author, *Masterful Coaching*

'*Become* delivers beautifully on its promise of enabling leaders and managers to generate meaningful results through critical coaching conversations. Sameer Dua brings a wealth of experience as a coach and leader to provide truly transformational insights not only for mentors, but also those who want to benefit from coaching relationships.'

Ashok Soota, executive chairman, Happiest Minds Technologies Pvt. Ltd

'This is an incredible book that will open up the eyes and mindset of every reader in a really different and a very powerful way.'

Klaus Trescher, MD and CEO, Siemens Technology and Services Pvt. Ltd

'Sameer Dua has written a remarkable book; he combines intellect with practice, insight with action, and depth of thought with ease of reading. The result is a powerful and inspiring book, for all who lead and coach, based in the arena of the challenging and caring conversation, at the heart of the exchange between us all. It is everywhere inclined towards informed and mindful action, and has many case examples of the techniques at work. Yet, the book is so much more, with interludes for the imagination, for reflection, and for meditation. It is hugely engaging to read and re-read.'

Professor Andrew St George, author,
Royal Navy Way of Leadership

'This thoughtful and passionate book is a fresh contribution to guidance for leaders. Sameer Dua takes the complexity of deep traditions in coaching, linguistics, somatics, and philosophy – and makes them practical and meaningful. People who want to build high commitment in their organizations will benefit from reading this book and putting the recommendations into practice.'

Pam Fox Rollin, executive coach and author,
42 Rules for Your New Leadership Role

'In his second book, Sameer promotes a crystal-clear message for leaders and managers about their individual responsibility to make things happen through others. If your team members are under-performing, then it's absolutely your duty to change perspectives and not engage in blame games. We are encouraged to use coaching conversations and generative practices to get unstuck through attentive listening to what people really care about, aligning personal, team and organizational goals. Sameer has a resilient approach to corporate, professional and personal life through the power of coaching conversations to generate actions.'

Dr Julie Davies, HR Subject Group Leader, The Business School, University of Huddersfield, UK

'This book can deeply impact the kind of conversations, and the way conversations are had in organizations. It will encourage you to keep aside your existing understanding and open new avenues of learning. Read this book and do adapt practices recommended by Sameer; it will help you with enormous value and put you on a path of transformational leadership. A new way, full of positive results and achievement!'

Dilip Kukreja, VP – IT & chief innovation officer, Bennett Coleman & Co. Ltd (BCCL)

'Sameer Dua's *Become* is a potent guide to the being and doing of exceptional leadership. At its core, *Become* is about the conversations leaders must have – with themselves, the people they work with and the world around them – to achieve exceptional results. Surrounding the core of key conversations, Dua has filled the book with valuable insights and powerful practices that, if applied, can become the foundation for positive, high-impact leading in any situation. Reading *Become*, itself, is a long, engaging and transforming conversation.'

Charles Feltman, executive and leadership coach; author, *The Thin Book of Trust*

'This is exactly what business leaders need to know to get the results they are looking for *while also* taking care of their people! Sameer gives helpful theory combined with practical advice so you can start leading differently.'

Terrie Upshur-Lupberger, MCC, executive coach and senior director, Altus Growth Partners

'Sameer's narration, based on the COACH principles has all the ingredients for leaders to imbibe, and therefore practise their leadership qualities, to productively engage the people, and the team. Sameer has very profoundly shifted the conversational skills from the head to the heart, which is the essence of his approach in this book. His story-telling style is quite gripping. "Taking care of what you care about" is the mantra for better commitment, to unlock greater possibilities and thus ensure greater results.'

Jagannath Vasudevan, CHRO for Hero Cycles, Caparo India and Dana India Corporation; head HR for JCB & PepsiCo units

BEC

The 5 Critical Conversational Practices
that Shift **WHO YOU BE** as a Leader

OME

SAMEER DUA

With Contributions by
Bob Dunham,
Umang Bedi and Sheeja Shaju

HARPER
BUSINESS

First published in India in 2017 by Harper Business
An imprint of HarperCollins *Publishers*
A-75, Sector 57, Noida, Uttar Pradesh 201301, India
www.harpercollins.co.in

2 4 6 8 10 9 7 5 3 1

Copyright © Sameer Dua 2017

P-ISBN: 978-93-5277-367-1
E-ISBN: 978-93-5277-368-8

The views and opinions expressed in this book
are the author's own and the facts are as reported by him,
and the publishers are not in any way liable for the same.

All rights reserved. No part of this publication may be reproduced,
stored in a retrieval system, or transmitted, in any form or by any means,
electronic, mechanical, photocopying, recording or otherwise,
without the prior permission of the publishers.

Typeset in 11/13.7 Adobe Caslon Pro Regular at
Manipal Digital Systems, Manipal

Printed and bound at
Thomson Press (India) Ltd

This book is dedicated to my first leader and coach, my father, Dr Giri Dua.

Bob Dunham,
Thank you for being such an inspiration, for your generous contributions to this book, and to my learning. It is an honour to call you my teacher and my coach.

This book is for those leaders and managers who are interested in learning the leadership conversational skills required to generate results.

CONTENTS

FOREWORD

Over more than thirty years as an executive coach, I have been fortunate to work with many powerful leaders whose influence shaped the world we live in. The assumption many people make is that, given these leaders' remarkable accomplishments and sterling reputations, their problems must be very complex.

And yet, leadership doesn't only happen in the realm of the complex – the big decisions, visions and strategies that get the most attention (although all of those things are unquestionably important). It also takes place in regular, daily interactions. The simple conversations we have every day can be incredibly powerful if we know how to harness them. In my view, any leader who wants to do that will find *Become* an invaluable tool.

That's because Sameer Dua is a talented coach and leadership expert who realizes that the way we talk to each other either sets the stage for our success or dooms us to failure. The five conversational strategies outlined in these pages contain key insights for anyone who wants to find that click of connection with co-workers and teams, and enable great results and innovation.

Not only that, this book is deeply practical. Sameer knows that intellectually understanding what to do is only the first step. Conversation is an art that must be practised in the real world, not just understood in theory. I agree wholeheartedly when he writes: 'Executive coaching is not a profession; it is a set of conversational practices', and 'You need to understand these conversations first, and then practise these conversations to gain mastery'. In some ways, leadership is a bit like learning a sport or playing an instrument. You have to practise to get good.

I have certainly found this to be true in my own coaching practice. I will give you an example of one simple technique I use to change the nature of my clients' conversations. I have observed that starting a conversation with two words stops the flow of conversation and ends any hope for productive discourse. Those words? 'No' and 'but'.

These words don't say, 'Let's discuss this' or 'I'd love to hear what you think about this' to people. They say, unequivocally, 'You are wrong and I am right.' If your conversation companion is also dedicated to his need to win at any cost, you will have a potential battle on your hands. The result? Nothing productive.

I advise you to start listening to colleagues – and to yourself! How many times a day do you start a sentence with no or but? You will likely be shocked at how common it is. If you drill a little deeper, you'll see patterns emerge. For instance, some people use these words to gain power. You'll see how much people resent it, consciously or not, and how it stifles rather than opens up discussions.

I use this technique with my clients, by keeping count of their use of these two little words. It's such an important indicator! If the numbers pile up in an initial meeting with a client, I'll interrupt him or her and say, 'We've been talking for almost an hour now, and do you realize that you have responded seventeen times with either no or but?' This is the moment when a serious talk about changing behaviour begins.

In this book and in his coaching work, Sameer brings his own forms of awareness to coaching conversations – and leaders at all levels would do well to pay attention. His techniques are non-judgemental, akin to his earlier work on declaring breakdowns. The powerful theme running through all of this work is to banish shame, accept that failure is part of life and walk with others in empathy. This is powerful stuff, and Sameer makes it accessible to anyone.

I suggest you try it – for the sake of your colleagues, your family, your friends and yourself.

Marshall Goldsmith
Thinkers 50 #1 Leadership Thinker and #1 Executive Coach in the World; #1 *New York Times* bestselling author of *Triggers*, *MOJO* and *What Got You Here Won't Get You There*.

Part I

Part I

1

GETTING STARTED

All results come from prior conversations. All of them: the good ones, the bad ones, and the so-so ones. They come from the conversations we have and the conversations we don't have; from the conversations we do well, and the conversations we do poorly. Our conversations don't just describe, they generate.

BOB DUNHAM

AN INVITATION

Become is an invitation to choose a powerful 'posture' in your leadership and in life. By posture I am referring to you taking a perspective and shaping yourself to see and acting in a way that fulfils your purpose.

It is an invitation to a posture:

- that we are responsible for generating any result we want in areas that matter to us.
- that the path from where we are to where we want to be is a path of conversations – (these missing conversations could be conversations that we have with ourselves, or with others).
- that if a few conversations do not generate the desired results, we will continue to search further for the right conversations. History is witness to the fact that the genesis of any result is prior conversations that shape its possibility, action and outcome.
- of responsibility rather than that of a victim. I will go one step further and state what I call a law: *'If we feel disempowered or de-energized with regard to a person or a situation, then we are being victims and are not taking responsibility with regard to that person or that situation.'*

The empowering view I have taken in this book is, 'If people around us are not delivering results, *we* are probably not having the requisite conversations with them.' The focus in this book is always on us – on what conversation *we* can have next, so that others can generate results that matter.

If you feel you are ready to live your life at this high level of leadership – where we are the source of results in our life, this book is for you! This book will help us identify the missing elements in five critical conversational domains and 'become' that impactful leader you have always wanted to be.

What is our choice?

From the way I see it, either we adopt a strategy to have the required conversations to generate results *that matter to us*, or we face the consequences of not having those conversations.

The most likely consequence? We become victims in areas we care about. The other choice is to give up on the results that matter to us.

However, if we give up on one set of results, by default we have another set of results that we want to generate. So, we are back to square one.

I invite you to a mood of 'playful wonder'. Here, the way we see the world is from the prism that states:

'I don't know what is going to show up next – irrespective of what shows up, I will enjoy myself.'

This invitation of being in the mood of wonder is not only while you are reading this book – it is also a great mood to live life in. In this mood, irrespective of what life throws at you, and what events take place, you remain ready to deal with them in a manner that still takes care of what matters to you.

As part of my coaching and training work, I work with several senior teams of global organizations. Let me share an example of the power of conversations that I experienced during a training programme organized by a €18-billion German company. The head of their largest manufacturing plant in India mentioned to me that he had a colleague in his management team who was not generating the results he was expected to. This was bringing down the performance of the entire plant.

I invited him to have the missing conversations (those that are elucidated in this book) with this person. He said to me that he had already had all the conversations that he could possibly have. None seemed to have worked.

In effect, he was stating that there was nothing more he could do, and for us to see some results, this colleague in question needed to take action. Sure, I thought, he needs to take action, but what about the critical conversations the plant head needed to have with him to generate action?

By the way, this is not unusual – most often people tell me they have had all the missing conversations, and these conversations haven't worked. (The invitation here for you is to see where this is true for you in your life.)

The plant head was disempowered, and he did not even know that he was disempowered. This is what I mean when I say 'acting like a victim'. He, at this stage, saw no action that could resolve things and was in the posture that something outside of him had to solve the problem. He no longer had choices.

To be a victim means you're not getting results because, according to you, someone else is not doing his or her job correctly.

So, I asked him, 'If it's not conversations, what else can you do?'

He responded, 'I don't know – that's why I am talking to you.'

I suggested, 'If you have had all the possible conversations, and the results are still not generated, why don't you ask him to leave?'

'I can't ask him to leave! There are other areas where he is critical to the organization. Even if I wanted to, the CEO would not permit me to let him go,' he said.

I finally said, in jest, 'Maybe you should leave this organization and your job!' We both laughed.

If you and I were in a similar situation, what choices would we really have? I assess there are only four:

a. we could ask the person to leave the job;
b. *we* could leave the job;
c. *we* could act like victims for weeks, months, years till one person left the job; or
d. we could have the required missing conversations.

Honestly, from the way I see it, we have limited choices. Either we have the conversations, or we live like victims.

After all, how many people can we fire? And how many job changes can we effect? Every new person, every new job, would have similar challenges. The solution is to have they missing conversations. And even if they don't work, ask yourself what other conversations you can have and continue to be in the search of that conversation that generates new result.

Anyway, I wrote down a few questions for the plant head and asked him to think about them over lunch: Here are the questions I asked him:

1. Are you willing to make a commitment to generate results for your plant?
2. Really? (This question gets the person to rethink their commitment.)
3. If you are making this commitment, and if one of your team members is not generating the result, what is it that *you* are not doing that would enable this person to generate the result?
4. What may be the missing conversation?
5. Are you committed to having this missing conversation?
6. What if this conversation did not work – will you give up on your commitment for the plant's results?
7. Do you trust your commitment?

He spent twenty minutes over the lunch break to answer these questions. After the lunch break, I invited him to the front of the room and respond to these questions in front of the group.

It became clear that the awareness he got from asking and then answering those fundamental questions was transformational. His embodiment shifted, and so did his energy and language. There was a change in the tone of his voice – he stood at the front of the room and seemed a lot more centered. He then stated, very powerfully, in front of a room filled with senior people from different departments of his organization:

I can now see that I was being a victim. I declare here that I am a stand for the results of my plant. I take responsibility for not having had the missing conversations, and for not supporting my management team members.

I commit to this group that I will distinguish the missing conversations, and have these missing conversations.

If one set of conversations does not work, I will try another. Because, honestly, I can see that if I care for my results, then this is really the only way forward!

The entire room stood up and gave him a standing ovation for the shift in his posture!

This book is an invitation to take this posture and make a commitment for your own power, leadership and ability to produce results that *you* care about. To have the missing conversations is to act out of commitment to generate results that matter to you. (You may not know what these missing conversations are. You may need to learn them. And the bigger question is: Are you willing to learn them?)

Pause for Reflection

Take a moment to answer the same questions the plant head responded to:

1. Is there a co-worker or a team member who is not generating results for your team / your organization?
2. Are you willing to make a commitment that you will be the source of generating results in this area of your life? (If your answer is 'No', find another area where you choose to take this posture.)
3. If you do make this commitment, and if one of your team members is not generating the result, *what is it that you are not doing* so that this person generates the result?
4. Introspect: what could be the missing conversations?
5. Are you committed to having these missing conversations?

6. What if this conversation did not work – will you drop your commitment for generating results? If your answer is 'Yes, I will drop my commitment', I invite you to reflect on your commitment to your results.
7. Do you trust your commitment?

WHY CONVERSATION?

The common-sense understanding of a conversation is speaking and hearing. Most people presume beyond speaking and hearing, there is not much going on in a conversation. This understanding of conversations is grossly inadequate and blind to the power that is latent in conversations.

The prefix *con* in Latin means 'together'; and *versatio* or *versationis* means 'a turning' or 'a changing'. In a true conversation, then, we 'change together'.

In my book *Declaring Breakdowns: Powerfully Creating a Future That Matters, Through 6 Simple Steps*, I quoted Bob Dunham's definition of 'Conversation':[1]

Conversation is the interaction of human beings that creates **action, meaning, listening, moods** and **emotions**, and the **future**.

Conversations are not just words, but the whole body reactions that are provoked when we interact in language; and when we interact and language is provoked.

Conversations include **language, moods** and **emotions**, **body reactions** and **experiences**, and the listening that is based on the history of the people in the conversation. Conversations are shaped in linguistic and cultural practices.[2]

According to Judith E. Glaser, in her book *Conversational Intelligence*:

We are now learning, through neurological and cognitive research, that a 'conversation' goes deeper and is more robust than simple information sharing. Conversations are dynamic, interactive, and inclusive. They evolve and impact the way we connect, engage, interact, and influence others, enabling us to shape reality, mindsets, events, and outcomes in a collaborative way. Conversations have the power to move us from 'power-over' others to 'power-with' others, giving us the exquisite ability to get on the same page with our fellow humans and experience the same reality by bridging the reality gaps between 'how you see things and how I see things'.

Glaser further adds:

> Words are not things – they are the representations and symbols we use to view, think about, and process our perceptions of reality and they are the means of sharing these perceptions with others. Yet few leaders understand how vital conversation is to health and productivity of their company.[3]

This book uses the broader meaning of the word conversation, and not the limited meaning of simply speaking and hearing. We recognize that it is through conversations that human beings interact with each other, and it is through these interactions that 'actions', 'meaning', 'listening', 'moods and emotions' and the 'future' get created. It is through conversations that we shape 'reality, mindsets, events, and outcomes in a collaborative way'.

So, if we want to get our co-workers and team members to take new and different action, or we would like to shift their realities and mindsets, we can do so by having effective conversations.

THE STRUCTURE OF THE BOOK

'Become', as per the Oxford Dictionary means, 'grow to be', or 'develop into'.[4] In my assessment, as a leader you never fully arrive. You are always in the making.

You may be a beginner, minimally competent, competent, expert or even a master – at each stage, you are in the process of 'becoming' the next stage.

A key attribute of a master is that it is the others who consider them to be masters. However, in my experience, most masters have the posture or the attitude of a beginner.

According to George Leonard, 'Mastery is not a really a goal or destination but rather a process, a journey.'[5] Masters are always in this ongoing process of 'becoming', by going deeper in their subject.

If you are not in the process of 'becoming', you reach a dead end. And that is the beginning of your decline. You don't 'become' by knowing more, you 'become' by shifting your practices, and in case of leadership, by shifting and creating new conversational practices. Which is why this book is not about understanding new concepts, but about learning new practices to shift 'who you be', moment to moment (this will further clarify as you read on).

This book is an invitation to you to begin and be on the journey to 'become':

- a 'new' leader;
- a coach of your teams (whether or not you are leading your teams you can have coaching conversations with your teams);
- a master who continues to operate as a beginner;
- anyone who you want to 'be', and in the process take care of what you care about.

This book is structured in a simple, easy to use manner, by using COACH as an acronym for the leadership conversational skills of:

C – Care
O – Observe (the observer)
A – Actions
C – Commitment
H – Holding Space of Conversation

Each of these are critical leadership conversational domains that need to be mastered for generating extraordinary results. In my experience, most leaders are found wanting in one or more of these skills. Although there is no hierarchy of importance, all five are as important as the other.

Each chapter includes 'what if' questions, generative practices,* reflection opportunities, myths and busting of myths around the topics of each of the chapters and other important points for the reader to remember and reflect upon. The idea, as stated above, is not only to make you more knowledgeable, but to also provide a platform for you to illuminate your darkness and to cultivate more skill and power in these crucial leadership conversational domains.

Umang Bedi, managing director, Facebook, India and South Asia has generously contributed several case studies at the end of each of the five chapters of Part II of this book. In addition to these, he has also contributed what I think is an outstanding case study, which I have presented verbatim in Chapter 9. This case study is titled 'Re-imagining and Reinventing Adobe Systems, India: A Case Study'. Umang provided these cases when he was the managing director of Adobe Systems, India.

Towards the end of the book we have as Appendix 2 an important leadership practice called 'Centering'. Appendix 3 contains somatic

---

* A generative practice is a practice that you choose, consciously, so that you embody a new habit or a behaviour.

Our bodies are always practising something, and it is easy to develop unproductive habits. To be involved in generative practices is to make a choice of how you want to see the world, and how you want others to see you. You choose a practice that supports what you care about; instead of letting old habits rule you.

practices for the chapter 'Holding Space of Conversation'. My colleague Sheeja Shaju has contributed both these appendices. Sheeja is widely appreciated as a somatic leader and a leadership coach at the Institute for Generative Leadership, India.

In Appendix 4, we have a glossary of all the distinctions used in the book. I hope you will find these useful to refer to while reading this book.

THE PROMISE OF THIS BOOK

The promise of this book is to provide the fundamentals of leadership coaching conversations to enable leaders to generate sustainable, extraordinary results. These are vital and non-discretionary conversations, and yet one rarely finds the skills of effectively having these conversations in an organizational setting. This book also hopes to help leaders and managers generate results that matter to them and support their teams to generate meaningful results.

Leadership is not just a job category. It is a set of conversational practices. You need to understand these conversations first, and then practise these conversations to gain a certain mastery over them. I know many leaders who may conceptually know these conversations, and yet do not have adequate practice for these to be a part of their repertoire in challenging situations. I'm not an expert either – no one ever is. Although I've been having these conversations over several years, I continue to discover new nuances that I hadn't seen earlier.

The idea of this book is to not only generate awareness of these conversations, but for leaders and managers to develop a level of skill in having these conversations effectively. For that, leaders will need to engage in practices that are provided in each chapter. You can only 'become' *by doing* the practices, and not by simply *knowing about* these conversations.

In the following pages, I've described several tried and tested distinctions and practices I've used at many global organizations

(John Deere India, Mercedes Benz, NetApp, T-Systems, Siemens, Schaeffler, Amdocs, BMC Software, amongst many others), the Indian Navy, and several large Indian multinationals (Endurance Technologies, Persistent Systems, Times Group and many others).

I also stand on the shoulders of giants from whom I have learnt much of what you'll read in this book. Besides, I am a part of a learning community at the Institute for Generative Leadership, USA, and members of this community have used these conversational domains with hundreds of their clients.

READING THIS BOOK AS AN EXPERIENCE

This is not a book you must rush and tick off on your reading list. *Become* will demand your time and patience. Engage with it as a conversation between you and me. Read it slowly and allow the conversations to settle in before moving to the next conversational domain. Take time out to journal your thoughts on our conversation through this book, and also journal what you learn from the practices. Let these conversations be about your leadership, your life, and your possibilities; not just understanding the content of the book.

Read this book – as if *you* were the coach for your co-workers, clients, your manager, the members of your family and everyone else you interact with closely. After reading my recommendations and practices, it may be tempting to assess what others may not be doing. Don't surrender to these assessments – they will only disempower you.

Become is about what *you* can produce in powerful conversations – not by becoming a critic to others. If you learn from this book, you will support others, not just criticize them.

If you distinguish some relationship that is not working for you as well as you would like, read this book to identify what conversational domain may be missing *from your* conversations.

This way of looking at relationship breakdowns will give you power to take new action, and generate new results.

If you read this book as I have suggested and engage with the practices, you will develop a new ability to not only generate extraordinary results, but also enable others around you to do so.

Every time you step outside your comfort zone, you unlock your potential for real learning. I invite you to 'look for' such experiences in this book. Moving quickly past these moments is an excellent way to protect what you already know and not learn anything new. In that case, reading this book would be a waste of time.

Read this book slowly – allow the learnings to settle in.

2

ONE KEY ROLE OF A LEADER IS TO COACH

Leaders must coach their teams. It's their team, who else is supposed to do it? The team's performance is a consequence of their conversations. There are key conversations that generate the team and its teamwork. The leader's job is to make sure that these key conversations happen and happen well.

BOB DUNHAM

How would it be if...

- the purpose of your organization and that of the individual team members in your team were fully aligned?

- you could generate extraordinary results in your team or organization with the right conversations?

- you discover greatness in each member of your team that had not yet been *discovered* by you? What results could be possible?

- you could create a culture of commitment in your organization, and everybody did what they said, and said what they did?

- you could create a space of conversation within your organization – of trust, openness, learning, expansion and of playing big games?

It is interesting how the word 'coach' came into existence. 'Coaching' as a term first appeared in 1830 at Oxford University as slang to mean a tutor who 'carries' a student through an exam.[1] It is like how a coach (train car in this case) 'carries' passengers from one place to another. Coaching, since, has become a widely used term, and it literally means that the coach, through his conversations with the learner, 'carries' the learner to a new place of 'seeing' and to being a new observer (we discuss 'Observe' in Chapter 4).

It is a myth that only professional coaches do coaching. One of the key roles of leaders and managers is to coach their team members and co-workers – they must 'carry' them to a different place of seeing the same situation, or to a new commitment.

It is through these leadership-coaching conversations that leaders and managers enable their co-workers to take new actions and generate new results. The idea of coaching is not to just get the co-worker to do more, or just take more competent actions, but to generate 'new' actions for the sake of generating 'new' results, those that may not have been available to the co-worker prior to the leadership-coaching conversation.

Let's understand this further. Amar Jain, the Indian branch head for a large German organization, realized that his team was not delivering results despite working hard. For him, the problem was not the intention of his teammates or any lack of willingness to work hard. His team was ready to give their 100 per cent – they just did not know what was missing. Amar realized that his job was to show his teammates possibilities that they could not see themselves. He invited them to 'new seeing' – and once they did, they started to take 'new actions' which generated 'new results', those that they had not even imagined earlier.

Amar's team had decided that a certain state in India was not 'worth winning', and hence they had decided not to take any actions in that state. When Amar challenged them, he asked them to clarify whether the state was not worth winning or were they not worthy of winning in that state? He showed them the impact on the sale numbers even if they could generate a 5 per cent market share in the first two years in that state.

The possibility of focusing on this state was simply not available to this team prior to this conversation with Amar. However, after this conversation, Amar opened a new possibility for the team. The team took new actions, in a market that they had historically never looked at, and indeed gained the 5 per cent market share within two years.

Jack Canfield in his article 'When we grow others, we grow ourselves' states:

'This is what Jeff Fettig, the chairman of Whirlpool Corporation, did to grow his organization. He fully committed himself to coaching people and to creating a coaching culture. He firmly believed that when he developed others, he developed himself and when he developed himself and others, he developed his organization.'

Canfield further adds in the article: 'Coaching people is so important to developing leaders that Jack Welch, the legendary former CEO and chairman of GE [General Electric], decreed that those who did not coach others would not be promoted. Welch knew that when his leaders grew others, they grew themselves and the organization.'[2]

I am not surprised at all that Robert Hargrove in his book *Masterful Coaching* states that 80 per cent of the best CEOs in the world spend their time coaching.[3] Your team is your team, and teams need a coach.

If not you, who?

Let's look at some of the recent captains of the Indian men's cricket team – Sourav Ganguly, M.S. Dhoni and Virat Kohli. Each of them was and is focused on ensuring that their teammates grow. Several players' flourishing careers can be credited to the opportunities and support provided by these captains. The same applies for leaders in the corporate world.

In a conversation with the head of manufacturing services at a large farm equipment company, he stated that he credits his manager for the growth he has seen in his career. While his role and designation did not change every year, the manager demanded a higher standard of work from him each passing year. This ensured he 'grew' in the quality of work he did, even if he did not grow in position in the organization (which of course happened in due course, because of high-quality work).

Pause for Reflection

As a leader or a manager:
1. Do you coach your team members?
2. If yes, what percentage of your time do you spend coaching them?
3. If you had to increase that percentage by, let's say, 15 per cent, what impact do you think that would have on the results of your team/ organization?
4. What skills will you need to make your leadership-coaching conversations more impactful?

LEADERSHIP-COACHING CONVERSATIONS

What do extraordinary leaders and managers *really* do? Observe carefully and you will notice that they spend most of their time having conversations. If their conversations are effective, the leader/

manager is considered competent. If it's otherwise, they are declared incompetent.

There are several conversational domains that are currently missing from the active awareness of the leaders in the corporate world. Some claim they 'understand' elements of these conversations, and yet, when you see them at work, you rarely find these conversational practices in action.

Having said that, there are leaders who actively practise these conversational domains – and if they do, they do so extremely successfully. By having the missing conversations that I've listed in this book, you will discover a more effective way of working with your co-workers and teams, instead of the now outdated command-and-control style of operation.

I am grouping these conversational domains and calling them 'leadership conversations' or 'leadership-coaching conversations'. These may not necessarily be new to some readers – many of you may already be regularly engaging in similar conversations. However, it's possible that you're blind to the fact that these conversations are, in fact, leadership-coaching conversations.

Prateek Sinha, CEO of a $300-million company once mentioned to me, 'Sameer, I am amazed at how ineffective my coaching conversations were with my leadership team and my unit heads. It is not that I speak disrespectfully to any one of them – it is just that my conversations were not generating the kind of results I wanted. A small shift in my conversations has had a big shift in the results we are now generating.'

The question, then, is, 'What makes a leadership conversation effective?'

This book uses the term COACH as a powerful acronym. If managers want to be successful, mastering these conversational domains is not discretionary. It is imperative for success in today's corporate world – a world that is soon going to be (if not already being) ruled by the millennials.

These five leadership-conversational domains are:

Care: Care is fundamental to being human. When you take care of the care of the other, you create value and open a space for magical results.

As an organization – or a team – are conversations, commitments, actions, practices and results inside of the care of the participants in the conversation?

Observe: When you observe 'the way you observe', you become aware that there exists a whole world outside of the way you observe; and when you become aware you give yourself new choices for what you pay attention to.

Are you observing your internal conversations that give you your external conversations and actions? As importantly, are you supporting your co-workers (including your reporting manager) in observing their internal conversations?

Actions: Action is central to generating results that matter to you. Only when you take action, do you get the desired results. Actions taken on a regular basis lead to practices, and practices lead to embodiment*.

---

* Embodiment: The process of embodiment puts more and more of what we pay attention to into the unconscious. Experts and masters who fully embody a practice have no conscious awareness of how they actually perform it. (Think of a time when you learnt driving or cycling or playing basketball or ballet or kathak, or any other sport, or dance or skill for that matter – it was difficult initially. As you practised, it became easier, and then came a time you became unaware of how your body moved while driving, cycling, playing basketball, doing ballet or kathak).

To embody a new behaviour is to achieve a level of skill that makes the behaviour automatic, habitual and effective even in chaotic situations. To embody means that the electrochemical pathways of the brain and the nervous system are modified.

This new behaviour, which you embody after engaging in generative practices, can then be used in any situation you find yourself in. To choose a generative practice is to choose a way of being in the world.

Are your conversations with yourself and with your co-workers generating new actions and practices to achieve the desired results?

Commitment: Look around you and you'll notice that the world operates on promises (or commitments). For example, there is a promise of the elevator; of your car, of the chair you may be sitting on while reading this book, of the security guard at your gate; of your colleagues, and so forth.

Results are a function of actions, and actions come from your (sometimes hidden) commitments. To generate new results, you need to make new, trustworthy commitments. Commitments are generated in conversations.

What are your current team commitments? Are these shared and accepted by all? Are these commitments being kept and managed? And if not, what is the impact? What new commitments are you making, and/or what new commitments are you soliciting from others in your conversations?

Holding Space of Conversation: For effective and authentic conversations, a safe space needs to be created and then held by the leader.

Are you having effective and authentic conversations where you create a secure space for the other person not to feel judged? Are you actively creating and holding such a space in your organization/team?

I use the term 'COACH' for leaders and managers. In my assessment, a good leader or manager is first and foremost a good coach. Conversations elucidated in this book are focused on shifting our own results first, and then those of others. These conversations are fundamental to leadership and management. The key role of managers is not to necessarily do everything themselves, but to get things done by others.

Further, in my assessment, a good coach is also a good leader. This book has been designed for leaders, managers or individual contributors who are a part of physical or virtual teams. It is for those who really care for generating results for their organizations, for themselves, and for their team members (*Honestly, every other way is short term and not sustainable*).

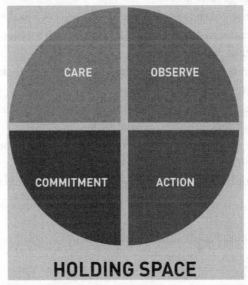

Figure 2.1: COACH: The five critical leadership-coaching conversations

What is a coaching conversation?

There's an interesting list I've shared, provided by Robert Hargrove and each of these points are covered in the five conversational domains listed in this book.[4] The reason I have referred to these points below is for you, as a leader or a manager, to see that these may be exceedingly relevant for your team and your organization in generating extraordinary results.

A coaching conversation is a conversation:

- that has a profound impact in the life of those coached (and sometimes even the coach)
- that interrupts the old patterns and opens our eyes to new horizons
- where we are touched with exciting new possibilities, and gain a greater appreciation of our own potential, or come to a revelation of our own foolishness
- where we somehow are left bigger than we were before and inspired to greater action
- wherein the coach is burning with intention to make an impact
- where the coach is speaking and listening from a total commitment to cause that person's success
- where the coach extends people an 'A' (you see their greatness), even when they disappoint you or make mistakes
- where the coach provides the kind of insightful feedback that rips the blinders off
- where people see new possibilities, and break through barriers showing up in an entirely new way
- where people walk away feeling inspired, empowered and enabled to act

THE COACH IS A MIRROR

The mirror has a role to play – it shows people what they cannot see themselves. That's exactly the job of a coach and a leader. As a mirror, the coach shows the coachee what they cannot see on their own. As a leader or a manager, your job is to show your co-worker or team member the observer he or she is and the different observers they can be.

Once those coached get the awareness of the observers they are, it opens new actions for them, and these *new* actions give birth to *new* possibilities of results (more on this in Chapter 4).

In other words, a coach or a leader is someone who can see things that the coached or the coworker is blind to, or may be oblivious to. This doesn't mean they are superior in any way, and the coach or the leader may not even have the skills in the same domain that the person coached has, but the coach's unique ability to show the coached what they cannot see on their own, can add immeasurable value for the coached.

According to Tracy Goss, 'Your role as a coach is to create an opening for action that allows people to get untangled from their structure of interpretation, and focus on the future to which they are committed.'[5]

My coach Bob Dunham once stated to me what he had heard from Humberto Maturana: 'There are no nouns – there are only practices.' For example 'stapler' is a noun. However, according to Maturana, a stapler is a stapler because it has a certain practice of stapling associated with it. Take that practice out, and the stapler becomes ineffective. Similarly, a leader is a noun – and a leader is not effective if he or she does not practise these fundamental leadership-coaching conversations. As far as my experience is concerned, a leader, a manager or even an individual contributor can practise these fundamental coaching conversations, and by virtue of mastering these conversations, they could wear the hat of a coach.

And hence, an effective leader or a coach is someone who has a deep skilful embodiment of these conversations, and regularly uses them to help others generate results.

THE IMPORTANCE OF AUTHORITY

This book is an endeavour for leaders and managers to understand the fundamentals first, and then have conversations using these fundamentals. Authenticity in the work of leaders and managers will come when they understand and embody these fundamentals first before they coach others. The generative practices listed after each chapter will support the leaders and managers to embody these conversations.

You do not get authority simply by your designation alone in the organization. Think of all the managers you reported to, and to how many of these managers you gave authority to tell you what and how to do things. Sure, thanks to their seniority, you may have heard them out, but internally, chances are that you filtered out a lot that was said by a manager whom you did not give authority to.

If you want to have a coaching conversation, you need to be given permission from that person. For example, every time I need to show a new perspective to my clients, or to leaders of organizations, I seek their permission to ask them a question. I ask them something on the lines of: 'Would you mind if I asked you a question pertaining to this conversation?' Most of the time I get a 'yes'. Only then do I proceed.

It's a myth that we cannot have a coaching conversation with someone senior to us. On many occasions, I have had 'coaching conversations' with senior people – senior by age or by work experience. The reason I am successful in these conversations – not always, but fairly often – is that I have been given authority to have these conversations and have built the skill in having these conversations.

Authority comes from two important things:

1. The person you coach needs to believe that you have depth in the area you are speaking in. Which is one of the reasons why I've recommended that you most importantly need to have these conversations with yourself first – that you need to embody the distinctions by doing the generative practices (this also creates trust in others and confirms that you have these skills).
2. Even if you have mastered the distinctions, you need permission from the people you coach to have these conversations with them. Imposing on them usually produces resistance.

When you do so, you open a space for magic.

PARADIGM-SHIFTING PRINCIPLES

Principle 1: Care is the foundation on which results are generated

Our predecessors have had a huge role to play in the shaping of today's world. We ourselves have a similar task for the generations to come. One of the drawbacks of the world we live in, especially in the corporate world, is that adequate importance is not given to a crucial concern of human beings: 'care'.

In this book, we use the model Anatomy of Action designed by Bob Dunham, which I've elaborated on in the third chapter on 'Care'.[6]

While Dunham calls this the Anatomy of Action, in my assessment, this is the Anatomy of Results. There is a clear framework to generate results, irrespective of the industry, function or domain, and that is what Dunham calls the Anatomy of Action. This model very eloquently brings out the relationship between care, conversation, commitment, action and results.

The proposition is very simple: When you care for something, the results that you generate will be significantly more than when you don't care for that something.

Interestingly, despite the simplicity, and the commonsensical value of this principle, one of the key missing domain of conversation in organizational settings are conversations around care.

In their fascinating book, *Ubuntu*, Stephen Lundin and Bob Nelson show us how Simon, through the South African philosophy of Ubuntu helps his manager John to transform an unproductive team to a productive one.[7]

Early in the story, Simon tells to John, 'The first step is to get to know your employees as people and not just as workers. That involves developing a sincere interest in each person. What is important to them? Do they have a family? What life experiences have shaped who they are? What are their interests? What are their goals? Where do they hope to be in five years? Are there hot buttons or things they would respond negatively to because of their past that you need to know to best work with them?'

Simon further adds in his conversation with John, 'You do not have to respect sloppy work, a bad attitude, or missed deadlines, but you do have to always be respectful of people who do the bad work even as you work to improve it.'

In his piece 'What Millennials Want in the Workplace (And Why You Should Start Giving It to Them), Rob Asghar quotes Jamie Gutfreund, chief strategy officer, for the Intelligence Group who states that 'a full 86 million millennials will be in the workplace by 2020 – representing a full 40 per cent of the total working population'.[8]

Gutfreund says that Intelligence Group studies of millennials have found that:

- 64 per cent of them say it's a priority for them to make the world a better place.
- 72 per cent would like to be their own boss. But if they do have to work for a boss, 79 per cent of them would want that boss to serve more as a coach or mentor.
- 88 per cent prefer a collaborative work culture rather than a competitive one.
- 74 per cent want flexible work schedules.
- And 88 per cent want 'work–life integration', which isn't the same as work–life balance, since work and life now blend together inextricably.

Clearly, the next generation, the millennials, is more aware of what they care for, and are ready to demand that their cares be taken care of. They are also aware, that when they act inside of their cares, they can generate extraordinary results.

In a *Business Insider* piece titled 'Facebook says its best managers exhibit these seven behaviors', Richard Feloni quotes Lori Goler, VP of People at Facebook: 'The most important thing is that we choose managers who want to be managers.'

What a seemingly simple thing, and yet, it misses the attention of many executives in organizations – Facebook chooses managers who want to be managers!

Some people have a love for leading teams and developing personal connections. They also want to see their juniors succeed. It is what they care for. Many others have no interest in leading teams – they want to do extraordinary work as individual contributors.

Goler and her team conducted a company-wide study of roughly 10,000 employees to discover which of the teams reported highest levels of satisfaction and engagement. They then checked with these teams on what it was about their team leaders that made their work experience rewarding. Interestingly, the first behaviour of these 'best managers' that stood out was that these 'best' managers 'cared about their team members'.

Here is something for you to consider:[9]

1. Care is critical for meaning in life; if there is no care, there is no meaning.
2. Care is critical for satisfaction; you cannot be satisfied till your cares aren't taken care of.
3. Care is critical to designing futures that matter; if there is no care, the future will not matter. What matters is determined by what you care about.
4. Care is critical to commitment; without care, commitments cannot be trusted.
5. Care is critical for value. When you don't care, it is not valuable.
6. Care is a source of energy. Irrespective of how tired you are, when you are taking care of something that you care for, your body is filled with energy; you are alive.
7. The reason someone is in a disempowered mood is that what they care for isn't taken care of.
8. When there is shared care, i.e., the cares of the organization, the team and individuals within the team are aligned, there opens a space for magic.
9. Care is that 'hidden ground' on which we stand. Only when we become aware of this hidden ground – ours and those of our teammates, can we attempt to take care of these 'hidden cares'.

Pause for Reflection

1. What may be the different domains of your cares (different areas of your cares)?
2. What may be the care of your organization?

3. What may be the care of your team – as a unit?
4. What may be the care of each of your individual team members?
5. Do you think you are taking care of what you care about?
6. If not, what may be missing?
7. Do you think you are supporting your organization and your team to take care of what the organization and the team care about respectively?
8. If not, what may be missing, as action, from *your* end?
9. Do you think you are adequately supporting individual team members to take care of what they care about?
10. If not, what may be missing, as action, from *your* end?
11. Anything else that may open up for you while considering these questions? Please journal your thoughts.

Principle 2: The observer you are determines what results you generate

I quote from Ken Burnett's blog a story now told many times in training programmes and shared in many books and articles. However, the relevance of this story, and more importantly, the simplicity of this story drives home the point of this principle very well:[10]

When I first visited Africa in 1978 I toured the wild north of Kenya. In tiny villages and markets along the way I kept seeing signs for Bata, the shoe company. When it came to indications of commercial product dominance in these flyblown, out of the way spots, Bata was in evidence far more than any other maker of anything. I vaguely wondered why at the time, and later was told this tale, in explanation.

At the end of the nineteenth century, just as colonial Africa was opening up as a market, all the manufacturers of shoes in Victorian England sent their representatives to Africa to see if there might be an opportunity there for their wares. All duly came back in time with the same answer. 'Nobody in Africa wears shoes. So, there is no market for our products there.'

All, that is, save for the Bata rep. He came back saying, 'Nobody in Africa wears shoes. So, there's a *huge* market for our products in Africa!'

And that's why signs promoting Bata appear all over Africa, even in the remotest of spots. It's why Bata's shoes are known as the shoes of Africa.

The way the Bata representative 'observed' the Africa market, i.e., 'Nobody in Africa wears shoes. So, there's a *huge* market for our products in Africa', determined what actions Bata took, and further determined what results they generated in Africa.

Similarly, the way the representatives of other shoe manufacturers 'observed' the market, i.e., 'Nobody in Africa wears shoes. So, there is no market for our products there', determined what actions (or inactions) they took, and hence directed what results (or lack of results) they generated in Africa.

In 2010, when I moved to Bengaluru with my family, I came across two individuals, both of whom were differently abled and had contracted polio at a young age. Both were wheelchair-bound. Physically, they were and are both as 'disadvantaged' as the other.

One of them found his physical state an impediment to his work and his life, and spent years complaining about his disability. In his opinion, his disability put him at a disadvantage compared to others. He generated no new results in his life in the three years of my knowing him.

The other person, Sunil Jain, now a dear friend, not for a moment observed his disability as an impediment. He continued to observe and actively look for possibilities, took action on them and generated some of the most fascinating new results I have seen *any* man generate. He has been instrumental in making voting centres disabled-friendly in Bengaluru, organized an All India Wheelchair Tennis Tournament and supported disabled athletes to train and win some international world tournaments. (I have also shared a few promises made by Sunil, and an example of the success generated by him, in the 'Commitment' chapter).

If you develop the eyes to see, you will notice people choose to see their environment either to empower themselves or feel disempowered (they may be blind to this choice they are making).

Last year, I delivered a programme for a large pharmaceutical company – same industry, same organization, same CEO. However, several people observed that certain results were not possible.

At the end of the year, these people did not generate the results that *they had observed* as not possible prior to even beginning action.

Interestingly, some other people in the same organization considered the very same results, described by the first group as impossible, as imminently possible and achievable. Guess what? They generated these results.

The way we see (observe) determines what we do (action), and what we do (action) determines, what we have (result).

As a leader, manager or a coach, our vital role is to show our teams and our co-workers the observers they are being, and how a shift in the way they observe can dramatically shift their actions, and hence results. For that, the leader or manager first needs to understand what it means to be an observer, and how to shift the observer they are.

In my assessment, one of the key roles of the manager is to be connected to the observer his or her team members are. If members in a team observe the world disempoweringly, there is a small chance (and I am being generous when I state 'small chance') they will achieve the results the team has set out to achieve.

Pause for Reflection

1. When was the last time you missed generating a result that you wanted? Was the observer you were then not aligned to generating the result you wanted to achieve? Every time you do not generate

the result that you want, the first place to look is 'what observer were you such that the results were not generated?'
2. Similarly, think of a time when you generated an extraordinary result and took everyone by surprise. No one expected you to deliver that result. What observer were you that you generated that extraordinary result?

We will discuss this further in the chapter titled 'Observe'.

Principle 3: To take action is to take care (if not you are engaged in meaningless activity)

The general understanding of action is 'to do something'. At the Institute for Generative Leadership, we define action, as 'taking care of what you care about'.[11]

If you are not taking care of what you care about, what exactly are you doing?

This is a question that I regularly ask my clients in organizations. The point of action is to take care, and if your action is not taking care of something that you care about, you are engaged in pointless or meaningless activity.

This is a paradigm-shifting principle, mainly because it forces people to ask themselves on a regular basis: 'For the sake of what care of mine, am I doing what I am currently doing?'

There are several activities that I was constantly engaged with, but with this question, I realized these activities were of limited or no meaning in my life, and hence I redesigned my activities. Now, every minute of the day, I try to be in action, i.e., taking care of what I care about.

Am I there yet? No.

Has there been a difference? Definitely.

For your information, these are a few examples of activities that I have given up or reduced:

1. Watching TV (Five years ago, I'd watch three hours of news every evening. Today, after having disconnected satellite TV at home, we enjoy a lot more family time together).
2. Going out 2-3 times a week for a drink with friends.
3. Significantly reduced watching movies. I still watch movies every now and then. However, now, the care I am taking care of is spending and enjoying time with my wife.
4. My phone conversations have become much shorter and crisper.

By stopping or reducing time on the above activities means that I have made more time for cares that matter to me, which are:

- Spending quality time with my family
- My physical and intellectual development – reading, writing, studying, resting and exercising
- My organization – offering consultancy, coaching and learning programmes, and serving my clients
- Promoting the cause of organ donation, and the Gift Your Organ Foundation

Pause for Reflection

In the last forty-eight hours, how much time did you engage in 'action', i.e., taking care of what you care about; and how much time did you spend in meaningless activity, i.e., that which does not take care of what you care about.

Please journal your reflections.

We will deal with this in greater detail in the chapters 'Care' and 'Actions'.

Principle 4: As a leader or a manager, you are a promise of being a coach to your teams

This principle, in my assessment, is more like a law. A law is not dependent on our acceptance; it has an impact on our life whether we know it or not, like it or not, accept it or reject it. Let's take the example of gravity – gravity has an impact on our lives. However, once we understand its impact, we can use it to our advantage. All the tall towers that we see, that seemingly challenge the law of gravity, have been constructed based on a deep understanding of gravity and physics.

Similarly, as a leader or a manager, you are a promise of being a coach to your teams. This is not dependent on your acceptance or liking. However, if you understand this principle, you can act in accordance with this principle and set yourself up for extraordinary success.

The consequence of not keeping a promise is that the following areas are negatively impacted. I call these the 4R impact:

- Respect (Self and others)
- Relationships
- Reputation
- Results

Let's assume that one of your team members looks up to you as his or her coach. And let's presume you are not aware of this, and you do not act as his or her coach. This person, considering the world view he or she has based on his or her historical assessments and life experiences, expects the manager or the leader to be their coach. For this person, this is obvious, and it needn't be explicitly stated.

Now, if this person is not appropriately guided and coached, in the eyes of this person, the following will be the impact:

- Respect
- Relationships (trust)
- Reputation (public identity)
- Results (success)

If you observe, the impact is like that of not keeping a promise. We will discuss this further in the chapter on 'Commitment':

Pause for Reflection

- Am I *really* a coach for my co-workers?
- If not, what are the consequences that I may have suffered – those that I may not have been even aware of till now?
- When I did coach my co-workers, what was the impact on the results, as compared to when I used authority over them? What was the impact on the results?

Principle 5: The space that exists in a relationship determines what results can be generated in and by that relationship

Imagine taking a walk in a beautiful garden by a river, listening to the sounds of the murmuring river adjacent to the garden. How do you feel? What does this set you up for?

Perhaps a smile on your face, some reflection time, maybe?

Now imagine walking past a road full of potholes with stinking garbage thrown randomly by the residents and commercial enterprises of that neighbourhood. How do you feel? And what does this set you up for?

Perhaps disgust and a frown on your face, maybe?

Similarly, every relationship evokes a certain feeling in you – that feeling has a great deal to do with the space that exists in the relationship. That space sets people up for a certain result and impacts how people feel and respond in that relationship.

The claim this principle makes is that a corrupted space in a relationship can generate limited or no results. The first step to generating extraordinary results in – and by – a relationship is to clean up the corrupted space that may exist. One of the ways this can be done is by using the first four conversational domains listed in this book. However, we will go deeper in this and bring out finer nuances that I believe are critical for holding space of conversations that will lead to the generation of extraordinary results.

MYTHS AND BUSTING MYTHS

There are a lot of myths around leadership coaching conversations, and in each of the five core chapters in this book, I have tried busting some of them. Leadership conversations are an integral practice – I am still struggling to find one person who can do without these conversations.

It's like saying 'I can live without looking at the mirror'. Only a person who lives without looking at the mirror, or is blind about his blindness, can state this. People who have been exposed to coaching want to, as often as possible, jump right back to 'see' what they cannot 'see' on their own – with the help of a coach.

Here are some myths:

Myth: Coaching is a distinct profession, and leaders and managers are not coaches

Busting the Myth: Coaching is not only a profession, it's a practice of having effective coaching conversations. For example, you may have seen a good parent working with their children on the latter's creative pursuits, keeping them well behaved, and yet give them the freedom that the child needs. This parent is not a designated coach, yet has mastered coaching conversations with their children. There are several other parents you may have seen who struggle to engage effectively with their children.

So, clearly, all parents are not acting effectively as coaches (while many would like to believe they are); only those who have mastered the conversations, and have authority from their children, operate as coaches with their children.

Similarly, there are managers and leaders who have embodied the leadership-coaching conversations listed in this book (whether they know this or not is a different thing altogether). In the eyes of their co-workers, these leaders and managers may be coaches.

If you want to be a successful leader or a manager, you need to embody these leadership-coaching conversations. You need to be a master in these conversational domains listed in this book. It does not matter what your title is.

Myth: 'As a leader or a manager, I don't have the time to coach!'

Busting the Myth: It is amazing how often I hear this statement. The question I ask such leaders or managers, 'Is it your job to generate results for your organization with the help of teams?' If the answer is yes, I tell them they have no choice – they need to either learn these conversational domains, or pay the price. (And the price is that they do not succeed as much as they'd hoped, had they known and practised these simple conversational domains.)

To state 'I don't have time to coach my co-workers', in my assessment, is akin to stating 'I have no time to generate results that matter or do my job as a leader or a manager'.

Myth: 'As a leader or a manager, I am a coach by default.'

Busting the Myth: Not at the least. 'Coach' is not simply a title; to be a coach you need to be in the 'practice' of having leadership-coaching conversations. As a leader or a manager, if you practise these well and have authority from your co-workers, only then are you a coach. Yes, as a manager, you certainly are a promise of being a coach; however, you need to actively practise the leadership-coaching conversational domains listed in this book to fulfil your promise of being a coach.

Myth: 'Authority is a function of seniority. By virtue of being the manager, I have authority over my co-workers.'

Busting the Myth: Authority is not a function of seniority. To have authority over someone means to have a certain degree of power over that person. And in this case, power would mean that that person grants you the right to present choices to them to make a decision, or in certain cases, even exercise choice on their behalf. Just because you are senior to a particular individual does not, by any means, signify that he or she has granted you that power. This power needs to be earned. Which is why many seniors (often blindly) grant authority to even people who are junior to them in heirarchy.

Myth: 'I don't have the time for new practices.'

Busting the Myth: Richard Strozzi Heckler in *The Leadership Dojo* makes the claim 'you are your practices'.[12] Many of us are blind to our subconcious practices that we repeat without concious choice. And it is these practices that lead us to our results (often, these results are not our desired results). To say that 'you do not have the time to adopt new practices' is to say that 'you do not have the time to generate results that matter to you in your life'. This also connects to people saying 'I don't have time for learning', and this is because for them, learning is academic and not related to work and results.

Leaders choose their practices because they understand the power of these practices. We embody new ways of doing things only through practices.

Now, if you say that the practices listed in this book do not resonate with you, that would be an altogether different proposition to consider. As expected, some practices will resonate with some, and some other practices with others. Try out the practices to see which ones work for you.

Myth: 'All my co-workers are my coachees.'

Busting the Myth: There is nothing inherently wrong with this statement. You could have the authority from all your co-workers to coach them, but you can't take this authority as a given. To be effective in your coaching conversations would mean that you have authority from each of your co-workers. That may or may not be true. And assuming that may just be the case, you can even have your seniors under your coaching – not formally – but you could have leadership-coaching conversations with them, and support them in generating results that matter to them.

Myth: To coach someone means there is something wrong with that person

Busting the Myth: This myth is like saying that mirrors are only for physically dirty looking people; clean and well-kempt people need not look at the mirror.

It's worthwhile to note that the latter use a mirror to ensure that they are clean and well kempt. Most people check the mirror in the morning after a shower before they set out for their day to see if they are ready, physically, in terms of their look for the day. That is the time, perhaps, they are the cleanest in the day. And yet they see the mirror to see how they can look better.

Similarly, the higher in seniority or more successful you are, the more you need a coach to support you. After all, as a senior in the organization, the way you see and the way you act impacts many people. Top performers in the world have coaches – professional athletes, public figures, musicians and leaders.

MOVING ON

Before you move on from one chapter to the other, I encourage you to engage with the practices listed at the end of every chapter. These practices are integral to building leadership muscle.

Having set the groundwork for the five critical leadership-coaching conversations, we begin with the first of the five conversational domains. The first of them, 'Care' is perhaps the most critical, and maybe the most crucial missing conversational domain in the corporate world today. You will see that care is also the basis of which all other conversations take place.

GENERATIVE PRACTICES

1. Journaling Practice

Extraordinary leaders take time out to reflect. They maintain a journal to have a regular conversation with themselves. Many see journal writing as an opportunity to open doors that they did not even know existed. It helps them understand how they observe the world, and the access to this understanding is available to them mainly through reflective thinking and writing.

The purpose of the journal is not to fill it, but to hone our attention to observe ourselves and others, and to introspect more deeply. Use this practice to provoke yourself into becoming a better observer of how life happens for you.

When you keep a journal, you begin a conversation with yourself. And like in a conversation with another person, you do not know what will come out of that conversation. Similarly, when you begin to journal, you do not know what reflections you will end up creating in that conversation with yourself.

I consider keeping a daily journal a powerful practice, and I encourage you to do so – certainly for the sake of your own leadership.

Begin by buying a new journal. Next, finalize a time of the day that works best for you to take out 15–20 minutes to write your reflections of the day. Finally, make sure you start writing.

Many people wait to know what they should write before they can begin to write. This is a mistake – this way you will end up writing what you already know. Journal writing is to begin writing first, without knowing what you will write, and then be surprised by what comes out.

This is when you really open up new avenues of thinking and doing.

2. Jack Canfield says, 'When we grow others, we grow ourselves'. Do you agree with this claim? Please reflect on the times when you grew others, and the impact that had on your growth as a leader. Journal your thoughts.

Please reflect on how much time you spend with your team supporting them to deliver results. Is this enough for your team to achieve results? If you spent even 10 per cent more, what could the impact be on your and your team's results?

Journal your thoughts, and any new commitments you make to yourself.

Part II

The Five Crucial Conversational Domains

3

COACH: CARE

Care is the essence of being human and our experience of life. It is the deep emotional foundation of our relationship with our future, our choices, our meaning, value, and satisfaction. It is the energy of our purpose, the music of the soundtrack of our lives, and the core of our commitment.

The tragedy of our era is that we are often blind and disconnected from our care, and so disconnected from our power. We have misplaced our birthright and diminished the fires of our care to petty personal desires. The journey of awakening and the path to power and a good life is to find your true care and choose to take care of what you care about.

BOB DUNHAM

How would it be if...

- members of your team cared for the purpose and outcomes of the team, and for being excellent at teamwork?

- everyone in the organization cared for each other and supported the other person to take care of what they cared for?

- the purpose of all individuals in your team was aligned with that of the organization?

- we could take care that our professional work is meaningful, valuable and satisfying to ourselves as well as a valuable contribution to others?

WHAT IS CARE? AND WHY IS IT AN IMPORTANT CONVERSATIONAL DOMAIN?

As humans, we are beings who have a future. We have a future we want, and futures that we don't want. We have emotional responses to these futures, and the foundation of these emotional responses is 'care'. We care about our future, having positive outcomes, and not having negative outcomes.

But care is not just a desire or preference. It connects to the depths of what resonates for us in life. It is the foundation of value, satisfaction and meaning.

What is crucial is that we can be connected to our care, or disconnected; clear or unclear about our care. It shapes our entire relationship with action, results and life.

Care is also part of action. We care, but we also 'take care'. Meaningful work, action and life is about taking care of what we care about.[1]

Let's look at some examples. Student A, who is appearing for his tenth-grade board exams, wakes up ambitious on the morning of the first examination paper. On the same day, student B wakes up dreading the day ahead, and has anxiety. Why does this happen – both these students have the same exam, and have exactly opposite feelings about the day ahead?

The reason this happens is because both students understand the importance of board exams and the impact its results will have on their college admissions. Both students care for the college they want admission in. Student A is ambitious because, given his preparations, he believes he will write a good paper. Student B believes he is not prepared for the examination (irrespective of the amount of time he spent preparing), and because he believes he is not prepared, he thinks he will not write a good paper. Hence he feels it will impact the college he gets admission in.

Given how these two students perceived the impact of the examination on their future determined how they were behaving in the present. Both have different opinions of their futures, but the significance of these opinions is that they care about what future will they create.

All this was happening in the present. The future had not happened. No one knew:

- what would happen in the future;
- how much of a role that day would eventually play in each of their futures; and
- whether Student A would have a good future or Student B would have a not so good future.

Despite the above, how each of them perceived the future governed how they were 'being' in that moment.

Let's look at another example: A few years ago, my family went on a vacation to Kashmir. About a month before our vacation, just after we had booked our tickets to Kashmir, there was great enthusiasm. Then we were a family of three (my wife, my daughter and I). All three of us were eagerly looking forward to the trip. Every time the three of us got together, that's all we would talk about – what we would do, eat, wear – and all of this was adding to the excitement in the house.

A month later, we did take that holiday – a fantastic ten days near snow-capped peaks, lakes and houseboats. The day before our holiday was about to end, my wife and I were at the Dal Lake, sitting in a houseboat – each such boat is popularly known as a 'floating palace'. It was a gorgeous evening and we were sipping awesome ginger tea (it felt like drinking sweetness and comfort straight from the mug).

Just then, my wife's shoulder drooped, and she said a bit disappointedly, 'That's it – our holiday is about to get over. We get back to our boring routine tomorrow.'

This is not about my wife, or me, or my family vacation – what I am attempting to do here is show you how each one of us is living inside of a future. While the Kashmir holiday was being planned, and we were at home – there was excitement – because in that moment, at home, we were living in a future of going to Kashmir. However, when we were in Kashmir, sitting in a floating palace, enjoying exactly what we had looked forward to – we were living in the future of going back to our so called 'boring routine'.

It's interesting how our present is determined by the future we live into. These reactions to the future can reveal what we care about and the new possibilities for taking care. This takes us to the possibilities to create value, satisfaction and meaning rather than to put up with our default expectations and opinions.

One Friday afternoon, a colleague and I were sitting at Starbucks in Bengaluru discussing a culture change programme at one of our client organizations. There was a group of two young men and a lady sitting right next to us talking about a seemingly big customer event their organization was planning the following day. One of the men and the lady were looking forward to the event and we could sense the enthusiastic energy. However, the second man seemed disinterested. He wasn't excited at all – he looked almost bored. And then we heard him say, 'I know this is a big event, and it means a lot to our organization – but why have it on a Saturday? It just messes up the weekend.'

All three of them cared for their future, but different futures. The two individuals who were excited cared for their organization, and were living inside of the future of having a successful customer event that would open up possibilities for their organization. The third person, perhaps also cared for the organization, but in that moment, seemed to care more for his weekend. For him, his weekend (what he cared for) was now incomplete, a 'mess' and therefore he wasn't exactly looking forward to it.

Each one of us has a future; and each one of us has things we care about. We also have an assessment of what we want and not want from our future. However, our present is determined by our assessment of whether or not the future that we individually see takes care of our care or not.

Care evokes other emotions

There is a great connection between your cares and the future that you live in. Not only that, how the future you perceive takes care of what you care about determines what emotion you live in, in the present.

Let's look at all the above examples:

- Student A: Had an emotion of *ambition*. Why? Because he thought he would get admission in a good college. He cared for getting admission in a good college, and that is why this examination mattered to him.
- Student B: Had an emotion of *anxiety*. Why? Because he thought he would not get admission in a good college. He also cared for getting admission in a good college, and that is why this examination mattered to him too.
- My family: Was *thrilled* because we cared for the holiday we were taking together after three years. Later, my wife and I were *disappointed* because our holiday was getting over, and we cared for that time we spent together – and wanted some more of it.
- The young man and the young lady: Were *excited* about the prospect of having a big customer event that would help the sales of the organization and that excited them.
- The other young man: Was *bored* because he cared for his weekend and hence was put off by the same customer event that was happening on a weekend.

Here is what I stated about 'care' in the introduction of this book:[2]

- Care is critical for meaning in life; if there is no care, there is no meaning.
- Care is critical for satisfaction; you cannot be satisfied till your cares are taken care of.
- Care is critical to designing futures that matter; if there is no care, the future will not matter. What matters is determined by what you care about.
- Care is critical to commitment; without care, commitments cannot be trusted.
- Care is critical for value. When you don't care, it is not valuable.
- Care is a source of energy. Irrespective of how tired you are, when you are taking care of something that you care for, your body is filled with energy; you are alive.
- The reason someone is in a disempowered mood is that what they care for isn't taken care of.
- When there is shared care, i.e., the cares of the organization, the team and individuals within the team are aligned, it opens the space for great possibilities.
- Care is that 'hidden ground' on which we stand. Only when we become aware of this hidden ground – ours and those of our teammates – can we attempt to take care of these 'hidden cares'.

Care is more than just an emotion – it is more like a master emotion that has a role to play in other emotions. Let's have a look at some emotions, and why we experience these emotions:

1. Shreya was angry that she was not promoted to the role of head of marketing in her organization, and that an outsider was brought in for the role. Her anger was because she thought this was unfair on that part of her organization and her eighteen years of committed service were not given due credence.

    Shreya cared for the role of the head of marketing, which is why she got angry. She cared about being valued, acknowledged and respected. She cared about succeeding and creating a bigger future for herself. She cared about being able to contribute in a larger way.

2. Marshall was anxious for a few days – he was to present to the global board of directors on his expansion plans for the South Asia branch. He felt his future depended on the acceptance of his plans by the board.

   There was uncertainty over whether the board would accept Marshall's plans, and that made his future look uncertain to him. He cared for his future and that made him anxious.

3. Samantha had just been nominated for the 'Business Leader of the Year' award by a coveted publication. She was delighted.

   Samantha cared for her public image, and she believed this award would significantly enhance her public identity – and hence she was delighted.

4. Rajesh was sad – he recently lost his key client who contributed 30 per cent of his overall sales.

   Rajesh cared for the sales at his organization, and hence he was sad. He cared about his identity and his success, and what impact this would have on his future.

5. John was resigned to the possibility of things changing in his organization. He had spent twenty years there, but when a new president of his business unit stated that he would like to change the culture of the organization, and make it more result-oriented, John wasn't surprised – after all, every new president wanted to do the same. John tried his best to support the first two presidents, but neither of them had succeeded. Hence John lived in the assessment that this president wouldn't either. John would love to be a part of the culture change in the organization, but did not think it was possible.

   John cared for the organization, and because his assessment was that there were no possibilities of the culture changing, he was resigned to the possibility of it ever happening.

6. Merill resented her line manager – she blamed her for the layoff of her best friend from their department.

   Merill cared for her friend, and for her friend's career, and because she held the manager responsible, she resented him.

Care is a fundamental dimension of all human action. We may be connected to it or disconnected from it, but in either case it has a fundamental role to play in shaping how it influences action, and the meaning and value of the outcomes produced. Despite its primacy, and its importance, interestingly, this is often the missing piece in organizational conversations. This is a common blind spot in our culture.

The evidence of this is available in the Gallup Survey of Employee Engagement, 2015 quoted below:[3]

> The percentage of US workers in 2015 who Gallup considered engaged in their jobs averaged 32 per cent. The majority (50.8 per cent) of employees were 'not engaged', while another 17.2 per cent were 'actively disengaged'. The 2015 averages are largely on par with the 2014 averages and reflect little improvement in employee engagement over the past year.
>
> The 2015 employee engagement average is based on Gallup Daily tracking interviews conducted with 80,844 adults working for an employer. Gallup categorizes workers as 'engaged' based on their ratings of key workplace elements – such as having an opportunity to do what they do best each day, having someone at work who encourages their development and believing their opinions count at work – that predict important organizational performance outcomes.
>
> Engaged employees are involved in, enthusiastic about and committed to their work. Gallup's extensive research shows that employee engagement is strongly connected to business outcomes essential to an organization's financial success, such as productivity, profitability and customer engagement. Engaged employees support the innovation, growth and revenue that their companies need.
>
> Yet, most US workers continue to fall into the 'not engaged' category. These employees are not hostile or disruptive.

They show up and kill time, doing the minimum required with little extra effort to go out of their way for customers. They are less vigilant, more likely to miss work and change jobs when new opportunities arise. They are thinking about lunch or their next break. Not engaged employees are either 'checked out' or attempting to get their job done with little or no management support.

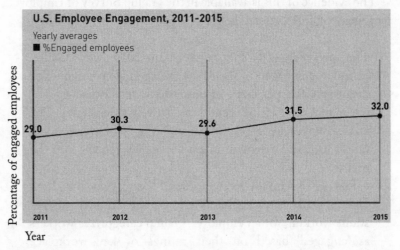

Figure 3.1: Gallup's yearly averages of US employee engagement, 2011–15

To generate extraordinary results in an organization, dare I say, the secret sauce of doing so is to create and establish shared cares – those of the organization and that of your co-workers.

TAKING CARE OF YOUR CARE

As humans, many of us are action-driven, and are exhilarated by taking action. Seldom do we stop and ask:

- What care is this action taking care of?
- Does that care *really* matter?

- If this action is not taking care of my cares, why am I doing what I am doing?

These are open-ended questions and do not have any correct answers. Please do not belittle or underestimate the power of these questions. You may not know the answer to these questions, and that is fine. In fact, even if you know the answer to these questions, try not to treat your answer as the final answer.

These are not everyday questions that we deal with in our organizational lives. By asking these questions, you may start to see the disconnect between your actions and your cares. For example:

- Alan claims that he cares about the mood of his team, and yet at the drop of a hat, he yells at a team member for the slightest mistake.
- Samantha claims that she cares about the growth of her team members, but rarely does she delegate the important stuff that will enable their growth.
- Ram is always talking to his children about the importance of speaking respectfully to seniors. However, Ram often speaks in a loud volume and almost disrespectfully to his own parents.

I have changed the names of Alan, Samantha and Ram, but these are real examples of people I know. On asking Ram, Alan and Samantha, 'Do you think you are taking care of your cares?' all three responded with an immediate 'yes' – almost without thinking. On deeper questioning, it occurred to them on how they have been inconsistent with taking care of what mattered to them.

These are fundamental questions and despite their importance, these questions are avoided in most organizational contexts. And these are not avoided for any other reason, except that organizations are blind to the importance of these questions.

As we will see in this chapter, and in the rest of the book, we cannot avoid the Care conversation – it is *the* most critical conversation.

TAKING CARE OF THE CARE OF ANOTHER

Paul Spiegelman, former chief culture officer of Stericycle stated in his article on inc.com:[4]

> Why do we care? Why do we care so much that we built a complete framework to enable different avenues and methods of caring in our business? Because, besides being the right thing to do, caring has been a cornerstone of our consistent growth despite the tremendous economic swings of the past ten years.
>
> Sure, we know that caring for our employees is smart. Caring creates trust. Trust creates loyalty. Loyalty lowers costs, and helps maintain a protectable profit margin. But I'm not here to present a business case for a note-writing program in the office.
>
> We care about our employees in the totality of their lives.

While Spiegelman states that 'caring has been a cornerstone of their consistent growth', what he perhaps means is that the company has been providing opportunities for employees to take care of their cares, and that has been crucial in giving them consistent growth despite the ups and downs of the economy for the past ten years.

To care for another would mean to show that you care, show you share the care, take care to the extent you can, and do what you can to enable the other to take care. This is the blindness in the corporate world. As a manager and a leader, you may think you are taking care of your people. However, to take care of your people and to enable them to take care of their cares are two completely different games.

In my assessment, often when people take care of another, they do so because it is not too inconvenient for them, and importantly it suits them. *To take care of the care of another* is, in reality, taking care of the other. This is when you get challenged.

Remember, you do not take care of the other's care at the cost of your own care. Taking care starts with self-care.

The role of the leader or the manager, as a coach is to:

- Be connected to your own cares. You can do this by asking yourself these questions:
  - For the sake of what am I doing what I am doing?
  - Why does this work have meaning for me?
  - To take care of what care of the organization does this team exist?
  - What support do I need from my team members in taking care of my cares, my team's cares and the organization's cares?
- Find out what the cares are of your co-workers or team members. You can do so by asking questions such as:
  - For the sake of what do you work in this team or in this organization?
  - Does this work have meaning for you?
  - Why do you think this work has meaning for you?
  - Where do you see yourself two, five or ten years from now?
  - How do you see what you are doing today helping you get there?
  - What support can I provide to you?
- Distinguish the shared cares, and generate action inside of these shared cares.

Here is an extract of an article that I read on Ashish Ambasta's LinkedIn page:[5]

This is a small story but with profound learning for everyone reading it. It was a great moment when Kotak Mahindra Finance got its banking licence in 2003. Obviously, everyone right from top management to the last person in the company was excited being part of a new bank. The hard work for the last eighteen years had paid off and the company was going to realize its dream of being a bank in Indian market.

Media, like all the great events covered the story with great fanfare. One of the leading business publications interviewed Mr Uday Kotak, the MD of the company, who created a massive story of ringing in a new era of Indian banking with a new private bank. Interview went off well and things were in place except for when the magazine sent the front page for his approval. In the front page, a very professional image of Mr Uday Kotak was printed and the title at the bottom was 'Creating History'.

Somehow, Mr Kotak didn't like that. He didn't like the fact that the entire credit for creating the bank should be taken by him. He didn't want to be on the front page alone. He instructed to the magazine if there is any way in which every employee of the Kotak group could be on the front page of the magazine as everyone here had created history.

After a lot of deliberation took place but no solution could be found about how 2500-odd people can find a place on the

front page of the magazine, Mr Kotak suggested that we click the photograph of each employee and put them on the front cover of the magazine and each copy's cover be customized to gift it to them and show people that every employee mattered. This is how it looked for me at that point of time (2003): See adjacent photo.

Today, twelve years later, when I look at Kotak Mahindra Bank and its performance, it doesn't surprise me that they have become one of the largest Indian private banks performing extremely well and creating a distinct positioning in the Indian banking industry.

I love this example shared by Ashish. Recognition, praise, respect and acknowledgement are all great ways to take care of people. Each of these are generally hidden cares of many, and when you take care of this, you take care of their care.

In her book *Conversational Intelligence*, Judith Glaser elaborates on this aspect very well:[6]

> When we receive public praise or support, we unlock yet another set of neurochemical patterns that cascade positive chemistry throughout the brain. Highly motivated employees describe the feeling of performing well as an almost drug-like state (because of the dopamine and endorphins released by these interactions, it is indeed quite similar). When this state of positive arousal comes with appropriate, honest, and well-deserved (sincere) praise, employees feel they are trusted and supported by their boss. They will take more risks, speak up more, push back when they have things to say, and be more confident of their dealings with their peers.

Gary Kirsten, one of Indian cricket's most successful coaches in an interview to *The Indian Express* stated:

> 'Relationships, for me, are everything … In any team, I want them [the players] to become better. But, for me, to build those solid connections with people is why I wake up in the morning. It's less about the results.'
>
> When asked about his favourite coaches, he said, 'The best coaches that I worked with were the ones I wanted to play for. They genuinely cared about my performances – and cared

about me as a human being. Duncan Fletcher, Eric Simons and Bob Woolmer – they weren't in it for their own glory. I took a lot out of their coaching style, because it worked for me. Their style was first, about the growth of a player, and second, about performances. It's more important to let a player become a better one than it is to have a great season.'

Between 2008 and 2011, the period when Kirsten was India's coach, almost every player under his watch grew in leaps and bounds. Average cricketers became good, and the good ones played like greats. Even the greatest, Sachin Tendulkar, saw some of his most productive years under Kirsten. While they became better individually, the cricketers also matured as a unit. The Indian team became Team India: the team came first.

'The Indian way is more flair and instinct. It's more individualistic, while South Africa's is more team-oriented. Over here, in India, it's the individual who stands out,' Kirsten recalled. 'Now, the concept of team was very dear to me. [It was] a very strong South African way [of doing things], and we introduced that in the [Indian] environment. The players really enjoyed it. It became a common belief for us that the team is more important than the individual.'

Kirsten's face lit up whenever he mentioned Dhoni. Kirsten–Dhoni had been the very embodiment of the coach's philosophy of trust and relationship. Frequently, we tend to imagine a perfect relationship as one where those involved are always on the same page. Kirsten and Dhoni often disagreed, but they trusted each other.

'I will never forget this one incident in Bangalore,' Kirsten said. 'We were going to the Indian Air Force base to meet up with a couple of guys there and do a bit of training with them. And we were three South African members in the support staff. They wouldn't allow us because we weren't Indians. And M.S. Dhoni stood up and said, "We are not coming if you don't allow Gary and Paddy (Upton) and Eric (Simons) to come as well."

'That's a value system. He is standing up for us. And that's what we were about. As an Indian team, we stood up for each other. I knew that MS had my back, because he trusted me, because he knew that I had his back. We are very close as people. I am very close to MS. I trusted him with everything in a game of cricket. So, when you got relationships like that, you can do anything.'

CARE: CREATING ACTION AND RECONSTRUCTING YOUR EXISTENCE

We hopefully now agree that care is fundamental to being human. All humans have some or the other care. Humans may be blind to what their cares may be, but that does not mean they do not have a care.

I have treated CARE as an acronym for: Creating Action and Reconstructing your Existence. Let's build a shared understanding of each of these words/phrases:

- Creating
- Action
- Reconstructing your Existence

Creating

Humans are constantly in the process of creation. We are creators. Whether we know it or not, we are constantly creating our thoughts – consciously or subconsciously. In November 2010, I read an article of a young twenty-four-year-old lady who underwent a successful heart transplant. She was a state hockey player and a musician in a rock band based in Bengaluru. Her story had a huge impact on me. She was probably about ten years younger than me, probably fitter than I was – she was a sportswoman after all – and she needed a heart transplant. Her story moved me so much that I spent the next few days researching about heart transplants, the process of organ donation, and the current state of organ donation in India.

The story had an enormous bearing on me and I consciously created organ donation as a care of mine. Inside of that care, along with another founder, Tina Budhrani and a co-founder, Reshma Budhia, we created the Gift Your Organ Foundation. Till November 2010, organ donation was not even in my conscious awareness. I may have heard or read of kidney transplants in passing – but never with any attention. However, ever since I 'created' organ donation and the Gift Your Organ Foundation as a care of mine, there was a shift in the observer I was.

I have done hundreds of workshops for all kinds of participants, and across a myriad variety of organizations. Many of these participants have come back to me a few years later telling me how they have created new cares, and started to take care of these new cares. Hundreds of them got reconnected to their care for their organizations, and just that one move (of creating and getting connected to their cares), according to them, hugely elevated their results.

While we may have some existing cares, we have a choice in creating or recreating our 'cares'.

Pause for Reflection

'How do I know what I care for?' and 'How do I create my cares?' are some common questions I'm asked often. The one way to get a response to this is to become more present to what actions and what results add meaning to your life.

That which is meaningful to you is what you care about. That which is not meaningful to you is what you do not care about.

For example, for some people, meaning comes from making more money, for others it may be recognition, and for some others yet it may be making a contribution to the organization's cause. You should determine/create what is meaningful for you.

This is a first, yet crucial step.

Begin reflecting this question: What may be the different domains of your cares?

Action

It is important to create a distinction between activity and action. Activity is movement and doing. In my consulting work with organizations, I interact with several people who come to work every day, are involved in certain activities, and they go home.

Action, on the other hand, is different. It is activity that makes you take care of something that you care for.[7] So, if you care for the results of your organization, and do activity at work to generate those results, you are taking action.

Here are some claims that we make:

- Care is the fundamental context of all action. Without care, action is mere activity.
- How action is carried out also is shaped by our cares – for example, the intensity and seriousness of our actions would depend on the intensity and seriousness of our cares.
- Whether an outcome has meaning or value is also dependent on whether we care for that outcome.

So, once organ donation and the Gift Your Organ Foundation was 'created' by us, as something that we care for, we designed new actions to take care of this new care of ours. These actions were not available to us till we had created organ donation and Gift Your Organ Foundation as our cares. And once we created this as a care of ours, every outcome that moved forward the cause of organ donation, and every small milestone achieved by the Gift Your Organ Foundation had meaning and value for us.

If your cares are not backed up by action, I question your commitment to your cares. To take care is to commit to certain desired outcomes and take actions to achieve those outcomes.

Reconstructing Your Existence

As I have stated earlier, humans are beings of care. You cannot take away the element of 'care' from a human being's existence. However, what you can do is recreate your cares, and by doing that, you literally reconstruct your existence.

Thomas Jefferson, one of the founding fathers of America, and the principal authors of the Declaration of American Independence stated, 'Do you want to know who you are? Don't ask. Act! Action will delineate and define you.'

It is interesting, isn't it, that according to Jefferson, action 'delineates and defines' who you are. At the Institute for Generative Leadership, we take this claim of Jefferson a step further – we claim that action is taking care of what you care about. And if actions define you, it is because actions define your cares and your cares define who you are.

Let me elaborate using the same example of the Gift Your Organ Foundation. Till November 2010 the Gift Your Organ Foundation did not exist. It came into being because we chose to create organ donation and the foundation as our cares. When that happened we acted inside of these cares. The act of defining these cares as our cares, and then taking action to take care of these cares – by default reconstructed who we were in our own eyes, and also our identity in the eyes of the others.

In my blog, 'Professor "Begs" in Local Train to Educate the Poor',I had written about how Professor Sandeep Desai quit his job as a teacher in a reputed management institution and decided to take up setting up and running schools for the underprivileged in India.

I have also shared Prof. Desai's example in Chapter 4. I quote from that blog post, 'People choose their problems. Some choose their maids and drivers to be their problems; while others like Prof. Sandeep Desai make the country's lack of education their own personal problem.'[8]

I use reconstruction here differently from the way you understand the common use of this word. I use it to invite you to your choice in this moment to create – *'What is it that you care for?'*

You can, at this moment, choose to reconstruct your cares, and when you start to take action inside of these new cares, you would have reconstructed your existence to the extent you reconstructed your cares.

The question is – how do we reconstruct our cares? You can create or reconstruct a new care by the act of declaration. In my book *Declaring Breakdowns: Powerfully Creating a Future That Matters, Through 6 Simple Steps* I had distinguished the term declaration (compiling elements from distinctions provided by several experts), and here is what I had stated: 'A declaration is a speech and a listening act, made by a person of authority to do so, where he or she, out of nothingness brings forth a new possibility, a new future into existence that they own.'[9] You create a new care when your body, your emotions and your language come together – like they did with the creation of Gift Your Organ Foundation as my care.

I was touched and moved by the story of the young hockey player who needed a heart transplant. There was a disharmony I sensed in my body, and there was anxious energy to do something about it. And then, through the act of declaration, in words, the founders of the Gift Your Organ Foundation stated that we were going to be at the cause of transforming the organ donation scenario in this country.

Gautam Buddha said, 'As we think, so we become.' This shows the importance of language in creation. Further, Mathew Budd and Larry Rothstein in their book *You Are What You Say* quote Fernando Flores, 'In language we build our own identities, our relationships with others, the countries that we live, the companies that we have, and the values that we hold dear. With language, we generate life. Without language, we are mostly chimpanzees.'[10]

What Fernando Flores asserts when he uses the word 'build' is that we are 'creating' 'the values we hold dear' and 'with language, we generate (create) life'. We are all in the constant process of creation – whether we know it or not.

Pause for Reflection

Begin to consider what may be the different domains of your cares, for example, your family, your health, your organization's vision, your learning and development and so forth.

Do you think you are taking care of your cares?

THE CENTRALITY OF CARE IN GENERATING EXTRAORDINARY RESULTS

The results that individuals, teams and organizations generate have a great deal to do with their respective cares and commitments.

As leaders, one of our key roles is to provoke the creation or awareness of a care, a new commitment in our co-workers, rather than tell them what to do. Let's understand the relationship between cares, commitments, actions and results a bit more deeply.

We also respect the power of questions like 'what do I care about?' and 'what do we care about?'. Often it is not about creating new cares, but discovering it through the process of conversation.

To understand the importance of and the relationship between cares, commitments, actions and results, it is important to understand the Anatomy of Results, i.e., what the underlying structure is that generates results. This has been created by Bob Dunham, founder of the Institute for Generative Leadership, USA. Bob calls this structure the Anatomy of Action.[11] For me, this is more the anatomy of generating results, and hence I choose to call this the Anatomy of Results.

Here are some fundamental claims:

1. **Outcomes or results are a function of actions.**
   Actions alone generate results. Once you act, you get results based on the nature of your actions. Without action, there are no results.

   Often, we also 'decide' that no intervention or act will produce what we want, so we take the action of abiding with what is happening anyway. It is an active choice. The problem is that we often see it as no choice, and we give up our power to choose in the story and emotions of resignation. For example, the assessments we make such as 'I cannot make a difference', or 'I cannot go against authority', or 'I am not good enough to act' are stories that create a mood of resignation and give us our choice of no action.

2. **Action is shaped by commitment.**
   In the 1940s, the philosopher John Austin at Oxford showed us that we perform acts in languages that are not descriptive, but that generate commitments and the future. He discovered that when we make a promise, for example, we are not describing something in the world. Instead we are making an act, and the act is one of commitment – showing what the speaker is committed to – for the future.

   Our actions are shaped by commitments – the commitments we make or don't make, the clarity of the commitment, and the ownership and importance of the commitment to the person or organization committing.

3. **Commitments arise through conversations.**
   That action is shaped by commitment is crucial for our understanding of action in organizations. However, the next question that arises is, where do these commitments come from? The short answer: conversations. Even commitments with

ourselves arise through conversations, or can be traced back to earlier conversations. Commitment is what shapes and drives action, and commitments arise from conversations.

4. **Our care determines what commitments have meaning for us.** The quality, power and effectiveness of all our actions depend on our relationship with care. We can bring our care and concerns to our conversations, or let our conversations turn into unfulfilling discussions of transactions and activities. Our commitments have meaning when they are inside of our care.

Care is the energy of meaning, importance and ownership that infuses our commitments and action. Action in which we care about the performance and result is very different than if we don't care. A multi-year research project done by McKinsey and Company, whose results they have described in the book *The Progress Principle* found that of all the events that can deeply engage people in their jobs, the single most important is making progress in meaningful work.[12] Our claim is exactly that – our care determines what commitments have meaning for us.

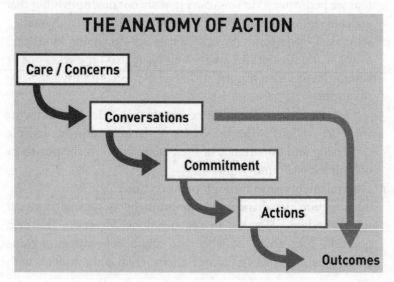

Figure 3.2: The Anatomy of Action.

The key claim of this diagram is that all results come from conversations. These conversations must integrate care and commitment into action.

POWERFUL QUESTIONS IN THE DOMAIN OF CARE

1. What are the different domains of your care? Have you identified them? What areas of your life give you a deep sense of satisfaction?
2. What is the desired outcome in each domain of your care?
3. What care are you taking care of at this moment?
4. What may be the different domains of care of each of your co-workers?
5. 'For the sake of what result' did you do what you did today/this week?
6. 'For the sake of what result' will you do what you will do today/this week?
7. Would you like to 'reconstruct your existence' by reconstructing your cares? If so, what may be your new cares?
8. Is your care aligned with the care of your team and your organization? Do you have a shared care?
9. What will you do this week to ensure that your care, your co-workers' cares, your team's care and your organization's care are aligned?

COMMON MYTHS

Myth: Care is not important in business.

Busting this Myth: Nothing can be further from reality than this. As stated earlier, care is the foundation of value, satisfaction and meaning. Organizations exist to take actions that are valuable and satisfying for their customers. They will cease to exist if they do not.

For a result to be valuable or satisfying for an organization – that result must take care of the care of the organization.

If the result is not inside of a care, that result is meaningless, and hence has no value.

Myth: 'I can generate results in areas I don't care for'.

Busting the Myth: Maybe you can generate results in areas that you don't care for. However, the question is not to generate any result whatsoever – the idea is to *generate results that matter*. The very fact that a result 'matters' is because that result is in an area of your care.

The claim of this book is to generate extraordinary results; these desired results must be cared for. When that happens, magic happens.

Look around you – there is adequate evidence. Millennials are generating extraordinary results in areas that a decade back would have seemed unlikely. They are producing billion-dollar ideas only by virtue of acting inside of what matters to them. In fact, there are thousands of others who are doing the same – acting inside of their cares, and achieving extraordinary success.

Myth: 'As a manager, I have nothing to do with the cares of my team members.'

Busting this Myth: On the contrary, as a manager, for you to be successful, it is critical that you are aware of the cares of your individual team members. Teams are made up of humans, and humans are beings of care. You cannot separate the cares of a human from the human itself. As a manager, when you connect to the care, you connect to the human – and when that happens, you create an opening for incredible results in your team.

The job of a manager is to choreograph actions with team members to generate results that matter to that team and the organization. To do so, leadership-coaching conversations are critical, and care is a key domain of leadership-coaching conversations.

Myth: 'As a manager, my job is to "manage" (to handle, direct, govern or control) my teams.'

Busting the Myth: A manager's crucial role is to be an effective coach of your team members. To better 'manage' their teams, managers need to have leadership-coaching conversations with them. If they are not equipped to do so (and most managers are not, while the irony is that many managers believe they are equipped to coach), this is one of the most critical skills they need to learn.

Myth: 'As a manager, my job is to get the work done, not to take care of the satisfaction of my co-workers.'

Busting the Myth: If you want sustainable results for the long term, as a manager you must ensure that your co-workers are satisfied and engaged. Imagine the levels of productivity and the kind of results a satisfied co-worker can generate, as against a co-worker who is frustrated, disengaged and generally dissatisfied. I have often come across managers who operate with the pre-set assumption that producing extraordinary results and having satisfied co-workers is not possible.

CREATING A SHARED CARE TO EXPONENTIALLY GROW BUSINESS
A case study by Umang Bedi

Here's an example of how connecting with the cares and passions of your employees can serve as one of the best retention tools for top talent within your organization. Interestingly, earlier on in our journey (at Adobe Systems, India) of building our digital marketing business in India, we found ourselves in a situation of trying to pitch a very large digital transformation project at one of the largest telecom operators in the country. During this process, we came across a woman on the customer side who was responsible for driving the online mobile and digital channels' business for that large telco, and that was about a billion dollars' worth of business at her hands. We found her extremely sharp, super creative and knowledgeable, and she spoke a language of digital and digital transformation with a certain maturity that we hadn't seen with too many other customers in the country.

Anyway, to cut a long story short, while the teams focused on driving that transaction and that project, and ultimately delivering customer success to that client, we started talking to her for an opening for her to join us as a leader for industry strategy. We found her refreshingly different and she spoke the language of business. And in a technology company, that's a really hard skill to find, because we are surrounded by geeks who love their products, love their technology, love what they create, and often live in this delusional world that it can solve world hunger. And here she was, with the knowledge of how technology can be applied to real-world business problems to solve real-world issues that clients have across diverse verticals. After a conversation that lasted over two to three months, we made an offer and she ultimately joined us as our leader of industry strategy.

What followed was three years of history in the making. Anjali was at the forefront of every strategic conversation that we were having with the largest brands in the country, with their CEOs, their CMOs, their heads of business, across banking, other telecom operators, Internet companies, mobile companies, media and entertainment companies, brands from diverse verticals, travel, tourism and hospitality. And she was at the forefront of the conversation – talking about digital transformation and how our technology could be used to deliver personalized, relevant, meaningful, contextual conversations, and for them to build digital businesses and drive digital transformation across the organization. Thanks to her, we had very large transactions taking place in the country.

She had been at the forefront of all those deals, all those discussions and negotiations with some of the senior-most strategic leaders in the country and had really delivered on her promise of helping organizations not only build the value of digital transformation but also drive digital strategy in the boardroom and associate key performance indicators (KPI's) and milestones along the journey for them to track on how their digital maturity and digital competency were actually improving across the entire process. She was one of the key individuals in whom we invested as key talent within the company, a rising woman leader within the company, and someone whom we deeply appreciated and valued.

One day, we had an interesting conversation with Anjali when she said she had decided that she wanted to leave it all to go back to her world of being a digital marketeer and running a digital business rather than assisting brands with that business. This came to us as a surprise because we should've seen it coming. It's just that we were living in our own world of happiness, because she was delivering such tremendous value for the company that we never saw what she deeply cared about, and that was running a digital business, owning the digital strategy, driving digital transformation and owning the business outcome. And we were kind of lost because we didn't see this coming, and this would have meant a tremendous loss to the company were she to leave the organization.

I think we understood her care, and we connected with it. We realized that the other side of our business – our digital media business, which is across our creative cloud and document cloud products – was going through a complete transformation in terms of routes to market because adobe.com, globally, had grown into a $1.5-billion-plus business and was growing at over 100 per cent, year on year. And that was a massive business opportunity to drive adobe.com and our overall marketing for adobe.com in the region. And we had this awesome candidate who would be brilliant at running that business, and we were struggling with that business because building an online business in India for software was hard.

But magic happened because we could relate with the care of Anjali. We understood that she was deeply passionate about building this online business, owning it as a business leader rather than just assisting brands build their own digital businesses. We quickly transitioned her to become the marketing leader for Adobe in the country. And that really did wonders because not only did it help retain her as key talent within the company, but it also helped us grow and transform our presence on adobe.com and grow that as a valuable route to market, which was an extremely profitable business for Adobe.

If you're able to connect with the cares of your employees, in time, you can use that as a retention tool. At times, some of their deep passions or interests, and their deep cares are where they can add value to other parts of your business, and it was better to have Anjali in that job than lose her to another competing company.

The best part about this was that on adobe.com Anjali was using all our digital marketing technology to grow the business, and today she is our number one customer within the company and serves as a reference with all customers who are evaluating our technology to embrace digital transformation. So, it was a bit like having our cake and eating it too. But she not only had transitioned into her role as the marketing leader building our dotcom business, but today stands as a reference customer testimonial in the market and talks to prospective clients on the impact of the technology in helping within her business.

This is a great example of how understanding an individual's care can not only lead to a great retention conversation but can also be invaluable in exponentially growing the business.

GENERATIVE PRACTICES

1. What may be the key domains of your cares or concerns? (For example: family, organization, health, personal development, social organization that you work for or volunteer, etc.)
2. Are you taking care of each of your cares? For each care, assess whether you are satisfied in how you are taking care of each care.
3. Where you are not fully satisfied, speculate on what may be the missing promises, and what actions can you take to take better care.
4. Have conversations with your co-workers on what their cares are. Get connected to their motivations to come to work, to do the project, to be a part of your team, the organization, and so forth.
5. Are you supporting your co-workers in taking care of their professional cares? Understand from them what you could do to support them in taking care of their cares. If there are areas you cannot support them, be honest with them. This is the beginning of a relationship where individuals can be open with each other, and build trust.
6. Keep the question 'For the sake of what' alive for everything that you do. Ask yourself this question several times in a day, and see if you come with an answer that works for you. This question is meant to test if the activity that you are doing is action inside of your cares, or meaningless tasks?
7. Journal your thoughts, reflections and what is opening up for you when you do the above practices. Make new commitments to yourself, inside of your cares.

4

COACH: OBSERVE

Everything we see is shaped by how we observe, what we pay attention to, and how we respond to it. We miss seeing the observer we are that enables us to see what we see. How we observe does not reveal reality, it reveals our history of learning how to observe.

The successful leader sees a different world than one that fails. The path of leadership is a path of learning what and how to observe for the sake of a future shared with others.

BOB DUNHAM

How would it be if...

- members of your team paused a few times during the workday, and observed *what* they were observing and *how* they were observing? What new choices could be available to them, and what would the impact of those be on your results?

- all members of your team recognized that they were being limited by their own blind spots, and became open to seeing the world with a new set of eyes?

- your team started to see new possibilities and actions, those that they had never seen before?

- your team was fully energized, moment to moment? What results could be possible then?

The world you see is a function of the observer you are. How you see your world determines your future, your possibilities and your actions.

This is one of the most important claims of this book. As a leader, if you understand and embody this claim, you will begin to lead your life, your team or your organization in a whole new manner and generate results that were previously unavailable to you.

I have a friend who lived in Mumbai and was in a high-flying banking job before he moved back to Punjab, a state in India where he had farms handed down from his ancestors. He took to organic farming as a profession. If he and I were to take a walk on his farmland (or any other land for that matter) and if we were to look at the same piece of land, do you think we would see differently?

Absolutely. He would try and identify potential for farming on that piece of land. Given his acquired expertise on the subject, he would possibly know what crops or vegetables would possibly grow there; while all I would see is mud, shrubs or stones.

Similarly, if my chartered accountant and I were to look at the quarterly numbers of an organization, do you think he and I would see differently? Without a doubt, we'd see different things. He would see the financial health of the organization, while all I would see is numbers.

The point is, as individuals, we may 'look' at the same thing, and yet 'see' different things. What we 'look at' is what is out there. What we 'see' is a function of what 'is in here'. The claim this section makes is that the world you see is a function of the observer you are. What you see is not just a function of what is out there, but is also always a function of how you see.

According to Brother David Steindl-Rast, 'It is no mere coincidence that the personal pronoun "I" in the English language cannot be distinguished by its sound from the word 'eye' for the organ of sight.'[1]

What a profound view! My understanding of this statement is that the 'I' and the 'Observer' are indistinguishable. In other words, 'you see what you are structured as an observer to see'.

The physical world out there is the same for everyone; however, the way we see the world or the way we perceive the world greatly differs from individual to individual. This is because each of us is uniquely structured biologically by our history to see our world and act in it.

In my book *Declaring Breakdowns: Powerfully Creating a Future That Matters, Through 6 Simple Steps*, I had distinguished between the physical world of facts that we live in, and the world that we observe.

Here are the important points recreated from that book:

1. One world is the physical world of facts the we live in.
    The other world is the world that we observe. We also live in this world like we live in the physical world.
2. The physical world is the same for all living beings.
    However, the world you observe is unique to you. It's exclusively your creation.
3. You can only describe the physical world – you cannot change it, or recreate it in the moment.
    Conversely, the world you observe is your creation – moment to moment (in your thinking and speaking). Most people are blind to this creation of theirs because it is usually automatic, and they hold what they create as 'the truth'. The moment they create the world they observe as 'the truth', albeit blindly, they give away their freedom and their ability to exercise choice. Awareness

creates choice. When we are aware we are an observer, we can begin to choose how we observe.[2]

4. In describing the physical world of facts, we talk about what's 'out there'.

But in the world that we observe, we reveal to others the way we see. Every individual sees this world differently, and what you see says more about you than what is 'out there'. For example, in interviews, questions asked by the interviewer are designed in a manner to get the interviewee to disclose the kind of observer he or she is. The more the interviewee speaks, the more he or she reveals the kind of person/the kind of observer he or she is. This is true everywhere, in team meetings, family conversations, strategy meetings – the more you speak, the more you disclose the observer you are (not necessarily [and rarely] to yourself, but to people around you).

5. In the physical world, the world comes first and then we describe that world in words.

Meanwhile, in the world we observe, the word comes first and then the world gets created (you speak and it gets created). For example, if we observe Ram to be unreliable, in the future we relate to Ram as unreliable. Ram is who he is. He is not who he is not. We create Ram as unreliable; and when we do so, we are disclosing our standards and the way we see.

6. Our moods and emotions do not impact the physical world of facts.

However, our moods and emotions greatly impact the world we observe. For example, when you're angry, the way you perceive your world and respond to it will be dramatically different from mine.

7. This physical world of facts is 'the' Truth. For example: Ram is the CEO of AAA Corporation. You cannot change this in the moment.

However, the world that you observe is 'your' Truth. For example: Ram is a brilliant CEO, or Ram is a terrible CEO. Depending on the observer, Ram is either a brilliant CEO, or

Ram is a terrible CEO (or as many different views as there are observers).

8. In this moment, the physical world of facts is the way this world is, and you have no choice in how it is.

   However, in the way you observe the world, you have all the choice. As a matter of fact, this world is the way it is because you exercise choice and observe it in the manner you do (whether you know it or not).

9. The way the physical world of facts is – is.

   The way you create the world you observe determines the possibilities that you have or the possibilities that you do not have. No wonder then, that in the same physical world of facts, some people see an abundance of possibilities, and yet, many others see an abundance of impossibilities.

10. The physical world of facts does not predispose you to any action.

    The world you observe not only predisposes you to action, it often propels you into action. The way you observe the world determines what actions you take.

11. The physical world of facts has no impact on your results.

    The way you observe the world has a great impact on your results. Because it is this world that predisposes you into action, and it is actions that give you results (see Table 4.1).

Table 4.1: Physical world of facts vs the world we observe

Physical world of facts	The world we observe
One world is the physical world of facts that we live in.	The other world is the world that we observe. We also live in this world like we live in the physical world.
The physical world of facts is the same for all living beings.	You are the only person living in the world that you observe. This world is exclusive to you.
You can only describe the physical world of facts – you cannot change it, or recreate it in the moment.	You create the world you observe – moment to moment (in your thinking and speaking).

Physical world of facts	The world we observe
In describing the physical world of facts, we are talking about what's 'out there'.	But in the world that we observe, we reveal to others the way we see. Each individual sees this world differently, and because of which – the way each individual sees discloses more about the person, than what is 'out there'.
In the physical world of facts, the world comes first and then we describe the world of facts with our words.	In the world we observe, the word comes first and then the world gets created (you speak and it gets created).
Our moods and emotions do not impact the physical world of facts.	Our moods and emotions greatly impact the world we see. For example, in the emotion of anger, the way I perceive my world, and the way I respond to my world, will be dramatically different from the way I perceive my world and the way I respond to my world in, let's say, the emotion of gratitude.
This physical world of facts is 'the' Truth. For example: Ram is the CEO of AAA Corporation. You cannot change this in the moment.	The world that you observe is 'your' Truth.
In this moment, the physical world of facts is the way this world is, and you have no choice in how it is.	In the way you observe the world, you have all the choice. As a matter of fact, this world is the way it is because you exercise choice and observe it in the manner you do (whether you know it or not).
The way the physical world of facts is – is.	The way you create the world you observe determines the possibilities that you have or the possibilities that you do not have. No wonder, in the same physical world of facts, some people see abundance of possibilities, and yet many others see an abundance of impossibilities.
The physical world of facts does not predispose you to any action.	The world you observe not only predisposes you to action, it often propels you into action. The way you observe the world determines what actions you take.

Physical world of facts	The world we observe
The physical world of facts has no impact on your results.	The way you observe the world has a great impact on your results. Because it is this world that predisposes you into action, and it is actions that give you results.

Pens, problems and possibilities

In my leadership programmes, I often speak about pens, problems and possibilities. There is a distinct difference in observing pens on the one hand, and problems and possibilities on the other.

Pens are physical entities. They exist independent of the observers. You can touch and feel pens. Either the pen is there, or not there – as a fact.

However, problems and possibilities are not like pens. You cannot touch and feel problems or possibilities with your hands. They do not exist independent of the observer. On the contrary they are wholly dependent on the observer. If the observer can see them, they exist, and if not, they do not even exist.

Interestingly, often when an event takes place; some observers see problems and yet there are other observers who see possibilities. Which means problems and possibilities do not exist 'out there'. If they existed 'out there', *everyone* would see either the problem or the possibilities, like everyone sees the pen. Which only means that problems and possibilities exist and only exist in the 'seeing' of the observer.

Problems and possibilities are not facts, like pens. They are a way seeing a fact (for example, an event takes place [which is a fact], and some observers observe the event as a 'problem', while some others observe the event as a 'possibility').

As leaders, we need to learn to observe our lives as always having an abundance of possibilities. We first need to develop the skill of 'listening for possibilities' ourselves, and then support our co-workers to do so too. If you listen for possibilities, you will find them. You just need to wear the lens to see possibilities, and develop the ears to listen to possibilities.

Remember, when you assess possibilities are over (and state something like 'it is not possible'), possibilities are not over (they never existed in the first place); it is from where you see (the observer you are) that those possibilities are over. If you tune yourself to listen for possibilities, you open a space for possibilities to show up. This fundamental stance that we can always create possibilities is our 'generative' context, reminding us that we can always invent possibilities and actions, not just be limited with ones from the past.

A COMPARISON OF ASSERTIONS AND ASSESSMENTS

An assertion is a claim of fact, which is either true or false, to a standard established by the community. Assertions can be substantiated or refuted through observation and evidence.

An assessment is a statement of evaluation, opinion or judgement. Assessments are neither true nor false. Instead they can be grounded* (supported by evidence) or ungrounded. Other words for assessments are stories, opinions, judgements, assumptions, etc.

When people speak, or think, they confuse between assertions and assessments and it is common for people to hold their assessments as facts. This is where the core of the difficulty lies. As I have stated in earlier chapters, we create our world (the observers we are) through our assessments, and then we forget we created this world – because we start to hold our assessments and assertions, as true, rather than perspectives and judgements.

This distinction of assertions and assessments, or of 'what is so' and 'what I am making of what is so' is critical. There are various statements that we make in passing and without noticing, that have an impact in the way we operate our lives.

Statements such as:

---

*   Please refer to the Glossary for meaning of 'Grounding of Assessments'.

- I cannot do this
- This is an impossible target
- The only way I can succeed is by doing this and this …
- This is a daunting task
- If only I had (this), I could achieve (that)
- I am not a morning person
- She is so annoying

All the above statements are assessments, and yet we say these as if these were assertions (and more importantly, we start to believe these are assertions). To get a little more rigorous, let's take this last statement 'She is so annoying' and discuss it:

The construct of the statement, 'She is so annoying', makes it sound like being annoying is a fact about that person. We make it sound like it is the same as other facts about her, such as:

- She is 5 feet 8 inches;
- She is a daughter of her parents;
- She is a sister of two brothers;
- She is a mother of one son;
- She is the general manager of a bank.

The above statements can be considered facts about her. Assertions are not dependent on the observer, and irrespective of who the observer is, the above statements remain as assertions.

However, when you say 'She is so annoying' – you say it like an assertion, which is like a claim of fact. It's almost like saying, 'She is 5 feet 8 inches tall.'

Once you have made this assessment, you subconsciously hold this as a fact and when you see her in the future, you continue to hold this true about her. You now have a present notion about this person and whatever she says will be seen with the lens of 'she is so annoying'.

Both these sentences begin with 'She is _____' making what comes after 'she is' a fact about that person. These sentences have been constructed similarly, yet, being 5 feet 8 inches tall is indeed a fact, and, being annoying is not a fact, it is your assessment of that person.

When you say, 'She is so annoying', you are actually saying:

'Given the observer I am, right now in this moment, I assess this person to be annoying.'

When you say it this way, you are now saying that annoying is not a property of hers. You are saying that it is *you* who assesses her as annoying at that moment and that you may change your assessment of her at a later date and time.

It is imperative to distinguish the distinctions between *assertion* and *assessment* and recognize that one is a claim of fact and that the other is just an opinion. Most often, we mix these up, and not create a distinction between these two terms. Let's see a comparison between Assertions and Assessments below (Table 4.2).

Table: 4.2: Assertions vs assessments

Assertions	Assessments
Assertions are claims of facts.	Assessments are opinions, judgements or subjective statements.
For example: Ram is the managing director of AAA Corporation.	*For example: Ram is brilliant at his work.*
Assertions belong to the thing being observed.	Assessments belong to the observer. Different observers will have different opinions. (Even if a group observes a thing in a certain way, the assessment still belongs to the group and not to the thing being observed. It becomes a group assessment.)

Assertions	Assessments
For example: Ram is the CEO of AAA Corporation. Here you are speaking about Ram's designation and the organization he works for.	*For example: Ram is brilliant at work. This is your assessment of Ram. There may be others who may not make the same assessment as you.*
Assertions can either be true or false.	Assessments cannot be verified to be true or false. However, assessments can be grounded or ungrounded.
For example: Rohit came late in yesterday's meeting by 30 minutes. If there was a camera recording the meeting, it could be proved whether Rohit came late or not. Which is the reason we state that assertions are claims of facts.	*For example: Rohit is unreliable. Rohit being unreliable cannot be generalized and cannot be proved true or false. However, you can give evidence of Rohit coming late for all meetings and hence you make a grounded assessment that Rohit is unreliable as far as coming to time for these meetings is concerned.*
Assertions reveal about the thing being observed.	Assessments reveal more about the observer / the standards of the observer than the thing being observed.
For example: John did not wish Peter or Anna 'good morning' on Monday morning.	*For example: Peter assesses John to be rude because he did not wish him 'good morning'. So, as per Peter's standard, that is being rude. John did not wish Anna 'good morning' too and as per Anna that does not mean John is rude.*
Assertions have to do with the past and the present.	Assessments set the context for the future.
For example: In yesterday's meeting Ram came late by 30 minutes.	*For example: Ram is unreliable and once you assess someone as unreliable, in the future you relate to that person as unreliable.*

Assertions	Assessments
Assertions are where language is most descriptive and least generative (the only speech act where language is descriptive).	Assessments are where language is extremely generative and creative.
For example: The dinner table is 10 feet by 4 feet. In this case I am describing a property of the table.	*For example: The table is big and we can play table tennis on it. In my language, I have created the dining table big enough for a table tennis match.*
Assertions are not influenced by moods and emotions.	Assessments are greatly influenced by moods and emotions.
For example: A stranger's elbow touches Chris.	*For example: In an angry mood, Chris assesses that the stranger 'should be keeping a safe distance' and yells at the stranger for not maintaining the distance. In a happy mood, Chris makes the assessment 'it's okay – it's a mistake' and smiles at the stranger.*
Assertions are 'what is so'.	Assessments are 'what you make of what is so'.
For example: The table is 10 feet by 4 feet.	*For example: I make this table big enough to play table tennis on it.*

Source: *Declaring Breakdowns: Powerfully Creating a Future That Matters, Through 6 Simple Steps*

Below are some examples of assertions and assessments (Figure 4.3).

Table: 4.3: Assertions vs assessments (examples)

Assertions (What is so)	Assessments (What I make of what is so)
Peter came one hour late to work.	Peter is not a disciplined manager.
My car had an accident.	I am now going to be inconvenienced and will find it difficult to get to work.

Assertions (What is so)	Assessments (What I make of what is so)
John dropped the bottle.	John is clumsy.
Susan's height is 5 feet 10 inches.	Susan is tall.
The temperature is 10 degrees' Celsius today.	It is cold today.
Karen to Angelica: 'Your target for this quarter is 2 million dollars.'	Angelica in her thoughts makes the assessment: 'This is impossible.'
I forgot my lines on stage.	I am shy that is why I forgot my lines on stage.
Husband to wife, 'Where is my book?'	Wife makes the assessment, 'You are so disorganized.'
Angelina did not complete the project on schedule.	Angelina is incompetent.
Father to his daughter (in a fit of anger) says, 'You are so stupid.' (That the father said this is an assertion, what he said is the father's assessment.)	The daughter, even five years later subconsciously, assesses herself to be stupid. She has now made this assessment her truth.

Source: *Declaring Breakdowns: Powerfully Creating a Future That Matters, Through 6 Simple Steps*

There are innumerable events that take place in our everyday lives. As humans, we by default pick and choose certain events and create our interpretations or assessments around them. In simpler words, we humans are story-making machines. As soon as an event occurs, we very quickly generate a story about it in our minds, and one of the traps we easily fall into is believing that this story is 'the truth'. Worse, we fail to recognize that we made up that 'truth'.

Let's see a typical day for Alan at work. Alan is a senior manager at a multinational bank. On one Friday, he enters his office premises totally engrossed in checking his emails on his phone. He does however hear the security man greeting and wishing 'good morning' to his colleague who is walking along with him. The security man does not greet Alan. Alan at that moment, very subconsciously assesses that the security guy does not respect him. He gives an angry glance to the security man.

> What was so (assertion) – The security man wished the other manager 'good morning'.
> What did Alan make of what was so (assessment) – The security guy does not respect me.

Alan goes towards his office, brushing off this seemingly unpleasant incident. At the coffee machine, he sees two women employees speaking to each other. Looking at them, he makes an assessment in his head: 'The weekend for them has already begun it seems ... they are wasting precious office hours chatting away.' He just shakes his head, makes a mental note about another point he needs to discuss in his weekly staff meeting about unproductivity, and moves on.

> What was so (assertion) – Two employees talking next to the coffee station.
> What did Alan make of what was so (assessment) – The weekend for them has already begun and that they are wasting their productive office time.

And the day continues.

This book is not about a hypothetical example of Alan. This book is for and about you. Human beings operate like I have described Alan above.

> An event takes place (what is so),
> human beings create a story, about what is so,
> hold the story to be the truth, and,
> forget that we created the story.

We then live our lives operating inside of a truth that we have created, having completely forgotten that we are the authors of these stories. We are empowered by these stories and sometimes we are disempowered by them. We become happy, sad, angry, frustrated, resigned, resentful and so on and so forth, all because of the stories that we create.

Pause for Reflection

What assessments may you be creating and holding to be the truth? (*This generally takes a fair amount of reflection. We hold our stories as facts, and it does not even occur to us that these can possibly just be assessments*).

OBSERVING THE OBSERVER: A KEY LEADERSHIP PRACTICE

Leadership is not about concepts – just being knowledgeable about concepts can make you arrogant. Leadership is about beginning with the practice of observing new distinctions, and then practising these distinctions. It is in the practising of distinctions that you become skilled. And leadership is a skill that needs to be developed through rigorous practice.

The key leadership skill that you as a leader need to develop in you first and then support your co-workers is the skill of 'observing the observer'.

Here, you observe the observer that you are; meaning that you develop the practice of becoming aware that you are always seeing from a perspective and context, and paying attention to 'seeing what you see'. It is markedly different from observing oneself (where you see yourself – in this practice you see what you see).

Before we go any deeper, let's ask ourselves: 'Why observe the observer?'

Short answer: To observe is to become aware.

Awareness means that something has been distinguished in our perceptual field, giving us the potential of paying attention to it and putting it into language. Awareness creates choice. Without awareness nothing exists for us. When we are aware we shape what we see, we can make choices about it. This is what we mean by observing the observer – how we see and observe.

Awareness is also the foundation of our power to act and interact with another. To be unaware is to be blind. By becoming aware, you are taking out the blindness that existed the moment before you became aware.

When we are unaware, we have no choice. The moment you become aware, you are presented with choice. The realization that awareness is the foundation of all action is behind the principle 'awareness creates choice'. We are literally aware only of what our bodies are trained to be aware of.

In a recent coaching call with John, a director of a successful consulting company in the US, he expressed his desire to write and share his knowledge with the world. He said, 'I have a lot of knowledge that I would like to share in the form of articles and blogs, but I am conscious of my reputation. I will not write any blogs or articles till I am convinced they will be of a very high standard.'

Take a moment to notice the observer John is: He sees that till his articles are not of high standard, he will not write articles; he perhaps sees that he may harm his reputation if his articles are not of high standard.

I asked him, 'How do you think your articles will be of a high standard, and what would you need to do to make your articles meet such standards?'

This question made John think. I could see a shift taking place in his mind, and suddenly, John had an 'aha!' moment.

He said, 'Good question! If I don't write, how will I get good at writing? For me to get good at writing, I need to get enough practice. The more I write, the better I'll get.'

Suddenly, we had a new observer in John. Just one powerful question, and the observer in John had shifted. He now observed that for him to get good at writing, he needed to practise writing. John went from what he would not do to what he would do in order to produce his desired result.

Let's presume you were John's manager and if you focused on the action domain, and not on the observer John was being – it would have been difficult to get John to take motivated action to generate the desired result. By shifting the observer John was, we automatically shifted his actions, and hence the results he could now generate.

ENERGY FOLLOWS ATTENTION

Yet another related claim is, 'Energy follows attention.'[3]

Just for a moment, pause and pay attention towards your breathing.

You are inhaling … and you are exhaling …

While reading, perhaps, you did not even notice that you were breathing. This process was going on, even while you were reading – but you may have been blind to your breathing.

To choose to observe is to choose to be aware of your awareness and attention.

When I asked you to pause and notice your breathing, did you observe that when you pay attention towards your breathing, chances are your breathing became a little deeper, and maybe even a little slower?

The moment you pay attention towards your breathing, you sent energy there, and with that energy, your breathing became deeper. With your attention, there you had choice and could shift what was going on.

Awareness and attention are the foundations of our power to act and interact with another.

OBSERVER–ACTION–RESULTS

All organizations and individuals are interested in results. But what generates results? Short answer: actions. Results are a function of the actions you take. And when I refer to results, I mean good and bad results, or desired and undesired results. A result is a result, no matter how good or bad. Also, when I refer to actions, I consider the absence of any action as an action too. So, if I do not take any action, I still have a result. However, that result may not be an acceptable result, but yet it is a result.

So results are a function of actions (results here include all results and actions include no actions). I take actions, and I get the results. If the results that I get are acceptable to me, I move on to new actions to generate new results. However, if I take actions and I do not get the results that I want, what do I do?

When I ask this question in my workshops, I get some of these answers:

- take better actions
- take more actions
- work harder
- take more refined actions

Let's presume I do all the above and at the end of it I still do not get the results that I want or my desired result. What do I do? Some people in my workshops have even said, 'Forget this result and move ahead.'

Sure, that's one possibility, which you may not be okay with (because this is a result you deeply care about).

This is where the Observer–Actions–Results model comes in.[4] Like I stated earlier, all results are a function of the actions that you take. Similarly, every action you take comes from the observer you are.

Different observers take different actions

While actions generate results, it's the observer you are that gives you the actions that you take. And if you are not getting the result that you want, by all means try taking more action, implement them better, work harder and if you still do not get the results you want, it may be time to question the observer that you are who is taking these actions.

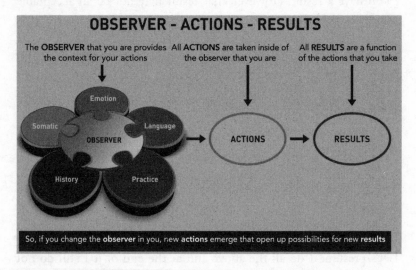

Figure 4.1: Observer–Actions–Results Model[5]

Above, we looked at how John became a new observer, and as a new observer, new actions opened up for John, and when he took the new actions, he generated new results.

New Observer = New Actions = New Results

Let's take another example of my experience with Prof. Sandeep Desai:

This was sometime in September 2012. I had a meeting with the health secretary in the Government of Maharashtra. I was hoping to meet him to introduce him to the concept of the Green Heart Driver's Licence*. I was trying to set up a meeting with him for a few weeks and finally got an appointment one evening at 6 p.m. I was already tied up in meetings in Andheri (a suburb in Mumbai, India) till 5 p.m. It was going to be impossible for me to drive from Andheri (north Mumbai) to VT (south Mumbai) in one hour at that peak hour. So, I decided to jump on to the Mumbai local train.

After many years, over 12–15 years maybe, I boarded a fast train from Andheri to get to Churchgate. What followed soon after I boarded the train was nothing short of fascinating. I was catching up on news on *The Times of India* Blackberry Application and reading about the resignation of one of the ministers in Maharashtra's legislative assembly. I then noticed a 'beggar' who was well dressed and who introduced himself loudly in the first-class compartment of the train in a deep, sure voice stating:

'Good evening Gentlemen, my name is Professor Sandeep Desai. I am here to seek your financial help'.

Just hearing the word 'professor' caught my attention. A professor? Begging? In a local train? Someone who spoke such immaculate English? He could get a job anywhere, I thought.

---

* Green Heart Driver's Licence is a project by the Gift Your Organ Foundation, of which I am one of the founders. This project commenced in Bengaluru, Karnataka, on 23 July 2012. Through this project, applicants applying for a driver's licence through select RTO offices are given an option to pledge their organs, and if they accept to pledge their organs, an 'Organ Donor' sticker is pasted on their licence.

I was now more interested in what he was saying than reading about the minister's resignation. The professor continued:

'Those who donate food to the poor, sort out their problem only for a day. But if the donations are made for their education, it can resolve their life.' He added, 'Education gives you the power to change your life. So, I decided to set up an English-medium school for the poor.

'So far, we have managed to start four schools in Maharashtra. The fifth school will be set up in rural Rajasthan. We have already bought land there and construction will start soon.'

He then took out a folder from his bag and started to show press articles that appeared in well-known Indian newspapers. He also claimed to have won the Real Hero award by the TV channel CNN-IBN (now called News18). Here was a 'real hero' begging in a train. (I made a mental note to see if he indeed had won this award, and yes he had! I actually checked.) After he had showed us these articles, he developed adequate trust in the eyes of the passengers of that train compartment.

Prof. Desai then took out a plastic donation box and went around to everybody in the train compartment seeking donations. Some people put in Rs 5, some put in Rs 10, some put in Rs 100, and I saw two people putting in Rs 500 in the donation box. Prof. Desai received all the money with the same amount of appreciation and gratitude, by bending a little forward and saying 'thank you'.

After receiving this, Prof. Desai got off at the next station. I suspect he boarded another compartment at the next station.

I just could not get the professor out of my mind. I went ahead to my meeting with the health secretary. It was a fabulous meeting. It was the first ever meeting with the health secretary that eventually culminated in us starting the Green Heart Driver's Licence project in Maharashtra too. However, despite that fabulous meeting, I was still reeling from the chance encounter with the professor.

So, I started to look him up on the Internet. His number was quite easy to locate. I got back to Andheri and called him. I introduced myself and asked him:

'Prof. Desai, what is it that makes you beg in local trains for money? Would it not be easier to go to organizations and seek sponsorships from them? Chances are you would receive a lot more money?'

I could sense him smiling at the other end. He responded, stating:

'Mr Dua, that's exactly what I thought earlier. I went to every organization that I could think of in the first year. I spoke to them. I made presentations to heads of the corporate social responsibility [CSR] departments of these organizations. I asked for money in different ways I thought was possible. But all I received was small change from them. This money was not enough to set up even the first school.'

'I asked myself this question,' he said, '"For the sake of what am I doing this work?" The answer that popped up was, "I am doing this for my country." The next question that came up for me was, "Who will benefit the most with the underprivileged of this country getting educated?" The answer that came up was, "My countrymen." Next, I asked myself, "If my countrymen would benefit the most, whom should I go to for seeking funds?" The answer was a no-brainer: "I should approach my countrymen for funds."

'And then the last question: "Where would I find the highest density of my countrymen to go and ask for funds?" Of course, it had to be Mumbai and its local trains. And guess what, I started to go to local trains and began seeking funding. As I mentioned in the train compartment, I have already set up four schools from the money that you call "begged" and am now setting up the fifth school.'

So, here, if you look at the Observer–Actions–Results model, the results that Prof. Sandeep Desai had after the first year, in his words, were 'small change'. His result was almost 'no result' – not enough to even set up the first school. When he became a new observer, he asked himself new questions, and the new observer looked at going to local trains to seek money. By being this new observer, he had a breakthrough result – he set up four schools and the fifth one was then being set up. He didn't just work harder at getting donations from organizations, he changed where he put his attention and actions.

I run a foundation too, and the observer I was, it was not even available to me, as a possible action, to go to local trains and seek funding. The observer I was, prior to this chance meeting with Prof. Desai, was that funding can be sought from organizations, doing fund-raising events, selling merchandise, etc. – all the standard ways an NGO raises money.

Here was Prof. Desai, who was a completely new observer, and as a new observer, took new actions (please note, I am not talking about 'better actions' or 'more actions'). And these new actions gave Prof. Desai 'new results' (again, please note, I am not talking about 'more results' or 'better results').

As a leader, when you practise observing the observer you are, you practise giving yourself a choice in the way you see a situation. This becomes particularly useful when you are not generating the desired results. You can choose to be a new observer then, choose to take new actions, and generate new results.

OBSERVER = SELPH

At the Institute for Generative Leadership, we use SELPH[6] (pronounced as SELF), as an acronym to explain what we mean by 'Observer'.

- **S:** *Somatics (The Body):* The term 'somatics' derives from the Greek word *somatikos*, which signifies the living, aware, bodily person. It posits that neither mind nor body is separate from the other; both being a part of a living process called the soma. The soma is often referred to as the living body in its wholeness; somatics, then is the art and science of the soma. Richard Strozzi Heckler has provided this understanding of Somatics in his book *The Art of Somatic Coaching*.[7] When there is a shift in the observer of an individual there is a shift in the body. Correspondingly, when there is a shift in the body, there is a shift in the observer. Your access to another person is through his or her body. A person's body exposes how he or she is feeling internally, and a good leader uses the signs shown by the body of the co-worker to understand what is going on with them. Similarly, your body is also your access to understanding how you are feeling.

  It is a leadership practice to listen to what one's body is stating. Many leaders 'think from their gut' – what these leaders are actually doing is 'listening to what their bodies are saying'. The more you practise listening to your body (and to the body of your co-workers) – the more skilled you will get at it.

  To be a new observer means to show up in a different body. For example, contract your body as much as you can, and then see your problems with this body. As against expanding your body, spreading your arms, opening your fingers, spreading your feet, and now see your world inside of this body. Our claim is that the body in which you observe the world impacts the way you see your world. Correspondingly, the way you see the world impacts your body too.

  You will notice some people live their lives in closed bodies; in contraction. Chances are, you will notice, these people do not see possibilities in their life. And then there are others whose bodies are generally in expansion – you will notice, chances are, that they have a high regard for their life, and for the possibilities in their life.

- *E: Emotions and Moods:* Emotions are our reactions triggered by events; and, moods are long-term emotional states and are not triggered by events. We have been led to believe that emotions and moods have no place in the corporate world. This is a huge misconception. You cannot disengage a human being from his or her emotions or moods. Imagine the productivity of an individual or a team in the emotion or mood of 'resignation'; as against an individual or a team operating in the emotion or mood of 'ambition'. The results each of these individuals or teams will deliver will be very different. A shift in the observer of an individual has a lot to do with a shift in the emotional state or mood of the individual, or that of a team.

- *L: Language.* Most people understand language to be descriptive. They are blind to the generative power of language. It is in language that they create their future and their present. When there is a shift in the observer, it means that the particular individual has shifted the way he or she creates his or her world. The job of the leader and the manager is to enable the co-worker to shift the way the co-worker is creating his or her world, and when that happens, there is also a shift in the way the co-worker shows up in the world.

- *P: Practice.* When there is a shift in the observer, it opens doors to let the individual take on new practices. It is only through practice that a person can change his or her embodiment. Charles Duhigg in his book *The Power of Habit* states, 'One paper published by a Duke University researcher in 2006 found that more than 40 per cent of the actions people performed each day weren't actually decisions, but habits.'[8] Through practice, we invite leaders to change their habits.

- *H: History.* We are all historical beings, and our history can deeply impact our present. When you become aware of how your history impacts your present, you give yourself a choice; one which you did not have till you had the awareness.

Said simply, when there is a shift in the observer of an individual, it means:

- The external environment in the world has not changed, however, the person has begun to observe the world differently;
- The possibilities they see change;
- Their emotions change;
- The way they comport themselves changes;
- The actions that emerge for them changes;
- And the way others see them may also change.

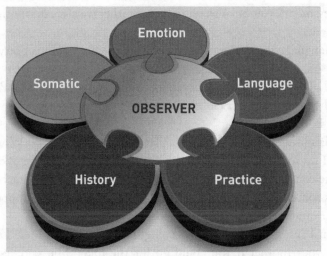

Figure 4.2: Elements of SELPH

OBSERVING BODY, EMOTIONS AND LANGUAGE

From the earlier example of John, you will note that John was not even aware that he was living in the 'assessment' that he would not write any blogs or articles till he was convinced they would be of a very high standard.

The moment he became *aware* that he was living in this 'assessment', automatically he created another 'assessment': 'If I don't write, how will I get good at writing? For me to get good at writing, I need to practise writing. The more I write, the better I will get.'

Like John, you (and our co-workers) are living in some assessment or the other, and are not even aware that you/they are living in this assessment. So, the first step is to distinguish, or become aware of the assessment you/they are living in.

Just the simple awareness of the assessment you are living in may give you a choice whether or not you want to continue living in that assessment. You realize that if you can observe in one way (create one assessment), you can also observe in another way (create another assessment).

Our language (assessments) is just the one element of the observer we are. As we discovered above, an observer is the coherence of SELPH. While we speak of each of these elements of SELPH distinctly, each of these is closely related and coherent.

Here is an example.

My daughter's skating group was planning to go on a hike. When I picked up my daughter from school at 3 p.m. that day, she asked me if she could go for the hike. I told her that I had no problem, but this was something that needed her mother's permission. I dropped her home and left to go back to my office.

When I returned home that evening, I asked my daughter, 'Did you ask your mother if you could go for the hike?' She said, 'Not yet dad, mom's been a little frustrated with the little twins and I am waiting for her to be okay so that I can get a yes.'

This statement made me think – how do you 'look at' frustration as an emotion in another person.

You cannot. What you look at is the body, and the body is a representation of the emotion you are in. What my daughter did was 'looked at' her mother, felt what was triggered in her own body from what she saw, and based on the body in which her mother showed up to my daughter, my daughter assessed the 'assessment' her mother was living in, and even assessed her emotion.

Similarly, you can hear the tone of the voice. The tone of the voice, which is part of body, will often enable you to assess the emotion of another.

If you see a man walking on the road, slowly, with his back slightly bent forward, and shoulders drooping – what emotion would you assess he is in? Dejected and sad, maybe.

Similarly, if you see a man walking with a spring in his step, singing along while walking, what mood would you assess he is in? Happy and cheerful, maybe.

Here are a few more examples of the coherence of the body and emotions:

- A smile may be the body response to happiness;
- A tear in the eye may be the body response to sadness;
- Gritting of your teeth may be the body response to anger or a similar emotion;
- An uneasy feeling in the stomach is the body responding to an emotion of fear.

Different people have different body responses to different emotions; I've listed above only the general observations for purposes of your understanding. For example, someone may even smile out of sarcasm; or have tears of happiness in their eyes.

However, what I am trying to stress on here is that you cannot 'look' at the emotion of another. What you can only do is 'look' at their physical self and assess their emotion.

Similarly, there is coherence between body and language.

There is generally a distinct body of a person speaking when they are:
- proud of something
- sharing good news
- sharing bad news
- declaring the vision of his/her company

Every moment, we are engaged in the process of creating our own world. Our inner voice is constantly communicating and reacting and making up this world. This internal conversation that we have with ourselves gives us our mood and the body in which we live.

When we alter our conversations, we alter our emotions and our body.

When we alter emotions and moods, we alter our conversations (internal and external) and our body.

When we alter our body, we alter our emotions and our conversations.

Our body, emotion and language are all braided together. While we do look at each of these individually, we are the coherence of all these elements.

Here is a table just to give you an indicative idea of the coherence between body, emotion and language (Table 4.4). To keep it simple, for each of the emotions, I am only stating 'open', 'closed' or 'neutral' as far as the body is concerned. The body is a whole new domain, and I am choosing not to go deep in this domain in this book.

Table 4.4: Coherence of Body, Emotion and Language[9]

Emotion / Mood	Language	Body
Ambition	I assess that there are future possibilities for me here and I am committed to take action to make them happen.	Open
Trust	Based on your past record (performance/actions) I assess that you will fulfil your promises to me.	Open

Emotion / Mood	Language	Body
Wonder	I don't know what is going on here. I see possibilities for myself here and I like it.	Open. If you made the assessment 'I don't know what is going on here. I don't see possibilities for myself here and I don't like it', you would easily move to the emotion of 'anxiousness' and a closed body.
Boldness	I will take the initiative to act even though I am unsure or scared.	Open
Acceptance	What is − is. I may not agree with it, but I accept this is how it is.	Neutral
Despair	I assess immediate negative possibilities for myself here. I assess no one can take action to change this.	Closed
Resentment	I assess that you have closed possibilities for me. I hold you responsible for this, and I am committed to not having a conversation with you about this.	Closed

Emotion / Mood	Language	Body
Confusion	I don't see what is going on here. I don't know what to do next. I don't see future possibilities for myself, and I don't like it.	Closed
Arrogance	I claim that I already know and my assessments are true. There is nothing else you can add here, and you should listen to me.	Closed
Anger	This is not fair and I don't like it.	Closed
Fear	There is danger ahead – either to my physical self, or to my identity.	Closed
Resignation	I assess that nothing is going to get better here; it has always been and it will always be this way; and there is nothing I can do about it.	Closed

I could list several more emotions, the associated assessments and body dispositions. However, the point here is to only show you the connections between body, emotions and language.[10]

Pause for Reflection

- What would you assess is the mood of your organization?
- What would you assess is the mood of your team?
- What would you assess is the mood of your family?
- What would you assess is the mood of each of your team members and family members?
- What would you assess is your mood?
- Based on the mood and body disposition, can you assess the story they/you live?
- What can you do to shift this mood, language and body disposition so that you shift the observer they/you are; to take new actions and generate new results?

OBSERVING PRACTICES

Your body is always in some practice or the other. And the way you operate today is the way you have practised operating for the past several years. Basically, what you are aware of is what you have practised being aware of.

This is a tall claim and I'm going to illustrate this with an example to make it convincing. One of my coaching programme participants, a senior manager in an IT-enabled services firm, had created for herself a world where she felt no one loved her and she believed that most people in her world even hated her. This was her 'assessment'. Every event, every twitch on the face of a colleague, every smile on the face of a friend was interpreted as a mock pointed towards her.

In my interactions with her, she discovered that the first time she ever thought like this, or felt victimized, was when she was seven years old. Her family had sold their house and moved into a small rented apartment to pay off the debts taken by the father for a business he set up and that went into losses.

She went up to her father, who by then had started to exhibit signs of constant frustration, to show him a poetry piece that she had written and that had won her an award in her class. Her father yelled at her: 'I'm not interested in you or your stupid poetry – leave me alone!'

Her father stated what he stated. However, what is of consequence is the 'assessment' she (subconsciously) created when her father said what he said.

We learnt soon that her first assessment was that her father did not love her. She then extended this assessment by convincing herself nobody loved her. Once she created this assessment, she subconsciously moved her attention to see who did not love her.

And then, like I stated above, every event, every twitch on the face of a colleague, every smile on the face of a friend was interpreted as a taunt aimed at her. This was the observer she became, and the world she created from that point of view.

If you practise focusing your attention on how much people dislike or hate you, what you will find is how much people dislike or hate you. It's simple because energy follows attention.

To get out of this dwindling spiral, this lady needed a generative practice to observe her habit of making up this assessment of how everyone hated her. When she discovered that she was making these assessments, and that it was she alone who was responsible for them, it suddenly dawned upon her of how she had been living her life. She had a huge breakthrough – awareness creates choice, after all.

It was not that she immediately stopped making such assessments. This was her practised way of life from a very early age. However, she developed a habit of observing that she was making these assessments, and gradually developed another practice of creating assessments that energized and empowered her. (The new perspective she brought forth on the incident with her father was that her father was going through a bad time in life, and that there was more than adequate evidence of him loving her – it's just that she had ignored all this evidence until then.)

The more she observed, the more she got skilled at it and trained her body to be aware. She developed a new way of being through designing new practices for herself.

Pause for Reflection

- Which of your practices may you be blind to?
- Which of your practices may not be working for you?
- What new practice would you like to create for yourself?

OBSERVING THE OBSERVER IN YOU AND OTHERS

In conversations with your co-workers, I am inviting you to observe two things:

- Observe the observer you are; and
- Observe the observer your co-worker may be.

Build a practice to observe:

- the automatic, habitual assessment that you create;
- the emotion that assessment predisposes you to (what possibilities and actions it opens and closes);
- the body that gets generated because of that assessment and emotion;
- what is your practised response; and
- what your history is that gives you this particular assessment, emotions, body and practices.

Each observer is predisposed to generate a certain set of results.

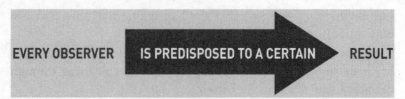

EVERY OBSERVER   IS PREDISPOSED TO A CERTAIN   RESULT

Figure 4.3: The direct relationship between the observer you are and the
results you generate

Once you observe the observer you are, what result are you
predisposed to generate?

Does that result work for you? If yes, great, continue being that
observer.

However, if that result does not work for you, give yourself the
choice to create a new assessment, choose a new emotion, and/or
choose another way to comport yourself.

You can be an effective leader, only if you are operating from a stance of choice

In a leadership conversation, every now and then, your own
assessments will get triggered, your emotions will get generated and
your body will produce certain reactions to comments of your team
members. In these moments, so that you do complete justice to your
co-worker, observe the observer you are and choose to be an observer
that duly serves the results of your team. (We will discuss more on
this in the chapter on 'Holding Space of Conversation'.)

Observe the observer your co-worker is

First, why observe the observer your co-worker is? For the same reason
why you should observe the observer you are. To become aware of the
way the co-worker is 'seeing' the situation. The way your co-worker
observes will determine what actions he or she will take; and the actions
he or she takes will determine what results he or she will generate.
These results will impact your team's (and organization's) results.

You can observe the observer your co-worker is using either one of these three doorways:
- Body
- Language
- Emotion

The co-worker's body, emotional state and language can give you an indication of the observer he or she is.

Sometimes, through the process of leadership-coaching conversations, you may reach an impasse, and every time that happens, and you do not know how to proceed forward, you can invite the co-worker to share their assessments, or their emotions or how they feel in the body. This will open up new access for you to take the leadership-coaching conversation forward.

POWERFUL QUESTIONS ON THE OBSERVER YOU ARE, AND THE OBSERVER YOUR CO-WORKER IS:

1. What actions do your assessments set you up for?
2. Will these actions generate the results you have committed?
3. If not, what new assessments can you make?
4. What emotion does the current circumstance cause in you?
5. Does this emotion support you in generating the results you have committed to?
6. If not, what new emotion may help?
7. What would you need to do to move into that emotion?
8. What do you think is the mood of your family, your team and your organization?
9. What is your hidden assessment driving your actions, and is it working for you?
10. If not, what new assessment would you like to create for yourself?

11. How can you see the world differently such that you give yourself an opportunity for a breakthrough in this area of your life?
12. Do you think you can frame your concern differently (be a new observer), so that new actions open up for you?
13. What could be a massive opportunity for you, or for your organization?
14. If you listen for possibilities, what may you see as possible for you and your organization?
15. What is the connection between the observer you are and your performance? What new observer can you be to significantly enhance your performance?

COMMON MYTHS

Myth: Language is only for academics and grammar teachers.

Busting the Myth: This is personal – I thought so too, till I learnt the real power of language in the creation of my world. Language is fundamental to our happiness and we are all linguistic beings. What we observe has a lot to do with the stories or assessments we create based on the event that has occurred. This rationalization lives in language, as an internal conversation, and it is this rationalization that is used to take action in the world.

When I use the word 'language' here, I certainly do not mean a particular language. It is the phenomenon of language, what language does, and is not restricted to any one or a few languages.

Myth: 'The world I see is the way the world is.'

Busting the Myth: Yes, to the extent you are talking about the physical world around us. But that's it. All your actions come from the world that you are structured to see, not from the physical world of facts. And this world is different for every human on this planet. Once you become aware of this, you have a choice to recreate this.

The world that we create comes from the coherence of SELPH, which is unique to each individual.

Myth: Emotions have no role to play in the corporate world.

Busting the Myth: It is critical to recognize that emotions shape actions. I have dealt with this in the body of this chapter. You cannot distinguish or separate a person from his or her emotions. Your co-workers are a coherence of SELPH, which is Somatic (body and mind), Emotions, Language, Practice and their History. If a person is in an emotional state that disempowers him or her, what actions and results can you expect from that person? It is the role of the manager or the leader to shift the stories of your co-workers that cause these disempowering emotions. Wishing that these disempowering emotions would go away on their own is living in a world of fantasy.

Emotions are contagious. If someone is in an empowering or a disempowering emotion, he or she could impact others with their emotions.

As a manager or a leader, it is our choice to support our co-workers in generating empowering emotions and moods – or we pay the price for not doing so (by compromising on the results that can be potentially generated).

Myth: Results come from hard work.

Busting the Myth: That results come from hard work is by itself an interesting story. If the observer makes this assessment, the actions he or she takes is that of hard work. Does that mean he or she generates desired results? Not necessarily. Results come from actions, and actions come from the observer you are. While action is critical, the lesser understood and known element in this is that of the observer you are. A lot of people work hard, and yet do not have results to show for the hard work they do. Which is why the 'observer' is the key. People, with increasing frequency are asking themselves, 'How can I or others generate an extraordinary result by doing the least amount of work?' It's about being perpetually in the search of this answer. The growth in industry, and the IT revolution is an example of people asking this question.

RECREATING THE STORY OF YOUR INDUSTRY
A case study by Umang Bedi

Brands like Facebook, Uber, Airbnb, and Alibaba began the process of disruption in their respective industries from within. Not only are they changing the rules of the game in their own industry – which they are literally creating from scratch – but their employees can observe such a large opportunity, that they are now beginning to disrupt associated industries as well. What's incredible is that all these firms are going about that journey with relentless passion and focus.

Think about it: Facebook is the largest media brand in the world today, yet it owns no media content or assets. None of the content is really theirs; it's been co-created and produced by all the consumers who are on Facebook as users. And then they are disrupting the news industry, the media and entertainment industry, the broadcast industry, and the video industry. They're literally going out with that disruption and owning mobile and owning social media as a channel like never before.

Facebook as an organization is an observer looking to connect every human being in this world, one connection at a time. And that mission has galvanized the entire organization to produce such disruptive technology.

Think about Uber. Today, it is the largest transportation company in the world and yet it does not own a single vehicle. What a unique observer again! Imagine the audacity of this story – to set up the world's largest transportation company, and yet not own a single vehicle. Uber has gone about this entire journey by disrupting not only the taxi market, but also the automobile industry. After all, people who are considering buying cars, or a second car, are now putting the idea on the back burner and opting for Uber.

The pattern is similar with Airbnb, now the largest hospitality portal in the world. It makes more revenue than the top three hotel brands put together, and they don't own a single real estate or a hotel asset. They too are going about this disruption by truly disrupting the revenues of the travel industry, and making homeowners giving out their homes on lease as a new option for travellers keen to explore the world.

Each of these companies, whether it's Facebook or Uber or Airbnb or Alibaba are going about this entire process by expanding the lens, broadening the observer, showing their organization and their teams what the future could look like, and driving total disruption, and digital transformation to create a completely new category of industries. In the process, they have disrupted other physical bricks-and-mortar industries that have been around since time immemorial.

That's the impact of being a new observer, and inviting your team to be a new observer. Each of these organizations have reconstructed what their markets are. For example, a typical taxi company's market would be people looking to rent a taxi. Uber recreated the story of the industry and expanded that market, to people not only looking to rent a taxi, but also those owning and looking to buying new cars.

GENERATIVE PRACTICES

1. Allocate a time daily and observe the observer that you are. Identify situations in your day where you could bring forth a different observer in you.
2. Think of someone you know whom you noticed in a state of excitement and enthusiasm: How did you know that that person was in this mood? What did you 'see'? Now think of the same

person in the mood of dejection and resignation: How did you know that that person was in this mood? What did you 'see'?

3. Also, take a moment to think of when you are in a mood that de-energizes you – how does the body feel when you are in such a mood. Also, think of when you are in a mood that energizes you – how does the body feel when you are in such a mood?

4. Observe the emotions and the body language of your co-workers. The physical self they show up in speaks a lot about the mood they live in, and the results they generate. The practice of observing your mood and your body, and that of others, will help you, as a leader, get a sense of the world your co-workers live in.

5. When was the last time you generated an extraordinary result in your professional or personal life? Was it because you took 'more action' or because you shifted the observer you were, or maybe both? Get your present to the times you shifted the observer you were, and your actions shifted – and hence your results shifted.

6. List assessments that you have about your co-workers, important people in your life, and any other key entities. Recognize that these are just your assessments and not the truth. The question you must ask yourself: Does it serve you to observe these people in the manner you do? If it does, great, and if it does not, give yourself the choice to reconstruct your assessments. Get your present to what opens up for you now.

7. Observe assessments that you automatically create when events take place. Notice that you are creating your world. Additionally, observe that despite the event being the same, others may create a completely different world (even if others create the same assessments as you – does not mean that these assessments are facts – it only means these are shared assessments). Give yourself the choice to create assessments that work for you, those that are aligned with your cares.

8. Get into the practice of living in the moment. Very often, we are either living in the future, or in the past. To get the best results, we need to be present in the moment. One way to do so is to practise centering.

We are centred when our body, mind and emotions are in a state where we can choose our actions. When we are not in a state to choose our actions, we are 'off-centre'; and our reactions choose for us.

In Appendix 2, we have provided a centering practice graciously contributed by my colleague Sheeja Shaju, who is a somatic leader and a leadership coach at the Institute for Generative Leadership, India.

MOVING ON

We've looked at the conversational domains of 'Care' and 'Observe'. For your better understanding, next we look at C – Commitment before we look at A – Actions.

5

COACH: COMMITMENT

The act of commitment is a generative act in conversation. It lives in you as an internal state that guides your external actions. It is a declaration you may share with others of a future outcome that you will produce. The act is specific and concrete and requires that you dedicate action, time, focus, and perhaps other resources to the outcome.

Commitment is to own the future you share with others, to own your power to create, to own the actions to produce the future, and to be responsible to yourself and others for the outcome.

BOB DUNHAM

How would it be if...

- you kept and effectively managed all the promises that you made?

- everyone in your team kept and effectively managed all the promises that they made?

- you and your team kept and effectively managed all the promises that you and they are (not only the explicit promises, but the implicit ones too)?

- you and your team continued to make bigger promises and were always looking to expand their leadership capacity?

A NEW GENERATIVE UNDERSTANDING OF SOME COMMON WORDS[1]

What is commitment?

In this book, I use the words 'commitment', 'agreement', and 'promise' interchangeably. Certain other discourses may create a distinction in these words – for example, commitment may mean the intention, while the promise itself may mean a guarantee towards a specific outcome. However, for the purposes of this book – they mean the same. Hence, commitment, when used in this book means the 'act' and not a confirmation of intention.

A promise is one kind of a declarative act that we make which internally organizes us to be in action for the sake of producing a specific outcome. It is also an act that we make externally and socially that produces an interpretation in others of what we will produce as outcomes of our actions. Promises are acts of coordination between people.[2] In making and managing promises, we are looking for the promise of an eventual future consequence that is of value for some customer (the person to whom you make the promise). We are not looking for a promise of engaging in some activity in which the result is not articulated or clear (unless the promise is itself to engage in an activity and not of a specific result).

What is fundamental for any promise is for the performer (the person who makes the promise) to produce a shared interpretation of the commitment with the customer (the person you make the promise to); and, to produce the assessment that this is a sincere

125

and authentic commitment, and that the performer will act towards fulfilling their promise.

Promise is taking a stand that you are responsible for the outcome. That is, you take the posture that the outcome can be produced and that you will produce the outcome. This means you do not act to 'do the best you can' (unless this is what you promised), or to 'do what is appropriate and see what happens' or 'do what you thought should do the trick' and or use breakdowns as excuses for non-fulfilment.

What is a team?

A team is a group of people with a *shared promise*. A team exists to make a *bigger promise* that one person alone can fulfil.[3]

What is an organization?

An organization can be understood as a *network of commitments* generated and maintained in a network of conversations to fulfil bigger commitments. 'Bigger commitments' in this context means commitments that individuals do not have the capacity to fulfil on their own, and hence group(s) of people come together to fulfil them.[4]

What is action?

Action is *taking care* of what you care about. If you are not doing so, you are only doing tasks, not taking action. In the world of generative leadership, we interpret action not as some disembodied activity that we have to organize 'out there', but rather as generated by acts of commitments by people who care about some concern.[5]

If you really get the depth of this distinction, it will transform the way you take action. For me, when I am *doing* something (generally, people would interpret I am in action) – I ask myself, *'What care am I taking care of with this doingness?'* If my response is that this doingness is inside of some or the other care and commitment of mine, then I assess that I am in action – otherwise I am indulging in meaningless activity.

To act is to take care.

TAKING CARE IS THE FUNDAMENTAL ASPECT OF ACTION THAT BRINGS MEANING, VALUE AND SATISFACTION.

What is a task?

A task is that which consumes human time and energy, but which is articulated by a description of what is being done. In other words, the distinction between a task and an action is that actions are inside of cares and commitments, while tasks are activities that take up time, and yet do not move forward a certain fulfilment of a promise.

Pause for Reflection

How much time of your day is spent in action (activities that are inside of your care and commitments) as against time that you spend on tasks (meaningless activity that does not move forward your cares and commitments)?

DISTINGUISHING MISSING CARE AND MISSING COMMITMENT

Care is the energy that brings meaning and importance in our lives; and it is through commitments that we take actions, thereby taking care of what we care about. We then need to, as a regular practice, distinguish 'for the sake of what commitment' we are taking this action.

This book began with the first chapter on 'Care'. Chances are by now you would have distinguished what your cares are, and those of your co-workers. If that is the case, it's time for you to distinguish your commitments inside each of these cares, and invite your co-workers to distinguish their commitments.

I did some intensive work for a global $15-billion group. I was invited by the CEO of its Indian office to conduct a series of seminars for all their employees in the sales and marketing team. Over tens of seminar-type conversations, I interacted with their staff – over 800 employees – right from the CEO down to the sales executives. The entire organization was focused on their commitment to increasing market share. On the face of it, this seemed pretty straightforward.

However, this was an interesting time in the industry – the industry size had declined by about 20 per cent in the previous two years, and the sales and marketing team had complained that the sales target in a declining industry was demotivating them, and hence the management of this organization had decided to change the target from a sales target to a market-share target. There was also a sales target, but as per the teams I interacted with, the market-share target was the one they were going by.

All teams did not meet their sales targets, and only a handful met their market-share targets. In my conversations with them, I heard many reasons (reasons are assessments that you believe in – but they are still only that – assessments) for not having met their targets.

Here are the most common ones that I heard:

- 'The overall industry has gone down and hence the targets were not met' (and yet, interestingly, there were individual branch heroes in several cities and regions who met their sales target – and hence their market-share target too).
- 'We do not have products in the segment the market grew. That is why we did not meet our market-share target' (if you do not have a product in a certain segment, that is not even your market. You should remain focused on your market).

- 'Our dealers are not as good as that of competition; they do not invest as much; they do not care.' (So, the dealers are to be blamed, eh? Who appoints these dealers? The same people who blamed these dealers.)

After I completed these seminars, I requested for a meeting with the CEO, and I shared the above comments, and many other similar comments that I had received from their teams on the ground.

I stressed on one point to them: *The problem was not only that the teams were having these conversations (making these excuses for failure); the real problem was that they believed these conversations (excuses) were 'the truth'. And in many cases, the heads of the regions, and area managers also believed that these conversations were 'true').*

If we go back to the lessons learnt from the 'Observe' chapter, if this is the type of observer they are, that their targets cannot be met, clearly their actions would be inside of this way of observing, and hence they have the results that they have.

The Game of Market Share

I had a concern, and I shared this concern with the management team of this organization.

If a region's industry size was, for example 100,000 units, and the target was to sell 15,000 units, then that would be 15 per cent market share. If I were a general manager of a region, it would be in my interest (not in the organization's interest) that the market fell by 30 per cent. And if that were to happen, my target would get reduced to 10,500 numbers from the original 15,000 numbers. In a declining market, it was in an individual's interest to have a market-share target, but that target is not in the interest of the organization.

Clearly, the way the game was set up, it did not work for the organization. Here, even if the general managers, the area managers, and everybody else involved met their targets, the company would lose money – and yet, the same people would get incentivized and receive increments.

Costs are recovered and profits are earned when sales happen, not when the market share grows. The market share should ideally be a result of numbers sold – it cannot be the target by itself.

As leaders and managers within organizations, if we indeed want to generate extraordinary results, we need to get people to stand in the future (stand in the commitment) of achieving the numbers, and then take actions to achieve those numbers. At best, employees within this organization were standing in a future (standing in the commitment) of achieving market-share targets; and, at worst, unfortunately, some were standing in stories of why 'even the market-share target was not possible'.

Our job, as leaders and managers, is to invite people to stand in the possibility of achieving their promises, and then take actions from that position; rather than from a position of why the promises cannot be fulfilled.

This organization not only started to operate from the position why the promises will not be fulfilled, they changed what the promise metric was – from sales numbers to market share. This further added confusion, and people thought they were doing better than they were actually doing. For me, this is one example of a missing commitment (more like a misplaced commitment in this case).

My work makes me interact with a lot of heads of organizations and heads of business units. Unfortunately, the above is not an uncommon situation at all. In a subsidiary of an Italian organization, the CEO stated that their Italian principal was not allowing them to grow beyond 5 per cent year-on-year (however bizarre this may sound). It took a short conversation to see through the claims of this CEO. Clearly, he was not ready to make a commitment to do what it took to increase the growth percentage in an industry that was growing 15 per cent year-on-year.

What is missing in both the above cases is commitment; what is commonly present is blame and excuses. *Blame and commitment do not go hand in hand.* Unfortunately, people in organizations are blind to this.

They claim to be committed, and I fully agree, they are committed – but to what? In the first case, the commitment was to a market share, and not to a sales number (which in my assessment is a misplaced commitment); and in the second case, the commitment was to 5 per cent growth and not to 15 per cent or more growth.

A missing commitment then is a commitment that is most of the times 'hidden' from the observer. It is missing because the observer is generally blind to the fact that it is this missing commitment, when made, will lead to actions, those that will generate the desired results. In the 'Care' chapter, we looked at the anatomy of results, and we saw that actions come from commitments, and when we make the missing commitments, we take the necessary action to generate the desired results.

For example, when a manager gets upset with his co-worker and starts to scream at him – that action of screaming comes from a commitment to either being right, or teaching the co-worker a lesson or some such thing. That action, more often than not, does not come from the commitment to organizational and team results (although that may be the claim of the manager). The objective of the manager is to help team members shape and own their commitments, not manipulate or threaten them. In this case, it is important for the manager to observe the observer he is, get present to the 'for the sake of what' (the care and commitment because of which the action is being taken), and then realign the action.

Leaders and managers need to invite their co-workers to see 'what really their commitment is' and whether their commitment 'takes care of what they care about'. When the co-workers discover this, through their own reflection and by being guided by an effective leader, you invite the co-worker to the missing commitments.

In the case of the Italian subsidiary, the missing commitment was the commitment to a minimum growth of 15 per cent, which was the growth of the industry. In the case of the global organization I referred to above, the missing commitment was a commitment to sales numbers, rather than a commitment to market share. In the case of the manager yelling loudly at his co-worker, the commitment is to being right and to exercising authority, the missing commitment is the commitment to the result which is to provoke ownership in the employees for the team and organizational promise.

A lot of people within organizations do not make commitments, because in their assessment, that result is not possible (they live in this assessment). The reason an individual, a team or an organization wants to generate a result is that the results take cares of their cares.

The question then is not whether this result is possible or not. (It is like asking if it's possible to take care of what you care about.) When you stand in this question, what you are 'looking for' are reasons for whether this result is possible or whether this result is not possible. The real questions to consider are:

- Are we committed to this result?
- What would it take to make this possible?

When you stand in the posture that you will achieve a result, you are 'looking for' what next can be done to achieve that result.

PROMISES INSTEAD OF TARGETS

In my interactions with organizations, I regularly ask people: Is this a target, or is this your promise? And pat comes a response: 'Oh, it's a target, I haven't made this promise.' The way a target is interpreted by many people that I have interacted with is, 'This is something that I need to go for, but if I don't achieve it, it's okay'. However, a promise is interpreted by these people as 'this is my commitment and I have to achieve this'.

Several organizations that I have worked with, and continue to work with, have stopped using targets. They now have decided to get promises of results from their employees.

This is not just a matter of semantics. This is a matter of how you show up to work every morning. If you must achieve promises, chances are, employees are a lot more connected to taking *action that helps them inch closer to achieving their promise.* What is also important to state here is that I have met many people for whom there is no difference in the words 'target' and 'promise'. For them, their target is their promise. However, on the other hand, I have interacted with many people in organizations for whom a target is something that *would be nice to achieve*, and a promise would be something that they *need to achieve.*

In the work of generative leadership, a target is a request by the manager to their co-worker. This request can be declined. It is in the manager's interest to recognize whether or not their co-worker has accepted the request and given a trustworthy promise to the manager. Often, co-workers accept 'targets' on the face of it, because their assessment is that they cannot decline the target assigned by the manager. When the performer accepts the target, and makes a trustworthy promise, that's when the manager can assess that the target-promise will be met.

The world operates on promises. Promises are what shapes what people do. It also shapes what customers expect in outcomes. When promises are missing or unclear, there is unproductive action and dissatisfaction. Individuals make promises to teams, teams to organizations, organizations to clients; clients to their clients; and so forth. This cycle breaks if you break a commitment. Unfortunately, a lot of people have not created an empowering context for why they do what they do. And because of this, they think it is okay to miss promises. This is where the manager or the leader comes in, and get their teams to recognize the promises of the team, and that of individuals within the team, and the impact of promises not kept.

A DECLINE IS A COMMITMENT

It is interesting in how many organizations, managers and leaders tell their team members what they need done, and presume that by simply stating so, it becomes the commitment of the other to do what has been requested. The general manager of the maker of a luxury cars once mentioned to me that in his organization, it is he who asks his team to tell him what annual target they should aim to achieve.

Interestingly, when speaking to his team, they said that the general manager gave the team their annual targets and asked them: 'Guys, is this target reasonable? If not, you need to tell me now.' And according to the team members, this was said in a manner and tone such that the general manager was not going to be negotiable. So, according to the general manager, in effect, he had a commitment from his team for a target.

Was this commitment a trustworthy commitment?

Not in my assessment. I say this based on my interactions with the general manager and his team. While I am writing this chapter, the annual financial year is not over yet – however, what is important to note is that this team has not even met the targets for the first three quarters.

I am not surprised.

Here's my perspective – when someone declines a target that you want him to take on – what that person is intrinsically saying is that *he cares for the relationship and does not want to let you down; and that he or she does not have the capacity, competence, or the intention to do what you want him or her to do.*

As a manager and a leader, to gain authority with your team, the first thing you need to do is make commitments that you will live up to. If you think you cannot live up to a commitment, politely decline. My coach Bob Dunham tells me, 'A decline is a commitment that I will *not* do what you have requested. It's a way of saying I respect you and do not want to let you down. Perhaps you can make a request to another person who has the intention, capacity or competence to fulfil your request. If I say yes and know that I cannot fulfil a promise, I am creating the eventual breakdown, dissatisfaction and consequences of the lack of fulfilment of the outcome'.

It is interesting to see how in our culture there is an assessment that if you decline a request, the other person will feel bad. And that is why several people sometimes make commitments they have absolutely no intention, competence or capacity to honour. Maybe, they are right. Perhaps the other person may feel bad that you declined his or her request. But what would happen if you make a commitment and then not keep it. How bad will that person feel then? What will be the impact to your relationship with that person? And more importantly, what will be the impact to the overall result of the team, or the organization? We are blind to this when we make a commitment that we do not intend to fulfil.

Bob Dunham, in his unpublished paper titled, 'The Generative Foundations of Leadership', states:[6]

Declines are an important part of coordination of action. Many managers and leaders have the mistaken interpretation that their role is to only give orders or to get people to say 'yes'. Yet if a person is committed to not perform or has a professional opinion that the request cannot be fulfilled, then a promise will be a lie or at least not produce effective outcomes.

If people feel they cannot decline, which is an assessment that pervades some organization cultures, they can only make shallow or uncommitted promises. Leaders and managers need to understand that the point of their requests and directions are to produce authentic commitment with ownership, not automatic 'yeses'. A decline is a commitment and just as valuable as a promise to clarify what future outcomes to expect from someone. In fact, a decline is a promise – a promise not to do something. A leadership challenge is to have the standard, listening, body and emotions to accept declines and move on to find the actions that are needed, to effectively negotiate, and to build a culture where declines have an appropriate place in coordination for the sake of better coordination and performance.

Declines are appropriate commitments in response to requests when they will produce more satisfaction for a customer than an accept.

MAKING TRUSTWORTHY COMMITMENTS

When you make a commitment, and at a later point you realize that you cannot honour that commitment, it's advisable to revoke or renegotiate that commitment.

It is critical to manage your promises. Later in this chapter, we look at the consequences of not managing your promises. With 'managing promises', we mean a specific set of actions to keep in agreement with the customer for the promise. This is to keep the customer of the promise informed and satisfied that the promise is still trustworthy. But it also means to alert a customer to risks and potential breakdowns with the promise, so that they can take prudent action with regard to the promise. When the promise is no longer fulfillable, for whatever reason, to manage the promise means to let the customer know, to give them the options you or they can take to deal with the consequences, or to renegotiate a new promise. Managing a promise builds trust with customers, while avoiding honest updates produces eventual distrust.

Often people make commitments, but they are blind to the fact that they have made commitments. For example, while in a meeting, a manager receives a call from his co-worker. The manager tells the co-worker that he is in a meeting and will call back soon after the meeting ends. The manager then forgets to return the call. This co-worker made that call because he needed support from the manager. The manager did not listen to him, and only said he'll call back. From the manager's perspective, this was trivial and so what if he forgot.

On the other hand the co-worker does not trivialize this. On the contrary, in his head, he may make a big deal of this. From his side, in this occasion of the manager not returning the call, there is a slight depletion of trust.

The more the trust depletes within the team, the lesser the performance of the team.

The greater the trust, the higher the performance of the team.

Making Trustworthy Promises

1. When you are making a promise, observe how your body may land on the customer – does this body in which you make the promise (the way you stand, the tone of your voice, the words you speak, and so forth) land as if your promise is trustworthy in the eyes of the customer?
2. Start becoming present to the promises you are making. Develop a practice of asking yourself two questions:
   a. do I intend to fulfil this promise?
   b. do I have the resources/means to fulfil this promise?
   If not, get into the practice of respectfully declining the request.
3. Another practice that I have found useful is before you go to bed, take a moment to reflect on which are the promises that you made in the day that you did not fulfil – to yourself and to others.
4. Make a note to either revoke or renegotiate those promises the following day. And then revoke or renegotiate those promises the following day.

SEEKING TRUSTWORTHY PROMISES

In the luxury-automobile company mentioned earlier, it may have been a better move for the general manager to request promises from his team. When each one of his direct reports gives him their promises for the year, what they are effectively doing is exposing the way *they see* the market for their products. If in the event, the promise given by his co-worker is as per his satisfaction, then that can be accepted.

However, if a promise offered by the co-worker is not as per his satisfaction, the general manager now has an idea of how his co-worker *sees* the opportunity (the observer the co-worker is). This opens a great space for a leadership-coaching conversation with this person and inviting him to see differently, and to see possibilities that they were blind to. This co-worker is making certain assessment, (which are different from those being made by the general manager – and that is why, as per the general manager, the opportunity is bigger than what is seen by his co-worker).

One important thing for leaders and managers to remember – you cannot wish that the co-workers will change his underlying assessment – the one that makes it appear to them that the target should be a certain number; you cannot even give them a higher target and hope they will achieve that higher target – because, inherently, the co-workers have assessments (that they hold to be true) that only this target (a certain lesser target) can be achieved. By giving them a higher target than what they assess is possible, merely leads the target not being achieved – like in the case of the general manager discussed earlier. As leaders, we must help them see how to authentically shift their assessment.

So, in the interest of generating results that matter to you, you need to have a leadership-coaching conversation – show them the mirror – show them their assessments; share your assessments with them in a manner that it is an invitation to them – rather than 'this is the only assessment and he has to accept this assessment'.

One of the ways of getting a trustworthy promise is to simply ask: 'Can I trust this promise?' I sometimes go a step further and ask: 'Really, can I trust this promise?' Often, this approach has worked. It's an indication to the other person that you mean business and it is important for you that he or she keeps this promise.

Seeking Trustworthy Commitments

People make commitments all the time. For example, I often request my daughter, 'Please keep your books back in your book cabinet.' She replies 'yes, dad' and gets back to doing what she was doing. The way she says 'yes, dad' will on most occasions be indicative of her intention to do what I requested of her. While she says 'yes, dad', meaning, I commit to doing what you requested me to do – her tone is more leaning towards 'not now, dad'. So, in this case, I do not have a promise that I can trust.

To understand whether you have a trustworthy commitment – you do not listen for a yes – only in words. People can say 'yes' and be committed to 'no' or 'maybe' or 'later'. You want to hear a yes – in emotions and in the body of the person committing. In our assessment, the emotion and the body give away more than what the words people say. Listening to a commitment is a full-body experience.[7]

It's a skill to recognize a trustworthy promise – and it is important that you develop this skill. After all, most of the times how the other person manages his or her promises significantly impacts your results too (remember, an organization is a network of promises to fulfil a bigger promise).

You develop this skill by being present to the requests you are making to people; observe the emotion and the body of the person accepting or declining your request. The more you observe, the more skilled you get.

When you get a commitment, I invite you to observe where in your body you feel the difference between witnessing a trustworthy versus an untrustworthy promise.

WHAT IS THE IMPACT OF NOT MANAGING PROMISES EFFECTIVELY?

People are blind to the impact of not keeping their promises or even managing their promises effectively. It is critical to effectively manage your promises (either keep your promises, or revoke or renegotiate your promise as soon as you find out that you are not able to keep your promise) – and if you do not, you need to face the consequences of not doing so.

The question then is, what are the consequences of not keeping and managing your promise.

I call this the 4R impact.

- Respect for self
- Reputation (Public Identity)
- Relationships
- Results

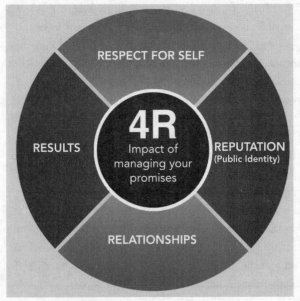

Figure 5.1: The 4R impact of not managing your promises

Impact on respect for self

One of the key areas that gets impacted by revoking or renegotiating promises is that there is a depletion in a person's self-esteem, i.e., an erosion in confidence in one's own word. I call this respect for self.

This is not a trivial matter – it's extremely significant. Your trust in yourself is of paramount importance to do or achieve anything of value in life.

A story one of my teachers told me when I was a little boy has stayed with me ever since. She told me that each one of us has a wheel with pointed triangles right next to our heart – just about touching our heart (please see Figure 5.2). Every time we lied, according to my teacher, this wheel would rotate a little bit – and when that would happen the triangle touching our heart would hurt our heart, causing pain. In the process, the pointed edge of the triangle would get a little blunt – enough for it not to touch our heart were it to come close to the heart again. With every rotation of the wheel, the next triangle would come and touch the heart.

The wheel shown in Figure 5.2 has twenty-four pointed edges, which means – assuming this was the wheel with the triangles touching our heart – we would get hurt the first twenty-four times when we lied. After that, every time we lied, the circle would rotate, but the triangle would not touch our heart, and hence it would not cause any pain at all. According to my teacher, those who are compulsive liars, the triangles on their wheel have all become blunt, and hence when they lie, it doesn't hurt them at all.

Figure 5.2: Circle with pointed triangles

I remember her telling me: 'Sameer, you need to ensure that you hurt if you ever lie – it's not good for the triangles on the wheel to get blunt.'

When I first understood about the impact of broken promises on self, after thirty years or so, I remembered this story of my teacher. The way I listened to each promise being broken, was similar to each lie being spoken – the wheel rotated. The triangle touching the heart hurt the heart, and with friction the triangle got slightly blunt. The more you broke promises, the more you got used to the pain, and eventually, all triangles got blunt – and at that stage, breaking promises becomes habitual for us.

We become what we practise. We can practise being trustworthy, or not.

In my coaching programmes, many people I interact with fall in this category. Given the observer I am, I can clearly see the direct connection between breaking promises and the lack of trust and respect they have on and for themselves.

One of my students, an architect, said to me, 'I know exactly what you mean when you say that promises have a direct connection with our self-respect. I don't make any promises to any one any more. I try and be vague, like, "This will be done in about a week or two", "I will try my best", "The project will be complete soon", and so forth. His question was, "What do I do now?"'

The response was simple, but not trivial (Figure 5.3).

- Make a promise to keep all your promises.
- Make only those promises that you can keep.
- If in the event, you make a promise that you cannot keep, revoke or renegotiate that promise and take care of the mess that this creates.

I also advised him to try this for only a week, and see the direct impact this has on his self-esteem.

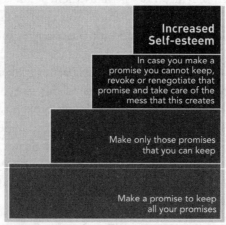

Figure 5.3: Access to increased self-esteem

This student came back a week later and said, 'It is amazing, I feel so good about myself.' Interestingly, just as an aside – for your information – his wife called a few weeks later and said, 'What have you done to my husband? He has started to keep all his promises to us. We did not know he loves us (the wife and the two kids) so much. We are so happy now! Thank you!'

Impact on relationships

Think of any of your relationships where trust is missing, and you will see the role of promises not being kept in causing the depletion in trust.

Furthermore, as we will distinguish later in this chapter, every relationship is constituted in an inherent promise. People may be blind to the promise of that relationship, but that does not mean the promise does not exist. If you look at any relationship that has stopped working, or is not working as well, and if you go deep enough, you will see a promise not kept or managed.

This is not rocket science. This is very simple. If a relationship matters, keep and effectively manage all the promises of that relationship, including expectations of the person in that relationship. If not, bear the consequences. My wife, whom I greatly love, walked out on me with my then five-year-old daughter. She did this not because I broke any explicit promises. It was because I did not meet her implicit expectations, and she was deeply hurt. It took me twenty months to get her and my daughter back in my life.

Often, in organizational settings, one gets to see strained relationships amongst peers, managers and co-workers, with clients, with partners, with associates, with vendors and so forth – and if you go to the bottom of this, there is a promise not kept or effectively managed.

I call this the missing explicit promise, which means, the promise exists in the eyes of the customer, except the explicitness of that promise and its agreement is missing for the performer. In other words, the promiser is blind to the existence of the promise, and yet, often, not released from the consequences of not keeping the promise.

For example, in an appraisal, the manager reviews the team member not only on the basis of the explicit promises, but also on his or her expectations that the team member met or did not meet. Effective managers ensure that there are as few as possible 'missing explicit promises' of the team member, and most, if not all, expectations are clearly expressed, and promises sought.

In such scenarios, there is rigour in the relationship, and yet relationships thrive.

The impact on your results

Commitment is an integral part of coordinating action with another person. The fundamental piece on which action is coordinated is a promise. Which is why, at the Institute for Generative Leadership, we believe that an organization is a network of promises, and a team is also constituted in a promise. If any member of the team does not keep their promise, the impact is borne by the entire team. Similarly, if a team underperforms, there's a blip in the organization's performance as well.

My organization recently conducted a programme for an organization in the IT-enabled services industry. The focus of the one-year-long exercise was to instill a culture of commitment in the senior managers of that organization. The management team believed that senior managers did not take their commitments seriously – including those to their customers – and it was starting to significantly impact the organization's success. The direct impact of not managing promises was visible in their results.

I was recently in a conversation with Claudio Toyama, a colleague in the Coaching Excellence in Organizations programme of the Institute for Generative Leadership, USA. He said to me that he was hearing from his clients in the US that several of them had tied up with business process outsourcing

(BPO) units in India, and they were not happy with the services provided. Some of them had already disengaged with these units, and some others were on the verge of doing so – waiting for the mandatory period on the agreement to expire. 'Not happy with the services' is another way of saying 'the promises to meet the standards were not kept'.

I can go on and on with examples. However, if you look closely, you'll notice that when there is dissatisfaction, you can be assured a commitment has not been effectively managed. This dissatisfaction impacts existing and new business – and hence directly impacts your results.

The impact on your reputation (public identity)

Your reputation or your public identity has a lot to do with how you keep and manage your promises. Amongst the least trusted people in India are politicians – they make big promises at the time of elections, and when they come to power, they fail to deliver on those promises. Take a moment and think of someone you respect in your area of work – perhaps a leader in your organization, or a leader in another organization, and ask yourself why you have a high opinion of that person. Chances are you will notice that this person keeps his or her promises to others and to themselves.

An interesting exercise we get people to do in our programmes is an audit of their public identity – we send our participants with a set of eight simple questions to ask 20–25 people they know. We request them to choose people from different areas of their life – colleagues (seniors, juniors, peers), clients, parents, spouse, children, friends, co-members of social organizations, neighbours, classmates, etc. The analysis of this audit our participants return with, very often, baffles them.

We ask them to look for places where promises were not kept, and that's when they notice – almost all places, it was the way they managed the explicit and the implicit promises that led to the results they brought in. If the feedback was positive in their assessment, it was because they kept and managed the promises; if the feedback was negative, it was because promises were not kept.

Now, for a moment, imagine, there is a person who has:

- low self-esteem – he or she has no respect for himself or herself;
- no trust in relationships with people around him or her;
- poor results – hence very limited success, and
- a poor public identity

What sort of a life do you think this person would be leading? This does not need any mental effort – there is nothing to the life of this person.

All of this can be greatly improved by making and managing promises well.

PROMISE EXISTS IN THE LISTENING OF THE CUSTOMER

When a promise is made – there is an interpretation of what the promise is in the eyes of the performer (the person who makes the promise) and there is an interpretation of what the promise is in the eyes of the customer (the person to whom the promise is made).

The question then is – whose interpretation is to be considered the 'real promise'? Our belief at the Institute for Generative Leadership is that the promise exists in the listening of the customer. It means the person to whom you made the promise is going to assess whether you fulfilled the promise based on his or her understanding of the promise (i.e., the customer's understanding of the promise).

Often, the conditions of satisfaction of the promise are unclear, and that is the source of many disagreements, even misunderstandings. This means that your role, as the performer of the promise, is to ensure that the customer understands what exactly the conditions are of satisfaction. Besides, what's the point of performing the action, if the action does not meet the requirements of the customer?

If I had to extend this further, we claim that it is also your role as the customer to ensure that your understanding of the promise is the same as that of the performer. The reason we say this is that, as the customer your results are at stake. If the performer is not aligned with you on the conditions of satisfaction, he or she will perform on the basis of his understanding of the promise.

So, while we claim that the promise exists in the listening of the customer, *you* (no matter if you are the performer or the customer) need to ensure the other party is fully aligned on the conditions of the satisfaction of the promise.

There are several things that need to be understood with this claim that the 'promise exists in the listening of the customer'. A case in point is illustrated below.

Customers have a certain expectation of the conditions of satisfaction of the promise. You need to fulfil that expectation. An example that works well here is of a client of mine, the owner of a well-known real estate company in Pune. One morning, he promised his daughter to take her to the park in the evening at 6 p.m. His daughter was obviously ecstatic – her father, who very rarely spends time with her one-on-one was going to take her to the park.

At exactly 6 p.m. the father got home to receive his daughter and the two drove to a nearby park. As soon as they got to the park, the father got on the phone to take his 6.15 p.m. conference call. This call lasted an hour and at 7.15 p.m. when the call got over, he went up to his daughter asking her if she was ready to leave and go home.

The girl was furious with him. He could not understand what was bothering her, and to make matters worse, she would not respond to any of his questions. Later, he discovered that she thought that he would play with her at the park, when what he had stated – and meant – was, 'I would *take you* to the park.' He thought he fulfilled his promise by taking her to the park. However, for the daughter, she interpreted that promise as, 'I will *play with you* in the park.'

There could be differing understandings of the condition of satisfaction – in this case the father had a different understanding and the daughter another. The same may happen in an organizational setting – the customer has one view of the promise and the performer has another.

We have already looked at the consequences of not effectively managing a promise above. If you do not fulfil the conditions of satisfaction of the customer, then you face the consequences of not keeping a promise – even though you think you kept it.

If the customer has an expectation of you, as a performer, that expectation of your customer is your promise. As a leader, this is a powerful way to operate and can generate great results. Many people find this contentious. I can understand why. The above is not necessarily a fact and is only a powerful perspective to choose to operate from. I can understand the discomfort resulting from a perspective that states someone else's expectation of me is my promise to them. It does not fit in one's frame of common sense.

However, here are some points for your consideration:

• If an organization did not meet the expectations of their customers, would they not face the consequences?
• These days, if an organization did not meet the expectations of their employees, would they not face the consequences?
• If a co-worker did not meet the expectations of his line manager, would he or she not face the consequences?
• If a spouse did not meet the expectations of the husband or wife, would she or he not face the consequences?
• If a child did not meet the expectations of his or her parents, would he or she not face the consequences?
• If a parent did not meet the expectations of the child, would he or she not face the consequences?

Take a moment to reflect how people are paying a price of a broken promise, only because they claim that they had not explicitly made it. However, if your customer has an expectation of you, you need to fulfil that or revoke that 'promise' by letting the customer know that you will not be able to honour it.

The question then arises: How can anyone deliver on such commitments? And before we answer this, it's worth asking: How often are you not aware of the expectations that others have of you?

When I ask this question to my clients and participants of my programmes, the answer that I get is – rarely. Several of us are present enough to be aware of the expectations others have of us.

And yet there are others that may not be aware of the expectations. And in that case – if you are not aware, clearly, there is nothing you can do. Awareness leads to choice and when you do not have awareness, you have no choice. However, that does not mean that you will not face the consequences.

Ignorance of expectations of you is not an excuse for not keeping or managing those expectations. However, often we are aware of the expectations that others have of us (we may choose to ignore them). We just need to be familiar with what those are.

The next section will help you further understand this claim.

YOU ARE A PROMISE

If you have made big promises and gone after them with sincere intent to achieve their outcomes, notwithstanding whether you achieved the result, I suspect you have high self-esteem. And the opposite is true too. There are people in the world who simply show up in their lives and go about their routine doing mundane tasks that are required of them, ignoring the promise they've made to themselves. (In the 'Care' chapter, we saw that' 68 per cent of US workers are not engaged or actively disengaged, as per a Gallup study.)

As humans, we were created to be unstoppable. I have evidence of this in my family. In 2014 my wife and I became parents to a pair of gorgeous twins. They were born premature, but have been unstoppable from the time of their birth (actually, from the time they were conceived!). I am seeing them grow week after week. First they would not recognize us, now they do; earlier, they could not hold their necks straight, now they do.

As they grew older, they first learnt to turn while lying down. Once they turned and lay on their stomachs, they were not able to go back to their earlier position of lying on their back. They yelled for help and one of us had to straighten them. But, they did not learn from this 'mistake' (thank God!). Imagine their audacity – they did not have the wherewithal to get back on their backs, but continued to turn on to their stomachs. They did the same thing again and again and again, till they learnt to turn back on their own. Nobody taught them this – they learnt on their own!

And then, they learnt to sit up, and then crawl. While crawling, they fell many times, hurt themselves, yet they did not stop. Eventually, they mastered crawling. Again, thankfully, that was not enough for them. They learnt to walk, and run; and I am sure they will learn to cycle, swim, etc., with the passage of time. And each time, they will fall and hurt themselves. Yet, they did not give up.

It is interesting that as we grow older, we think we become smarter and this smartness goes against us. We start to attribute reasons and make decisions that don't help us. If we fall (read fail), we give ourselves such convincing reasons for not attempting again.

In a workshop that I conducted recently for a large multinational organization, there was a practice that I asked the participants to complete first thing on the morning of day three. A senior manager in that organization could not complete the practice. He 'decided' that he was 'slow' and hence he could not complete it.

To me, however, he did not seem slow at all – he was active in the conversations during the programme. It was clear that the other participants had high regard for him and his achievements.

However, it was evident that he believed that he was 'slow' and his being slow was the reason for not completing the practice. My guess is that the practice was not completed because subconsciously he was proving himself to be right – that he was 'slow'. But in his view, since he was slow, he did not make big promises.

For you to grow, you need to have a promise that is bigger than the last one you made. When my twins learnt to crawl, they were a promise for walking. And irrespective of the number of failures, they continued to try to walk – till they began walking.

This experience opens a path of lifetime learning. Too many people fall into the story that they have learned and now they are fixed the way they are. But brain science has shown that we can continue to learn throughout the course of our lives. We can continue to open possibilities, become aware, make new choices, and fulfil them. And we can learn to do so, with fascination, to take care of what we care about, not learning as a burden of tasks. We can be designers in our life, not just drifters.[8]

You need bigger promises for your own sake; your family needs you to make bigger promises; your organization needs bigger promises and the world too needs bigger promises!

Are you ready to do so?

In 2016, I attended a fascinating event called 'Ideas on India'. It had some big names from the present and previous government speaking about their ideas on India. The programme also had some well-known and senior ex-servicemen as speakers, who shared the kind of idea India is, in their assessment. (P.S.: I love the concept of India being an idea.)

Without a doubt, the discussions at the event provoked a range of ideas and thoughts amongst participants and each of them was left with some question or the other in their minds. The question that got triggered in my mind was, 'What does being Indian mean to me?' and 'What is my relationship with my country?'

And to answer that question, I looked closely at the meaning of the word 'relationship'.

A relationship is a promise

I am the father of my children, not just because they carry my genes, but also because I choose to be in this relationship with them and uphold the promise of this relationship. There is a certain set of expectations that my children, my wife, my parents, my children's school and the society have of me as a father. And it's only when I meet *their* expectations do I truly become a father in their eyes.

My brother, meanwhile, has two adopted sons. Although they don't carry his genes, his promise as a father is by no means any less than mine. So, my claim is that being a father is not about blood, but about a promise.

My relationship with India, and with being Indian

If I had to take the same logic to my relationship with my country, India, I am not Indian because I was physically born in India or because I was born to citizens of India. Being Indian is a promise, the same way being a father is a promise.

The question then is: What is my promise to my country because of which I can choose to call myself an Indian?

Simply because I was born in India does not give me the right to call myself Indian. Being in any relationship has a set of duties, and similarly, being in a relationship with my country, and calling myself Indian has a set of duties – and these duties are my promise to me being an Indian.[9]

While the state does not punish me for not fulfilling my duties towards it, clearly that does not absolve me or anyone else from our duties. However, in my assessment, I am breaking the promise of being Indian when I do not comply with these duties.[10]

Coming back to the comparison of my relationship with my daughter, and my relationship with my country, there are certain unspoken expectations of each of these relationships. For example, the unspoken promises of my relationship with my daughter are to encourage her, to promote her, to support her, to respect her, to honour her, to hold her to account, to love her, to provide her with the dignity that she deserves and so on.

There are certain 'duties' that I have as a father and then there are certain 'unspoken expectations' that my daughter has of me. Both these are as important for me to keep and manage. Often, people may choose not to manage these expectations, which is perfectly okay, as long as you are ready to pay the price of doing so (the 4R impact).

Similarly, I see my relationship with my country as no different. I have a certain set of duties towards my country, which are explicitly stated in the Constitution of India; and then the country also has a set of expectations of me, which are not explicitly stated, yet are important for the fulfilment of my promise as an Indian. These unspoken promises of my being Indian, in my assessment, are to promote her (India), to support her, to respect her, to honour her, to hold her to account, to love her and so on (similar to the expectations of my daughter). To have the right to call myself an Indian, I must first fulfil my duties and the expectations the country has of me.

This is not about the country, or my children. This book is about you as a leader, and as a coach. I am inviting you to reflect what promise may you be as:

- The CEO / vice-president / director / manager (or whatever your designation may be) of your organization
- As a father / mother / son / daughter / spouse / brother / sister / friend / any other relationship that matters to you
- Co-worker / team member / member of a committee / and so forth
- Yourself

As stated earlier, *someone else's expectation is your promise. However, for the sake of coordinating action effectively, an explicit promise with clear conditions of satisfaction is critical.* Coordination of action has been dealt with in greater detail in the chapter on 'Action'.

THE LEADER AS A PROMISE OF BEING A COACH

The five domains in the acronym COACH provide a great basis to look at the promise the leader or the manager is – as a coach (remember, as a leader or a manager, you may be a coach in the eyes of the co-worker). So, whether you think you are a coach or not, it doesn't matter. In the eyes of the co-worker – and to generate results that your organization expects you to – they may expect that you operate as a coach and show your co-worker the mirror every time they need to see the mirror.

Let me clarify here – many co-workers of managers and leaders do not 'see' their line managers as coaches. And this is primarily because these managers have already not kept the promise of being a coach (and to be fair to these managers and leaders, they did not even know that they were to have these coaching conversations with their co-workers).

As a COACH, you are a promise in these five domains:

Care

- Have distinguished your own cares and are committed to taking care of these cares.
- Understand that the co-worker has his or her cares too and that your co-worker may have different cares than the ones you have – and you respect this distinction.
- Be connected to 'for sake of what result' are you doing the actions that you are engaged with.
- Enable the co-worker to see – 'For the sake of what result' are they taking their actions.

Observe the observer

- Most importantly, observe the observer that you are (refer to the 'Observe' chapter).

- Support the co-worker to observe the way the co-worker is observing. Remember, awareness creates choice.
- Offer alternative ways of observing, and give the co-worker a choice to observe differently for the sake of opening authentic possibilities.
- Show up to work with a mood that the results are entirely possible to achieve – and it is upon the team to take the requisite missing actions.
- Show up to work in a body that inspires, rather than a disempowered and closed body.

Actions

- Constantly observe your own actions and practices.
- Co-create actions and practices with your co-worker.
- Focus on 'what's missing' and 'what's possible' (solution) rather than on 'what's wrong' (problem).
- Understand that irrespective of how good individuals are and what they do, breakdowns will happen – the leader commits to enable the co-worker to navigate through these breakdowns.
- Respectfully, support the co-worker to discover whether he or she is operating as 'the safe person', 'the busy person', 'the jerk' or 'the performer' (as elaborated in the TAP Matrix in Chapter 6).

Commitment

- Keep and manage your commitments to the co-worker and to the organization, and support the co-worker to keep and manage their commitments.
- Stand totally committed to the co-worker, and to their results.
- Work backwards from the promise, and support the co-worker to work backwards from the promise to see the actions that are needed, rather than moving forward from the history of the group/individual (past).

Holding space of conversation

- Create and hold a space of mutual trust and respect.
- Stand in people's greatness, particularly when they cannot see their greatness.
- Speak from a stand to achieving the promise, rather than from reactions.
- Be open to receiving and giving honest feedback.

TO CHANGE YOUR IDENTITY, MAKE BIGGER PROMISES

One of the 4R impacts of not managing your promises effectively is the impact on your reputation. I have also referred to reputation as your public identity. The claim that I make in this section is that you can change your identity in your own eyes and in the eyes of others by making bigger promises, and by keeping these bigger promises.

As I have stated above – you are a promise. How big you are is a function of how big your promises are, and how big is the impact of your promises. I have examples of two people that I want to use to further elaborate on this point.

The first one is Sunil Jain, who is a chartered accountant by profession. Sunil was struck with polio when he was about a year old, and ever since he's been wheelchair-bound. However, the world (people like me and other people in his circuit) do not relate to Sunil as a wheelchair-bound person. We see Sunil as a man who makes big promises, acts on these promises and achieves desired results.

Sunil set up Astha Foundation in 2010, about the same time as we set up the Gift Your Organ Foundation. I have had the good fortune to see the foundation grow, and its impact multiply year after year. Annually, around World Disability Day in December, Astha organizes an event called Jugalbandi, literally meaning 'entwined twins' where he has musical performances by artists who are bodily abled and bodily disabled. The abled and the disabled perform together, creating magic on stage.

In December 2015, the fifth year of Jugalbandi, Sunil declared that in the Paralympics of 2020, India would have four gold medals, and his foundation would train all these winners. Soon after making this declaration, Sunil got into action focusing particularly on two sports, viz., para-swimming and wheelchair tennis. Astha trained Vishwas, an upcoming para-swimmer, who went on to win a championship in Canada; and then a year later, Astha organized India's first ever ranked wheelchair tennis tournament. About thirty-six wheelchair tennis players participated in this tournament, setting up the platform for each of them getting ranked, and opening doors for participation in international tournaments, representing India. What the sports ministry and the All India Tennis Association could not do, Sunil Jain did single-handedly.

These are huge first steps in fulfilling his declaration of getting four gold medals for India in 2020 Paralympics.

In all this, Sunil has remained the same – humble and down to earth as ever. However, his identity in the world – in the eyes of his friends, family, All India Tennis Association, Indian and international tennis stars, the citizenry of India – has gone through a huge shift.

The reason for the huge shift in his reputation and public identity is that he made a big promise, and he is on the way to fulfilling his promise.

Look around you, at the people whom you hold in high esteem – chances are, they are making and keeping big promises.

The second example is that of Parag Agarwal. Parag has a wide history of working in different industries – trading in shares, real estate, hospitality, IT hardware and networking, security, farm equipment to now water. Here's a man who never shied away from making big promises, who tried hard to fulfil these big promises and struggled. Till the day when he finally set up Janajal (clean water for all).

Not that he has stopped struggling hard to take his enterprise to the next level. However, his commitment is to fulfil a huge promise of providing clean water to the citizenry of this country. He has created a for-profit model that operates as a social enterprise. It works for all, i.e., the public at large, the government and his company's shareholders.

Parag's public identity, like Sunil's, has shifted dramatically in the last five years. As a person, he hasn't changed; however, the way people see him certainly has, and so has what people expect from him. He is now a more respected person, and importantly, the value of his 'word' has changed. Not only have Sunil's and Parag's public identity changed, my guess is that the way they see themselves has considerably shifted too.

I have chosen examples of everyday people only to show you that thousands of people around the world are shifting their public identity by making and keeping bigger promises.

This is not rocket science. It's quite simple: If you want to shift your public identity, make promises bigger than the ones you last made and go all out to fulfil those promises. You will significantly shift the way the world sees you.

The way the world sees you has a huge role to play in your success.

POWERFUL QUESTIONS ON COMMITMENT

1. What may be your commitments inside each of your cares?
2. Are you committed to your commitments?
3. What may be the missing commitments in your life, which when made will enable you to better take care of your cares?
4. Do you need to revoke or renegotiate any commitments that are not relevant for you any more? If so, which ones?
5. What is the 4R impact in your life for not having effectively managed your promises?
6. Are you ready to give up your excuses for your commitments? If so, which excuses will you give up today?

7. What new promise can you make, inside a care of yours, when made, will dramatically shift your public identity?
8. What is the impact on your self-esteem when you do not keep and effectively manage your promises?
9. Where are you making untrustworthy promises so that you may not be held accountable for these promises?
10. What promise are you going to fulfil today?

COMMON MYTHS

Myth: 'My promises are only those that I explicitly make.'

Busting the Myth: Generally, most of us make several promises every day, even when the use of the word 'promise' is missing. Many people are blind to the promises they make on a daily basis. Even if you are not aware of the promises you make, if the listener or the customer assesses your statements to be promises, those are your promises. If you do not keep and manage them, you bear the consequences of not doing so (the 4R impact).

Further, as I mentioned earlier, you *are* a promise. Every relationship, every role (including your role in your organization), and also your relationship with yourself – is a promise. Most of these are *not* explicit, but implicit. Awareness of these implicit promises, and keeping and managing these promises enables people to navigate through life more successfully.

Myth: 'I cannot find out if the promise I receive is trustworthy or not.'

Busting the Myth: If what others do impacts your promises and your results, you have a choice to ensure that you have a trustworthy promise. Listen not only to the words being spoken, listen also to the emotion of the words being spoken, and the body in which these words have been spoken. The emotions and the body give away more than the words by itself. Try and develop a practice to 'listen to the intention' of keeping the promise.

Further, if you are unsure, simply ask – can I trust this promise? If the answer does not satisfy you, check again.

Myth: A decline of a request is unacceptable.

Busting the Myth: A decline is a commitment to *not* do what has been requested. In an organization that would like to instill a culture of commitment, a decline is not only acceptable, it is encouraged when the promiser does not have the intention, competence or the capacity to fulfil the promise. This at least gives the person making the request an opportunity to ask someone else to get the job done, rather than have someone who has no intention, competence or capacity to say yes and then not do the job.

Myth: 'If I cannot keep a promise, I revoke the promise. My job is done at that stage.'

Busting this Myth: While it is imperative to revoke a promise, as soon as you find out that you cannot keep the promise – what is of as much importance is that the performer also supports the customer of the promise to find alternatives in dealing with the promise and help the customer with the consequences of the revoke, or face any consequences that may emerge.

Imagine a ball being handed over to you when you accept a request and make a promise. This ball needs to be taken to a certain destination, like a goal, and when you do so, you fulfil the promise. Somewhere during the process, when you cannot take the ball to its destination any more, you cannot simply drop the ball and go your way. You need to let the customer of the promise know you cannot any more do what you promised, support the customer in finding someone who can, and if not, face the consequences of simply dropping the ball.

INVITATION TO A BIGGER COMMITMENT
A case study by Umang Bedi

Here's a fun example of how you can understand your employees' cares and what they are deeply passionate about, and yet challenge them with what they think is impossible in a manner that enables them to fulfil their deep commitments.

When I joined Adobe in 2011, it was largely a very small-focus business. We didn't do large deals.

When I met with a small team of around six individual contributors, their whole goal in life was to become stellar performers, do large enterprise sales deals. They requested my personal support, in mentoring and guiding them to shape their career in terms of being individuals who could drive large volumes of business for the organization.

Well, that was easy the way I looked at it. We implemented a policy that I don't know of ever being implemented by any other organization in the country. We saw their commitment to generating large volumes for the organization, and their commitment to their own growth. And we wanted to see if they had the mettle to deliver.

So, we told them that we understood that Adobe was a popular software, there was a demand for it in the market from various customers across individuals, small and medium businesses and enterprises alike. There was a lot of pull that we got from the market because we were the market-leading de facto standard for a lot of the creative and content-creation technologies. Now, what we did was that a lot of this pull demand reached us via the distributor, and the distributor helped fulfil that demand. There was not too much of a role for Adobe to play, except to ensure that the hygiene of the transaction was conducted by the norms and the rules that have been laid out by the corporation across the globe.

What we did was we told these six individuals that the largest deal that we had ever done in our lives was around $100,000. We then discussed their target for the year. However, the caveat was they could only meet their target from single transactions whose minimum value was greater than $100,000. Of course, we would help them with all the tools and value propositions, and the executive commitment and the support to go out there and meet CXOs to make it happen.

It was magical because we invited these six gentlemen to not only see differently, but to a whole new commitment – for the sake of the growth of the organization and their careers. This invitation to a new commitment generated what is called in management, 'goal-congruent behaviour'. It was kind of humorous to see the way these individuals' behaviour changed, because 50 per cent of their compensation, the variable part of it, was linked to their goals that they had signed up for with the company. Except now, we just added one small clause in that every single transaction that they needed to do was to be greater than $100,000.

Of course, they thought we were crazy, but it led to a fascinating change in behaviour where they were now looking (being new observers) for larger opportunities, talking to more strategic customers, driving a more solid value proposition, engaging our business leadership and country leadership to engage with CXOs, and CIOs, and CFOs, and CEOs within the client organization to start building stronger and deeper value propositions.

What was interesting was that every single transaction that we did via this team for the next four years was greater than $100,000. In 2013, we grew our business across this phase exponentially. That year we did more business in terms of revenue and units than we had done in the last five years put together. From 2013 to 2016, we've had very steady, large, double-digit growth across this business year-on-year, quarter-on-quarter, and interestingly, all six sales representatives have achieved greater than 100 per cent of their quarterly targets across the last five years. No one has ever missed a goal or target that was set out for them.

Of course, the leadership team did whatever they could to provide them with all the support, infrastructure, technical guidance and the business commitments that they needed.

GENERATIVE PRACTICES

1. Get the present to the promises that you are making in your day-to-day life.
2. Make a note of the promises that you have not kept or managed in each of the important relationships in your life. For example:
   a. Your customers
   b. Your co-workers
   c. Your peers
   d. Your line manager
   e. Your spouse
   f. Your children
   g. Your parents

3. What has been the impact on the 4Rs in your life if you have not managed your promises effectively in the above relationships?
4. Revoke or renegotiate the unkept promises. Observe the impact on the 4Rs while you are revoking/renegotiating. You will notice in certain cases that despite not having kept your promise there is an upward movement in each of the 4Rs, just by revoking or renegotiating the promise.
5. You are a promise. What does this mean to you?
6. Please write down in your journal: 'What promise are you in each of these relationships?' (Refer to the list of relationships in Practice 2 above.)
7. Write down your reflections in your journal of what is opening up for you while doing the practices listed in this chapter.

6

COACH: ACTIONS

To act is to make something happen. Yet our interpretation of what is action can be blind to powerful acts. Action happens first in language with acts of language. It shapes every other kind of action we take as a consequence.

Our power and skills in action have been learnt and embodied through practice. You don't learn a performance art by understanding, you learn through practice. Understanding the concepts is not enough. Leadership is a performance art that can only be learned through practice.

BOB DUNHAM

How would it be if...

- everyone in your team was a high performer, not just a busy person, or a safe person, or a jerk?

- the team constantly generated new actions and new practices to generate results that mattered for your organization?

- the practices of your team that did not support generating valuable results were eliminated, and new practices created – those that supported creation of extraordinary results?

- your team operated with a commitment to success, overcoming breakdowns instead of being blocked by them, and working with high satisfaction and ownership?

ACTIONS GIVE YOU RESULTS

Eventually, it is actions that give you results. You must 'get on the court' and act and enable your co-worker to do the same. There can be any number of excuses that you may give yourself or your co-worker may give you for not taking action, and yet none of them lead to performance.

Remember, it is actions that you take that lead to your performance. History is testimony to the fact that no one has ever won a game by being on the stands. One of the key roles of a leader or a manager is to empower the co-worker to take and coordinate action with others to generate extraordinary results.

What does 'Action' mean?

The common understanding of action in our culture is that it means 'movement'. However, Bob Dunham claims that all action is shaped by language, and the generative acts of language are the actions that shape subsequent actions that lead to your results.

So, in effect:

Action = generative acts in language that shape subsequent physical action (behaviours, activities and physical acts) for the sake of an outcome agreed upon that takes care of our cares.

COORDINATION OF ACTION

All of us coordinate action all the time. However, we may either be doing it well or poorly. Our results depend on our skills in coordination. Becoming aware of the distinctions of coordination of action, and using these distinctions effectively can significantly enhance the results we generate. Whether we know it or not, coordination of action has a cost and it also creates value. We want to reduce the costs and increase the value.

We coordinate our actions to bring about something specific in the future by clarifying and making certain who is committed to doing what and by when. We make requests of specific people for specific outcomes in specific time frames and for seeking trustworthy promises.

The conversation for action is a non-discretionary structure. It is not just a technique, but a structure you will find in the world if you have the eyes to look for it. Conversations for actions are happening all around us. The question is, 'Are the conversations happening effectively and are these conversations generating the desired results?'

There is a clear structure to this conversation, and it is there for you to see, if you develop the eyes to see it, and a practice to embody it as a part of coordinating action and generating results.

Mastery in the conversation for action will enable you to get things done, some of which you may never have earlier imagined were possible. There are seemingly simple elements to the conversation for action, however, my experience as a leadership coach has been that very few people are competent in these areas.

The conversation for action involves two parties, in the roles of what we call the 'customer' and the 'performer', who work together to negotiate a condition of satisfaction (COS) to which both commit. *The customer is a person who makes a request, and the performer is the one who responds to the request and makes a commitment.*

The key milestones in the conversation are shown below:

1. **Request**: The customer makes a request and outlines the conditions of satisfaction to the performer.
2. **Negotiation**: The performer does one of four things: accepts, declines, counter-offers or commits to commit (defer). In the event of a counter-offer that the performer makes to the customer,

the customer has the same four choices of: accept, decline, make a counter-offer or commit to commit.

3. **Promise**: After the negotiation, the performer makes a promise to perform.
4. **Execution**: Performer performs.
5. **Declaration of completion**: Performer declares completion to the customer.
6. **Declaration of satisfaction**: Customer declares satisfaction (or dissatisfaction).
7. **Revoke/cancel**: During this process, the customer can revoke the request, or the performer can cancel the promise. (See Figure 5.1.)

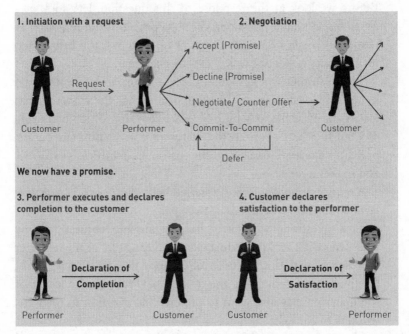

Figure 6.1: Conversation for action

When I first heard about the conversation for action from my coach Bob Dunham, I couldn't believe that this was all there was to it. It looked much too simple! While conceptually this may seem simple, its practice is not trivial at all. Each of these moves has been discussed in detail in my book *Declaring Breakdowns: Powerfully Creating a Future That Matters, Through 6 Simple Steps.*

Here are some questions, first for you to consider for yourself, and for you to have in your repertoire to ask your co-workers. These questions are an invitation to reflection for the leader or the manager and their co-workers.

1.   Request

a. What may be a missing request to generate the desired result? Before we look at the response to this question, let's look at a more fundamental question: Why do people make requests? A request is made because, left on its own course, the future that may emerge may not be okay for the customer.

The customer would like a different future to be created, and hence a request is made. It is important that the customer has clarity on what the new future looks like – that which takes care of what they care about. If the customer wants a different future, or a different result to emerge, the customer identifies a performer and makes a request.

Requests are profoundly generative acts; they bring into motion actions that otherwise would not take place.

This question, 'what may be the missing request', in my assessment, is a very powerful question. The leader or the manager is presented with this choice to reflect upon this question regularly, for the sake of generating the desired new future. The leader or the manager may also want to present this question to their co-workers to consider.

However, one of the biggest blind spots in organizational culture is 'missing requests'. In many organizations, whenever there is dissatisfaction, chances are there is a missing request. It is crucial to recognize that when there is dissatisfaction in an organization, you can either play victim or take responsibility and begin a new conversation for action by simply making a request.

b. What future would unfold if the customer does not make the request?

This is a powerful question too, because it invites the customer to become aware of what future may unfold were they to avoid making a request. By becoming aware of this future and its possible impact on the customer, you open a space for missing requests.

c. What are the possible responses to the request of the customer?

As elaborated earlier, there can only be four committed responses to a request (there can be thousands of non-committed response types, usually with excuses and justifications). These are:

- Accept
- Decline
- Commit to commit
- Counter-offer or negotiate

If you do not have one of the above four responses, it is important as a customer to clarify with the performer what their commitment is. Often, the response one gets is, 'I'll try'. 'I'll try' is not a committed response. The entire objective of the request is to get a commitment to an outcome. 'I'll try' does not give you a commitment to the outcome, but a commitment to action.

When one gets an 'I'll try' kind of a response, the customer does not know whether to reach out to another performer for the outcome or trust this performer.

What is important to note is that the point of the request is not to get a 'yes', but to get a trustworthy commitment to an outcome. For that matter, a decline is a trustworthy commitment.

d. Was the request an effective one, or a sloppy one? The first move in coordinating action is making an effective request. Here are the elements that make a request effective:

- **Who?** Is the customer committed to making the request and generating the outcome?

  Often, customers make requests without adequate commitment. Performers 'listen' to the entire body of the customer, and not just the customer's words. Committed customers have a body that displays commitment to the request.

- **Whom?** Is the performer a committed listener?

  Was the request made to a specific performer or did the customer in a conference room state, 'I would like such-and-such a thing to be done' – hoping one of the members attending the conference would do that task.

  If a request is made to a performer who is distracted or disinterested, the very purpose of the request is defeated. The idea is to generate an outcome through the performer, and if the performer is not fully with you, that outcome will certainly not be generated. A committed customer ensures that the performer is committed to listening to the request and understanding the conditions of satisfaction (and not talking on the phone while the customer makes the request, or doing some other work, while the customer yells out the request).

- **What?** What are the clear conditions of satisfaction of the request?

  For every request, it is important that the customer lists out the conditions of satisfaction. Conditions of satisfaction are a clear description of the standards of the outcome that will satisfy the customer. The objective of describing the conditions of satisfaction is to arrive at a shared understanding between the customer and the performer of the future outcome.

  If the conditions of satisfaction are not clear, the performer may fulfil their understanding of the request, but the customer may still be dissatisfied. This depletes trust between the customer and the performer.

- **When?** What is the timeline for fulfilment of the request?

One of the elements of the conditions of satisfaction is the timeline by when the request needs to be fulfilled. This is a big concern in organizations – requests and promises without timelines for fulfilment. This leads to overcommitment and eventual failures.

- **How?** What was the emotion of the person making the request?

  Every customer has an emotion in which the request is made. If that emotion is not appropriate to the request, chances are the request may be declined. Even if the request is accepted, the chances of fulfilment are less.

  While it is important for the customer to be in an appropriate emotion while the request is being made, the customer also needs to be cognizant of the emotion of the performer. Further, the customer must also listen to see what emotion the request generated in the performer. That will help the customer judge if he or she can trust the response of the performer.

- **Why?** For the sake of what care is this request being made?

  When the purpose of the request is articulated to the performer, the performer gets a lot more connected to the 'why' of the request. This element, as fundamental as it may be, adds a lot of power to the request.

A request 'act' is effective when the above elements have been included in the request. When you make the request with all these elements, the chances of your request being accepted and, more importantly, the outcomes generated, are greater. However, this does not guarantee that all your requests will be accepted and the outcomes will be generated as per the conditions of satisfaction.

e. As a customer, are you getting stopped from making the request?

  As a coach, I have seen people refraining from making requests, which means they have stopped themselves from action and participating actively in the causation of the future (taking care of what matters to them). One of the reasons for doing so is that they assess the request as unreasonable.

'Unreasonable' is an assessment you make, without realizing that this is your assessment, and that it is this assessment that stops you from making a request to the performer.

There are several other automatic assessments that stop people from making requests, such as:

- It's going to be declined any way, so why make this request?
- I will come across as demanding and overstepping if I make this request.
- I don't make these kinds of requests!
- It is obvious that I need this. I don't need to specifically ask.
- They are busy and do not have the time for my requests.
- I have my requests being declined. It's insulting!
- And many more.

When a person makes a request that they have not historically made, there is a certain expansion that takes place in that person. This expansion does not only happen if the request is accepted. It happens when the request is made, and is irrespective of the response to the request.

Pause for Reflection

1. Take a moment to get the present to the 'unreasonable requests' you made of people, and when they accepted these requests, the impact it had on your life and on your success.
2. Now, think of the requests that you are currently not making of anyone – colleagues, seniors, spouse, parents, children, customers – that if you made, would enable you to generate an extraordinary result for you.

One of my favourite quotes of George Bernard Shaw is: 'The reasonable man adapts himself to the world; while the unreasonable one persists to adapt the world to himself. Therefore, all progress depends on the unreasonable man.'

f. Is the customer taking the responsibility for having effective conversations for action with the performer?

If the performer accepts the request, he/she will be acting to support the future the customer wants to create. The customer has a choice to let the performer be, once the request has been accepted, and hope that the performer fulfils the request; or alternatively, the customer can continue to have effective conversations with the performer, offer support where required to the performer, in the interest of the fulfilment of the request.

2. Negotiation

a. Was there a counter-offer made by the performer? Did the customer accept the counter-offer?

In an organization, where there is a culture of commitment, the performer is allowed by the customer to decline a request if the performer does not have the intention, competence or the capacity to fulfil the request. The key reason for this is that the customer wants a promise that is trustworthy, not a promise for the sake of getting a promise. This is the framework of the negotiation – if the performer cannot accept a request, the performer has the choice to decline, negotiate or counter-offer to arrive at a commitment that is trustworthy.

It is important that the customer either then accept, decline, commit to commit or further make a counter-offer to the performer. This continues till there finally is a commitment – a commitment to an outcome that has been requested by the customer; or a commitment not to generate the outcome requested by the customer (decline). The key objective of this is to ensure that the customer and the performer get on the same page, and that there is an *actual commitment* that both can share (a decline is a commitment too).

b. Did the customer stop because there was a decline, or because the counter offer was not acceptable?

Interestingly, in my consulting assignments in organizations, I regularly see customers stop because they have a decline, or a counter-offer that is unacceptable to them. A decline is a decline to the request, not a decline to the customer. Customers often forget this distinction.

Customers stop because of their blindness – the whole generative frame is to build a future with trustworthy shared commitments, and if the one you want is not available, you take other actions to get to the future. The idea is not to insist on promises that won't happen – but to build a path to the future through trustworthy promises.

Pause for Reflection

1. What does a decline to your request mean to you? Do you generally consider this to be a decline to you personally, or simply a decline to your request?
2. Get present to a time when you made a 'decline to your request' personal to you.
3. If you considered a decline, 'only a decline to the request', and not to you personally, what new requests would you make?
4. How would that impact your performance?

---

3. Promise

a. Does the customer have a clear promise from the performer?
    It is critical that the customer and the performer have a shared understanding of what the promise is between them.

b. Are the conditions of satisfaction clear and shared amongst the customer and the performer?

To have a clear promise is to have clear conditions of satisfaction between the customer and the performer.

c. Can the customer trust that the performer will keep the promise?

This is critical. The customer may get an 'accept' to the request that he or she made to the performer. However, the performer may not have the capacity or the intention to fulfil the request. In that case, the request will not be fulfilled. It is in the customer's interest that he or she makes an assessment whether or not they can trust the performer's 'accept'.

d. If not, what may be a missing conversation?

This is what a negotiation is for. A competent customer helps the performer make the moves to produce a shared commitment, and vice versa. If in the event the customer cannot trust this 'accept', the customer, in the interest of the fulfilment of the request, must let the performer know of his or her concerns and be open to getting satisfied by the performer's responses.

e. Is the performer taking the responsibility for having effective conversations for action with the customer?

As explained in the previous chapter, the performer's results, relationship, respect and reputation (4R impact) are at stake every time he or she makes a promise. So, it is in the performer's interest – to have any additional conversations for action with the customer.

You don't have to have a customer competent in the conversations for action, if the performer is. The performer can then guide the conversations. Similarly, you don't have to have a performer competent in the conversations for action, if the customer is. In this case, the customer can guide the conversations.

4. Execution

Does the customer need to follow up with the performer/does the performer need any support from the customer in the fulfilment of the request?

Once in the stage of execution, the customer and the performer need to be in regular touch with each other to ensure that the promise is on track and not at risk.

5.   Declaration of Completion

a. Did the performer declare completion?

The execution stage is completed when the performer assesses that he or she has fulfilled the request. The performer then declares completion to the customer. The declaration of completion is an invitation to the customer to review whether the fulfilment of the request was up to the satisfaction of the customer.

b. What may be the cost of not declaring completion?

By not declaring completion, the customer continues to wait for the performer to fulfil the request, while the performer, in his or her assessment, has already fulfilled the request and moved on to other assignments. This impacts the way the performer gets listened to in the future. In the eyes of the customer, the request is fulfilled not when it is actually fulfilled, but when it is declared to him or her by the performer that the request is fulfilled.

6.   Declaration of Satisfaction

a. Did the customer declare satisfaction?

The whole point of declaring satisfaction is that the customer has assessed that the conditions of satisfaction of the promise have been fulfilled. The declaration of satisfaction may often just be a 'thank you', or another form of acknowledgement. The conversation for action does not complete at declaration of completion, rather it gets complete when the customer declares satisfaction.

b. If the customer is not satisfied, are there any new requests to ensure the satisfaction of the customer?

In case the customer is not satisfied, a request is made to the performer to fulfil what remains undone, pending, or not done to the satisfaction of the customer – this request re-initiates the conversation for action cycle.

7. Revoke/Cancel

The point of these moves is to ensure that the customer and the performer are on the same page at all times. And for that, there can be a cancellation or a revocation.

a. Did the customer cancel the request if the request was no longer relevant? If not, what may be the impact on the relationship with the performer?

If the request is no longer valid, and the customer does not cancel the request – the performer continues to execute a request even though it is no more relevant. When the performer discovers this, it causes damage to the relationship between the performer and the customer. The customer will find it difficult to get the same performer to accept his or her request in the future.

b. Did the performer revoke the promise if the performer did not intend to keep the promise or not keep the promise on time? If not, what may be the impact on the relationship with the customer?

If the performer's intention has changed, or something else comes up that is more important in the assessment of the performer, and that threatens the fulfilment of this promise – the performer needs to revoke the promise made to the customer. If the performer does not revoke the promise, the risk is the 4R impact (pl. see Chapter 5).

Who is finally responsible for Coordinating Action – the Performer or the Customer?

This is a common question that I get asked frequently. Who is eventually responsible for coordinating action: the performer, or the customer? A lot of the people I interact with have great reasons why the performer is finally responsible; and similarly, as many of them have as good reasons why the buck stops with the customer. The person who is finally responsible for coordinating action is: *YOU* (whether you are the customer or the performer).

This is a leadership book for leaders. And hence, this claim is an invitation to you to take a stand to ensure that you will do what it takes to generate the results that matter to you. For me, responsibility is looking towards the future (unlike blame, that considers history and attributes reasons for things having not worked). Responsibility, then, is a posture you take in the moment, to generate a future result that matters to you.

There are two ways to show up – one, being the victim, claiming that it was the other person's responsibility to coordinate action. This generates emotions of frustration, resentment, resignation and other disempowering emotions.

The other way to show up is to take responsibility and do what is necessary to ensure that action is effectively coordinated, for the sake of generating the desired result. This approach generates resolution, compassion, confidence and other empowering emotions.

This is a stand of leaders. You own what happens.

We need to first embody this ourselves, and then invite our co-workers into this way of life – own the conversations, and own the promises, help others to own them as well. So, irrespective of whether you are a customer or a performer, you are responsible for coordinating action and generating the result.

At the Institute for Generative Leadership, Bob Dunham has created these roles of the customer and the performer. If you are the customer, for the sake of generating results that matter to you, you:

- begin by making clear requests, those that have clear and concrete conditions of satisfaction, and those that answer the specific question, 'What does it look like when the promise is fulfilled?'
- are fully committed to the fulfilment of the request
- are committed to be satisfied with the fulfilment of the request
- declare satisfaction and dissatisfaction
- declare breakdowns and ask for recovery plans
- take responsibility for effective conversations for action with performers
- are committed to mutual satisfaction with performers
- assess the trustworthiness of performer's promises – do they have teams, plans, promises and practices of coordination that assure fulfilment?
- are proactive and also:
  - make regular assessments of fulfilment and share the assessments with the performers
  - cooperate to resolve breakdowns
  - inform performers of changes in conditions of satisfaction; make new requests and negotiate new promises

And, if you are the performer, for the sake of generating results that matter to you, you:
- act out of commitment to satisfy the customer by coordinating the making and fulfilling promises of value to the customer
- negotiate promises you can fulfil
- decline or counter-offer requests you cannot fulfil
- take responsibility for effective conversations for action with customers
- are committed to be satisfied in the fulfilment of the agreement – mutual satisfaction with the customer
- maintain trust by communicating and keeping the assessment of fulfilment with the customer up to date
- announce breakdowns early, assess their consequence to the promise, and take actions to resolve them, developing recovery plans
- ask for help to fulfil the promise, if needed

- revoke or renegotiate a promise that can no longer be fulfilled
- offer to help take care of the consequences to the customer of changing a promise
- listen to the concerns of the customer and make offers to take care of them
- build a relationship of teamwork with the customer.[1]

THE RELATIONSHIP BETWEEN PROMISES AND ACTIONS: TAPPING YOUR FULL POTENTIAL

In this section, I have categorized people into four kinds, based on their orientation to promises and action. This is best understood through the TAP (The Actions–Promises) Matrix. However, before we move to the matrix, it would be prudent to understand some terms used in this context.

The TAP Matrix asks the question – 'Are you TAPping your full potential? But first we need to have a shared understanding of a few distinctions.

What is capacity?

Your capacity is your ability to make and fulfil promises.

What is potential?

While the dictionary meaning of potential is similar to that of possible (as against actual) – I am taking a slightly different perspective here. In my assessment, 'When you operate at your full capacity such that your capacity itself expands, you operate at your potential.'

You will see in the TAP Matrix diagrams (Figures 5.2 to 5.7) that there is a quadrant called the 'Safe Person'. Even the safe person makes and fulfils promises. But the safe person is not operating at his or her potential, because he or she can make more promises and still fulfil those promises.

So, while your capacity is your ability to make and fulfil promises, your potential is the ability to operate at full capacity. When you operate at full capacity, you keep increasing your capacity, and hence your potential and the value you create for others and for yourself.

What is the difference between action and task?

We discussed this in detail in the earlier chapter. However, in the interest of rigour, it is important to get reconnected to the generative meaning of the words *action* and *task*.

Action is taking care of what you care about. If you are not doing so, you are only doing tasks, not taking action.

To 'take care', you need to take action inside of promises, those that are inside of your cares.

Task, on the other hand, is activity that consumes time and energy, but does not move forward the commitment and care of the individual. In generative leadership, we assess this to be meaningless activity.

Figure 6.2: Action is taking care of what you care about

We often find tasks masquerading as actions. In my assessment, often people are busy doing tasks, believing they are taking action, and hence – despite a long, hard day of work, they may not feel satisfied. This is because they are no closer to fulfilling their promise, or taking care of what they care about.

The TAP Matrix

The TAP Matrix is 'The Actions–Promises' Matrix, which enables the reader to make an assessment whether or not they are performers.

On the Y-axis of TAP Matrix, we have Promises; and on the X-axis we have 'Actions' (Figure 5.2).

Results are generated through commitment and action, and hence we use these two elements in determining whether you are a performer or not. The matrix has four quadrants – 'safe' person (Figure 6.4), 'busy' person (Figure 6.5), 'jerk' (Figure 6.6) and 'performer' (Figure 6.7).

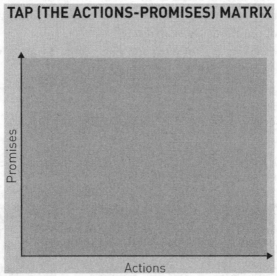

TAP (THE ACTIONS-PROMISES) MATRIX

Promises

Actions

Figure 6.3: The axes on the TAP Matrix

This is a self-assessment matrix. You are requested to review whether you are 'safe', 'busy', 'jerk' or a 'performer'. Some of my clients, whom I coach, assess which quadrant they belong to, on a weekly basis. This assessment generates a new awareness, and hence choice for new action.

The objective is to be in the performer matrix. The performer is the only one of these four categories of people who is taking care of their cares. In the description of the four quadrants below, we have looked at what may be the blindness of people in each of the four quadrants. Blindness is a state when you don't know that you don't know. It is a state of no choice (when you know that you don't know, you have choice, when you don't even know that you don't know, you have absolutely no choice). The objective of revealing the blindness of each of the other three quadrants is to open new choices for people in these three quadrants.

What is important is that other than the performer, people in all other quadrants may be blind to their cares, and hence either they do not make commitments inside of their cares, or their commitments are disconnected from their cares.

Our emotions predispose us to actions and hence we also look at the possible emotions people in the four quadrants may be living in. Along with the emotion, I have also tried to articulate hidden assessments that give us these emotional states. If you stop and assess your emotion or your assessment, you may get an insight of which quadrant you may currently be living in.

Inside of this context, let's have a look at the four quadrants of TAP Matrix.

Quadrant 1: The Safe/Complacent Person

The safe person makes few promises, but acts to fulfil them. They can be trusted, but perhaps not for bigger promises. They respect the status quo, and operate inside of the boundaries of the status quo. They may claim that they are satisfied, but on deeper questioning, it becomes clear that they are waiting to emerge, and make big promises.

The safe person is also the complacent person. They always think small and make modest commitments, and take action only when required. They are also averse to learning and growing – they consider it threatening or too cumbersome.

Roger Martin in his article posted online on *Harvard Business Review* on 2 May 2014 speaks about the top three human urges, and he states that the urge to succeed is the third strongest human urge (after survival and procreation). He spoke about how people play only those games that they can succeed at, thereby not risking their life and liberty.[2]

The safe person or the complacent person may not be as 'safe'. They are actually risking their 'life', their expansion, and their growth in being 'safe'. The complacent person has no ambition, and also has no desire to do more. They are contracted and are drifting, with limited control on their own life.

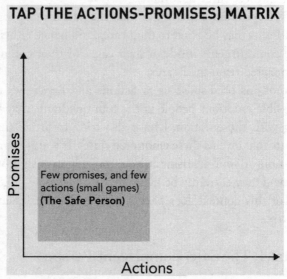

Figure 6.4: TAP Matrix – The Safe Person

Blindness

The safe person is blind to his or her own generative power (power to create new futures, generate new actions). They are blind to their untapped potential. The emotional tendency is towards fear and contraction, rather than attraction towards growth. They are blind to new possibilities, and hence new avenues of action to achieve these new possibilities.

Possible emotions

- Resignation, with an underlining assessment that states 'I cannot do this' or 'this is not possible'.
- Naivety, with an underlining assessment that states 'everything in life is good, and there is no need to take any new action'. They may ignore that they perhaps are not taking care of what they care about.

- Fear, with the underlining assessment that 'life is dangerous and taking on bigger possibilities will expose me to negative consequences'.

Quadrant 2: The Busy Person

The 'busy person' is very busy. They enjoy being that way. For businessmen, this is 'busy-ness', and not business. One of the biggest problems people have in tapping their full potential is that their calendars are full of tasks, or actions that are not inside of promises. The busy person is trapped in a small world. The busy person has no problem with taking action or doing hard work. The irony is that they consider themselves to be good performers or they even do a lot, yet they are limiting their potential.

When you question them why they are taking that action, they are dumbfounded. Although they are good at taking action, they are still in the 'drift', and not in 'design', because they are busy with what shows up as a to-do at that moment.[3] They live in the world of 'I don't have time' and are most often overwhelmed and exhausted.

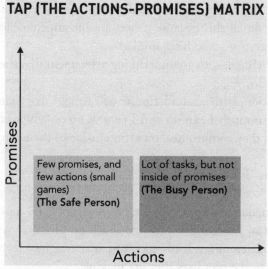

Figure 6.5: TAP Matrix – The Busy Person

Blindness

The busy person is blind to what their cares are; or their commitments are disconnected from their cares. They do a lot of work, but a lot of that work is not inside of what they care for. The advantage with the busy person is that they are not afraid of hard work, but they are blind to the results they can generate if their actions would be in the service of commitments and what really matters to them, rather than just some tasks to be performed.

Possible emotions

- Resignation, with an underlining assessment that states, 'I have no time'.
- Frustration, with an underlining assessment that states, 'what I am doing now should have been done by someone else' or, 'what I am doing now should have been completed by now. I am already late with this task'.
- Cynicism, with an underlining assessment that states, 'I distrust others to do this job, so I have to do everything'.
- Feeling victimized, with an underlining assessment that states, 'I have to do all this because others are incompetent/do not have the interest/or something similar'.
- Overwhelmed, with an underlining assessment that states, 'I have a lot to do'.
- Exhaustion, with an underlining assessment that states, 'There is only so much I can do and I cannot go on any more'. (In the bargain, they compromise on action inside of their cares.)

Quadrant 3: The Jerk

The 'Jerk' makes a lot of promises, but does not fulfil most of them. They want to think big, but do not back up promises with action. There are different levels of jerks, and at the highest level, they are even blind to the promises they are making.

The jerk has a low self-esteem, because they cannot trust themselves. Others also cannot trust the jerk, because historically, the promises made to others were not fulfilled. This lack of keeping promises, to themselves and to others, impacts the success the jerk can achieve.

This person can also be the pleaser who wants to please everyone by saying yes to every request, and they end up not keeping most of their promises. They are dreamers thinking big possibilities, yet do not take actions to make these dreams come true. They are also victims, who blame others and the world around for not fulfilling their promises.

Jerks often make promises that are not clear and the conditions of satisfaction not specific. It gives them the excuse to interpret the promise in a manner that suits them.

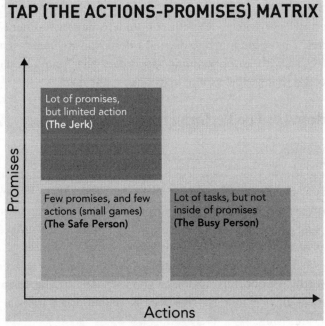

TAP (THE ACTIONS-PROMISES) MATRIX

Promises

Lot of promises, but limited action
(The Jerk)

Few promises, and few actions (small games)
(The Safe Person)

Lot of tasks, but not inside of promises
(The Busy Person)

Actions

Figure 6.6: TAP Matrix – The Jerk

Blindness

As mentioned above, the jerk at the highest level is blind to the fact that what they say is interpreted as a promise by others. They are blind to the impact their broken promises have on their reputation, results and relationships (4R impact). They are also blind to what really matters to them, and that they are not taking care of what really matters to them.

Possible emotions

- Resignation, with an underlining assessment that states, 'I cannot do this' or 'this is not possible'.
- Confusion, with an underlining assessment that states, 'I don't know what to do next' and gets paralysed into not taking new action.
- Getting overwhelmed, with an underlining assessment that states, 'I have too much to do, and I don't know where to start'.
- Bravado, with an underlining assessment that states, 'I need to pretend that I can do more than I can really do'.

Quadrant 4: The Performer

The performer makes promises, and backs them with action. They may not always know what action needs to be taken, and yet makes promises, and does whatever it takes to fulfil those. When the performer is not able to fulfil their promise, they let the customers know and support them in finding alternatives. They even keep them posted on the status of the fulfilment of the promise.

The performer generates results, has high respect for self, enjoys trustworthy relationships, and has a good reputation. The 4R impact is positive and all four Rs (Respect, Reputation, Relationships & Result) are rising.

In learning to make bigger promises, and backing these promises with action, the performer is expanding their capacity.

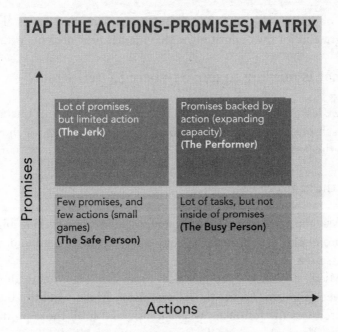

Figure 6.7: TAP Matrix – The Performer

Possible emotions

- Ambition and resolution, with an underlining assessment that states 'there are possibilities here and I am going to act on them now'.
- Commitment, with an underlining assessment that states 'this project needs and deserves my attention, and I will take whatever action required to be taken to see this project through'.
- Wonder, with an underlining assessment that states 'how would it be if I fulfil this commitment – I don't know how yet, but I will figure it out'.
- Boldness and courage, with an underlining assessment that states 'I will take the necessary action, even if I am unsure or scared'.
- Enthusiasm, with an underlining assessment that states 'I am enjoying what I am doing. It takes care of what I care about'.

- Gratitude, with an underlining assessment that states 'I am grateful for the opportunities that life has presented me with'.

What is missing to move to being a performer?

As we learnt above, the objective is to be in the performer quadrant, in each of our cares. Here are some recommendations for moving into the performer quadrant.

For the 'Safe Person'

- Ask the question: 'What is stopping me from making bigger promises?' Get present to your assessments and ground your assessments.
- Make slightly bigger promises from the one you made last week/month. Fulfil those promises. Make slightly bigger promises the following week/month, and fulfil those promises too. Very soon, you will assess yourself to be in the quadrant of 'the performer'.

For the 'Busy Person'

- Ask the following generative questions:
    - For the sake of what result am I doing this task?
    - If I had to make a promise for this task, what would that promise be?
    - Who would be my customer for this promise?
    - How can I have more meaningful actions taken?
- Make new promises inside of your cares, and take actions to fulfil those promises.

For the 'Jerk'

- Make promises that you can fulfil.

- Get present to an assessment that you may have around declining requests others make to you. Start realizing that it is better to decline a request rather than accept a request and then not fulfil it.
- Promises exist in the interpretation of the listener. Be present to the promises that are being listened to.
- Renegotiate promises that you cannot fulfil.

For the already 'Performer'

If you are already a performer, here are a few things you need to keep in mind:

- Be aware that a performer today can be a busy person, or a safe person, or a jerk tomorrow. Keep making new promises and managing these promises.
- Be mindful of your capacity, and make only those promises that you assess can be fulfilled.
- You can expand your leadership impact as a performer by making bigger promises, but not necessarily taking 'more' action. Please see the next subsection on 'Expanding your leadership impact growing value'.

Please note:

- The same person can be in different quadrants in different areas of his or her cares. For example, a person may be a performer in his professional care, and a jerk in the care of family. And this can keep shifting, depending on what actions you take and how you keep and manage your promises.
- You can be a performer on one day, and a jerk, or a safe person, or a busy person the next. Your actions inside of your promises day on day determine which quadrant you are in – on a particular day.

Expanding your leadership impact and growing value

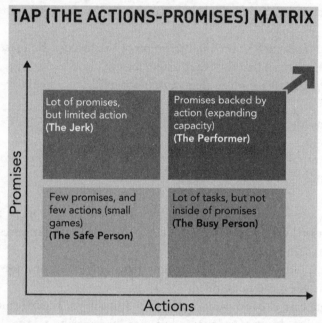

Figure 6.8: TAP Matrix – Expanding your leadership impact

Once you are a consistent performer, you have an opportunity to expand your capacity for the sake of growing value. You can do so by making bigger promises, for bigger results, without taking 'more' action. To grow value, you need to:

- Engage in ongoing embodied learning
- Expand your skills through practice
- Become more self aware
- View concerns as a different observer.

Table 6.1 presents a detailed comparison of the characteristics of the persons occupying the four quadrants of TAP Matrix.

Table 6.1: A comparison of the four quadrants of TAP Matrix

	The Safe or Complacent Person	The Busy Person	The Jerk	The Performer
Introduction	Few promises, limited action	Limited promises, more tasks (meaningless action)	More promises, limited action	Big promises, backed by action
Emotions they live	Resignation, with an underlining assessment that states, *'I cannot do this'*, or *'This is not possible'*. Naivety, with an underlining assessment that states, *'Everything in life is good, and there is no need to take any new action.'* They may ignore what appears unpleasant or ugly.	Resignation, with an underlining assessment that states, *'I have no time'*. Frustration, with an underlining assessment that states, *'What I am doing now should have been done by someone else'* or, *'What I am doing now should have been completed by now. I am already late with this task'*. Cynicism, with an underlining assessment that states, *'I distrust others to do this job, so I have to do everything'*. Feeling victimized, with an underlining assessment that states, *'I have to do all this because others are incompetent / do not have the interest / or something similar'*. Exhaustion, with an underlining assessment that states, *'I cannot go on any more'*.	Resignation, with an underlining assessment that states, *'I cannot do this'*, or *'This is not possible'*. Confusion, with an underlining assessment that states, *'I don't know what to do next'* and gets paralysed into not taking new action. Getting overwhelmed, with an underlining assessment that states, *'I have too much to do, and I don't know where to start'*. Bravado, with an underlining assessment that states, *'I need to pretend that I can do more than I can really do'*.	Ambition and resolution, with an underlining assessment that states, *'There are possibilities here and I am going to act on them now'*. Commitment, with an underlining assessment that states, *'This project needs and deserves my attention, and I will take whatever action required to be taken to see this project through'*. Wonder, with an underlining assessment that states, *'How would it be if I fulfill this commitment – I don't know how yet, but I will eventually figure it out'*. Boldness and courage, with an underlining assessment that states, *'I will take the necessary action, even if I am unsure or scared'*. Enthusiasm, with an underlining assessment that states, *'I am enjoying what I am doing. It takes care of what I care about'*. Gratitude, with an underlining assessment that states, *'I am grateful for the opportunities that life has presented me with'*.

	The Safe or Complacent Person	The Busy Person	The Jerk	The Performer
Blindness	The safe person is blind to his or her own generative power (power to create new futures, generate new actions). They are blind to their untapped potential. The emotional tendency is to fear and contraction, rather than attraction to grow. They are blind to new possibilities, and hence new avenues of action to achieve these new possibilities.	The busy person is blind to what their cares are; or their commitments are disconnected from their cares. They do a lot of work, but a lot of that work is not inside of what they care for. The advantage with the busy person is that they are not afraid of hard work, but they are blind to the results they can generate in the service of commitments, rather than just some tasks to be performed.	As mentioned above, the jerk at the highest level, is blind to the fact that what they say is listened to as a promise by others. They are blind to the impact their broken promises have on their reputation, results and relationships (4R impact). The jerk is also blind to his own generative power.	As humans, all of us have blindness. The performer could be blind to how he could shift the complete game and expand his leadership impact. This is an ongoing process.

	The Safe or Complacent Person	The Busy Person	The Jerk	The Performer
What possibilities are available to them?	The only possibilities that are available to the safe person are those that he or she can fulfil easily. Possibilities that will expand or challenge the safe person just do not show up in the awareness of the safe person	The busy person sees possibilities for tasks, but not necessarily for promises. For him or her, new promises just do not show up as possible.	The jerk sees possibilities for promises; but does not see possibilities for action. In this person's world *it is not even possible to fulfil all promises*.	The performer sees all kinds of new possibilities. Performers listen for possibilities. When they listen for possibilities, guess what they find? New possibilities!
Are they connected to their cares?	No	No	No	Yes
Are they taking care of what they care about?	Definitely no.	Definitely no.	Definitely no.	Yes

	The Safe or Complacent Person	The Busy Person	The Jerk	The Performer
What do they need to do to move from the current quadrant to the performer quadrant?	If you assess yourself to be the 'complacent person', ask the question. '*What is stopping me from making bigger promises?*' Get present to your stories and ground your stories. Make slightly bigger promises from the one you made last week/ month. Fulfil those promises. Make slightly bigger promises. the following week/ month, and fulfil those promises too. Very soon, you will assess yourself to be in the quadrant of the 'performer'.	Ask the following generative questions: For the sake of what result am I doing this task? If I had to make a promise for this task, what would that promise be? Who would be my customer for this promise? How can I have more meaningful actions taken? Make new promises, and take actions inside of these promises.	Make promises that you can fulfil Get the present to an assessment that you may have around declining requests others make to you. Start to notice that it is better to decline a request rather than accept a request and then not fulfil it. Promises exist in the listening of the listener. Be present to the promises that are being listened to. Renegotiate promises that you cannot fulfil.	Continue to make and fulfil promises – those that expand them and their impact.
Are they acting inside of choice?	Claim to, but not really.	Claim to, but not really.	Claim to, but not really.	Yes, absolutely!

POWERFUL QUESTIONS ON ACTION

1. What action – till now missing – can be taken to keep and effectively manage your commitment?
2. What actions of yours currently are not inside of any of your promises? Can you drop these actions? Or can you make a promise around these actions inside a care of yours?
3. What new learning would you like to commit to, in order to expand your capacity for action, and hence your capacity to generate results?
4. What practices may be blind to you – but if you altered those, they could bring about a big change in your life?
5. What are the missing requests or offers that you need to make to take care of your commitments?
6. Are you open to new learning, to new practices? What new learnings or practices are you committed to?
7. What action will you take today to achieve your promise?
8. If no new actions are taken, how similar is your future to your past?
9. Where do you see yourself in the 'TAP Matrix'? What do you need to do to move to the 'Performer Quadrant' in each area of your care?

COMMON MYTHS

Myth: Action is movement or action is doing something.

Busting the Myth: Actions are generative acts in language that shape subsequent physical action (behaviours, activities and physical acts) for the sake of an agreed-upon outcome that takes care of our cares.

You first take action in conversation, through generative acts in language, and these generative language acts (for example, request and promise) shape your physical action. The key here is to recognize that action is done for the sake of taking care of some care that matters to you.

Myth: 'I am a performer when I am busy working.'

Busting the Myth: You are a 'busy person' when you are busy working. A 'busy person' does not equal to a 'performer'. To be a performer, you must be a promiser, fulfilling promises, generating outcomes, creating value, and taking care of your cares while doing so.

Myth: A decline means the customer cannot make the request again.

Busting the Myth: This is such a widely held, yet such a subtle, hidden myth. People often say, 'What can I do - he said no!' And this decline becomes the reason (read excuse) for inaction in the future.

Nothing stops you from making:

- the same request again to the same performer
- the same request to another performer
- a different request to the same performer (inside of your commitment to the same future)
- a different request to a different performer (inside of your commitment to the same future)

There is always a missing request or a missing promise to fulfil any future that you would like to create.

Myth: 'To do something, I need to know how to.'

Busting the Myth: This is another big one that stops people. What comes first – 'doing' or 'knowing'? It is critical to understand that 'knowing' happens only when you 'do'. Here are some examples:

- You 'know' cycling only after you take a cycle and attempt to cycle (do)
- You 'know' swimming only after you go into the water and attempt to swim (do)

- You 'know' speaking in front of an audience, only when you go up there and put yourself on the mat (do)

Myth: Learning happens when you understand the concept.

Busting the Myth: Learning does not happen when you understand the concept – it happens when you embody the concept – it becomes a part of you. You embody something with regular practice. Remember:

- Understanding concepts without practice leads to arrogance
- Understanding concepts with practice of the concepts leads to learning

MOVING ON

Having gone through the four key conversational domains, let's now look at the container conversational domain, which is, 'Holding Space of Conversation'. In the next chapter, we look at what 'space' in this context means; we then go on to define ten points that help create and manage the space of conversation using the acronym 'Space First'.

We also look at a common blind spot of leaders, managers and co-workers, a topic that is not widely spoken about: invalidation, something that's rampant and negatively impacts performance, and yet, most people are blind to this.

And finally, we look at the 'GREAT' model, which provides access to building a trustworthy relationship with your co-workers.

GENERATIVE PRACTICES

1. Action vs meaningless activity
   Develop a practice to observe, at least once every week (if not every day), and to assess how much of your time was spent in the

week taking action (taking care of what you care about) as against meaningless activity (where you were busy, but were not taking care of what you care about).

2. Observe where effective coordination of action is missing in your team meetings.
    a. Are effective requests being made?
    b. Are the promises explicit, and are these promises trustworthy?
    c. Are commitments revoked and renegotiated when the fulfilment of the promise is at threat?
    d. Is completion and satisfaction declared?

3. What new requests and promises can you make to take care of what you care about?

4. Make it a weekly practice to assess:
    a. Where are you in the TAP Matrix?
    b. Where is your team in the TAP Matrix?
    c. What may be your and your team's blindness?
    d. What is your/your team's underlying emotion?
    e. What missing move will help you to become a performer – individually, and as a team?

7

COACH: HOLDING SPACE OF CONVERSATION

To hold the space of conversation is to take responsibility for orienting yourself in your presence and engagement to create an invitation to conversation where another can engage honestly without fear. It is also taking responsibility to bring possibilities to whatever may show up for the sake of a shared future. It includes a readiness to accept declines and cope with breakdowns or reactions. This is a skill of embodied presence, connection, and producing a resonance in conversation with another.

BOB DUNHAM

How would it be if...

- there were high degrees of trust in your team and in your organization?

- you and your team members were not afraid of failure and played big games for the sake of generating results for the team and the organization?

- there was no invalidation in your team, and everyone supported each other?

- the environment in your team was open, and everyone had the freedom to share what they wanted to – for the sake of the results of the team and organization?

WHAT DOES SPACE MEAN?

To understand 'holding space of conversation' in the leadership context, we first need to understand what 'space' means. According to the online Oxford Dictionary, the two meanings relevant of the word 'space' in this context are:

- A continuous area or expanse which is free, available, or unoccupied; and,
- The freedom to live, think and develop in a way that suits one.[1]

While the first definition above of space indicates physical space, in the leadership context, it clearly is not physical space. Space in the leadership context is a 'free', and 'unoccupied' *emotional* space that you create for yourself and your co-worker.

And because this is not physical and is emotional, for your co-worker, this 'free' and 'unoccupied' space either exists or does not exist in *their* experience. As a leader, you can state that you created the space; however, if the co-worker does not experience it, the space didn't exist for the co-worker. At a very subconscious level, if the co-worker experiences this space, he/she will show up in the leadership-coaching conversation without the fear of being judged.

The other definition of space as per the Oxford Dictionary defines space as 'the freedom to live, think and develop in a way that suits one', and this, in my assessment is also as relevant. The keyword here is 'freedom', i.e., the feeling of no restriction and the ability to move unreservedly – in thinking and developing that suits them.

For the co-worker to experience freedom and safety in a leadership-coaching conversation, they should be able to:

- say what he or she would like to;
- feel any emotion;
- share his or her deepest fears, anxieties, frustrations or anything else without feeling any restriction;
- engage without the fear of being judged.

When this sort of openness exists in a team, or in an organization, where people put out on the table all their concerns – it creates access to deal with these concerns. When you don't even know the concerns of your team, there is no way you can deal with their concerns. A mature team or organization is one that is together playing the team or organization game, rather than playing the game of one-upmanship within a team/organization.

WHAT DOES FREEDOM MEAN IN THIS CONTEXT?

Freedom is one of those intriguing distinctions. Many leaders and managers claim that their co-workers have freedom in how they want to act, respond and behave with them. However, on many occasions I have found co-workers feel stifled. Let's attempt to distinguish freedom in the context of holding space, and in the context of generating extraordinary results. (I am not discussing freedom from the point of view of being free from slavery, detention or oppression.)

What is freedom?

In the world of generative leadership, we always begin with the 'what' question. So, the question here is: 'What is freedom?' Freedom comes from two words – 'free' and 'dom'. To be free means to not be affected or restricted by a given condition or circumstance and, 'dom' denotes a state or condition.

So, if we take the literal meaning of freedom, it means being in a state that is not affected or restricted by a given condition or circumstance.

Further, in my assessment, freedom is a *felt experience* of being *unrestricted* in a particular moment. You may experience freedom in one moment, and not experience it in another And it could be the other way round too. You could experience restriction in one moment and then the next moment you could experience freedom too.

You have a huge role to play in whether or not the co-worker experiences freedom in any conversation. We do not give as much importance to the experience of freedom in organizations. Some organizational cultures do not make employees feel free, but only to do what is required of them by the organization, i.e., be a good human resource.

One of the greatest ways for you to support your co-workers in experiencing freedom is understanding and accepting that they may have different cares and commitments than those of yours. And that this is okay. Leaders need to understand that each team member is different, has different cares and commitments, and are unique observers. What is most important for leaders to recognize is that this is an asset, and not a problem.

Hence:

Freedom experienced by co-worker = positive impact on conversations = greater results

Limited freedom experienced by co-worker = minimal impact of conversations = negative impact on results

It is the responsibility of the leader to ensure that their co-workers experience freedom. For that to happen, the co-workers must experience they have choice in the moment.

To experience freedom = to experience choice, moment to moment, in a conversation

WHAT DOES IT MEAN TO 'HOLD SPACE'?

Every relationship has some space or the other. What may be the space between you and your co-workers? In certain relationships, because the space is so good, the manager can say one word and the co-worker can interpret it perfectly, and not only that, the co-worker gets into action with a shared understanding of the conditions of satisfaction. In certain other relationships – especially where the space is so toxic – even the most harmless words said by one person is misinterpreted by the other. There is just no trust in such relationships.

In its definition, space means 'empty space'. If it was not empty it would not be called space in the first place.

To 'hold space' means to 'hold the free or unoccupied emotional space' – a space where nothing exists. None of your past assessments, your opinions, judgements or your views exist there. To hold it that way would mean that every time an automatic assessment or opinion or judgement came up during a conversation, you set that aside and do not allow that to corrupt the space.

Also, often this space may be already occupied with different kinds of disempowering emotions (resignation, resentment, frustration, anger, boredom and so forth), and in such a situation, the role of the leader is to recognize what exists in the space and open it up for something new to emerge with new empowering emotions, assessments and choices.

Further, to hold space is to acknowledge the dignity of your co-workers, to hold them lovingly and yet firmly to the standards that they are capable. This, in my assessment, is another important part of 'holding space'. To hold space does not mean that you do not hold them to the high standard that they can achieve, on the contrary.

To hold them lovingly means that you are willing to walk alongside your co-worker in whatever journey they are on without judging them, making them feel inadequate, or trying to fix them. When we hold space for other people, we open our hearts, offer unconditional support, and let go of judgement and control.

Holding space is about respecting each person's differences and recognizing that those differences may lead them to make choices that they would not make otherwise. For example, they may choose something based on cultural norms that we can't understand from within our own past experiences and cultural practices. As long as these do not impact the results of the organization, encourage your co-workers to make choices that work for them.

When we hold space, we release control and honour differences.

Richard Strozzi Heckler in his book *The Art of Somatic Coaching* states:

> 'I saw that acknowledging their [co-workers'] basic human dignity increased their capacity to be self-educating, self-healing, and self-generating. I was shown over and over that the human spirit steps forward when people are held lovingly, and firmly, to the standards of which they are capable. There's an innate intelligence at our cellular level that rises to the foreground with the slightest encouragement.'[2]

SPACE FIRST

'Holding space of conversation' is a container inside of which all leadership-coaching conversations take place. If this container didn't exist, the leadership-coaching conversations would not be effective. One way of looking at space is the context that drives conversations for individuals.

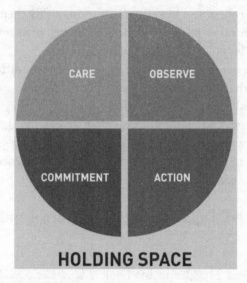

Figure 7.1: COACH: The five critical leadership-coaching conversations

To make an extremely appetizing and delicious chicken biryani, you need a container in which you add all the ingredients. You do not throw all the ingredients on the gas and hope that your biryani will get cooked. Instead, you soak basmati rice in a container with water and gradually keep adding additional ingredients. Gradually, they all come together and the resulting product, the biryani, takes shape within the confines of the container.

So every action in the cooking process is carefully thought through with clear intentions. What gets created eventually is significantly greater than the sum of all the ingredients used.

Similarly, if you want to generate extraordinary results in your organization, your conversations need to be held well, inside of a space that you generate – with choice and with intention. The container needs to be created consciously from the first conversation onwards. If the container has been created well, you will succeed even when the conversations are tough and uncomfortable. However, if the container has flaws in it, even basic non-controversial conversations may turn ugly.

At the Institute for Generative Leadership, we claim that leadership is all about conversations. Judith Glaser too agrees. She says:

'To get to the next level of greatness depends on the quality of the culture, which depends on the quality of relationships, which depends on the quality of conversations. Everything happens through conversation.'[3]

If it is all about conversations, and everything happens through conversations, the space in which these conversations take place needs to be held in a manner that supports these conversations.

I have identified ten points that mean to 'hold space' for the co-worker (and for any other relationship that matters). Holding space is not about tips and techniques – it is about the co-worker's experience. You could presume you have followed all that is listed below, and hence you are holding space. That may not be true. Unless the co-worker experiences this, it was not present.

This is the key – *space either exists or does not exist in the experience of your co-worker*. If you recognize that this space is corrupted, you must take responsibility for cleaning it up, so that effective conversations, as listed in earlier chapters, can take place.

Learning to hold space cannot be an academic exercise; there are practices listed at the end of this chapter, and only after you actively engage with these practices will you get skilled at holding space for your co-workers. Simply put, this means that your co-workers will gradually feel more and more comfortable with you.

Before we go to the ten points, let's take a short pause for reflection:

Pause for Reflection

Take a moment to think of a time, when you thought the conversation was going to be straightforward and yet it turned out to be not so pleasant.

Now, take another moment to think of another time when you thought you were going to be in a tough conversation, and you – or someone else you know – took sufficient time to set up the conversation well – such that the tough conversation did not seem tough any more.

What space existed in each of these conversations between you and the other person?

To define the ten critical points that hold space, I am using the acronym: SPACE FIRST

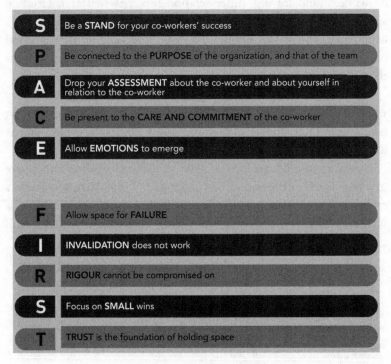

S Be a **STAND** for your co-workers' success

P Be connected to the **PURPOSE** of the organization, and that of the team

A Drop your **ASSESSMENT** about the co-worker and about yourself in relation to the co-worker

C Be present to the **CARE AND COMMITMENT** of the co-worker

E Allow **EMOTIONS** to emerge

F Allow space for **FAILURE**

I **INVALIDATION** does not work

R **RIGOUR** cannot be compromised on

S Focus on **SMALL** wins

T **TRUST** is the foundation of holding space

Figure 7.2: SPACE FIRST

Be a stand for your co-worker's success

Robert Hargrove describes 7 Masterful Coaching 'Come Froms' and one of which is: 'A masterful coach stands in people's greatness even when they fall from it.'[4] I find this an extremely useful 'come from' – it states that you come from a place where you see your co-worker as great – even if he or she does not see himself or herself as great. Interestingly, if you look for the greatness in your co-worker, you will find greatness. The question is not whether your co-worker is great – the real question is: 'What are you looking for?' or 'Are you looking for greatness?'

In their book, *The Art of Possibility*, Rosamund Stone Zander and Benjamin Zander state:

> Michelangelo is often quoted as having said that inside every block of stone or marble dwells a beautiful statue; one need only remove the excess material to reveal the work of art within. If we were to apply this visionary concept to education, it would be pointless to compare one child to another. Instead, all the energy would be focused on chipping away at the stone, getting rid of whatever is in the way of each child's developing skill, mastery, and self-expression.
>
> We call this practice 'giving an A'. It is an enlivening way of approaching people that promises to transform you as well as them. It is a shift in attitude that makes it possible for you to speak freely about your own thoughts and feelings, while at the same time, you support others to be all they dream of being. The practice of giving an A transports your relationships from the world of measurement into the universe of possibility.[5]

Further, to stand for your co-worker's success is to state that you will not accept anything less. In my book *Declaring Breakdowns*, I have stated:

> Another way of declaring that I am taking a stand is to state 'I commit to', and perhaps this comes from the battlefield

analogy, where it may be stated for symbolic reasons for someone or a group to hold a particular piece of ground in the face of adversity. Generally, you take a stand when there is adversity or great opposition, and it is easy to give in to what you are not committed to.

When you take a stand for your co-worker's success, you effectively state that you are making a commitment to making that success be real, and you will do what it takes to make that happen.

You don't say to your co-worker repeatedly: 'I am taking a stand for your success' – this is, of course, the underlying context that drives your actions in your conversations with them. When your co-worker sees the context in which you operate, a new space opens up inside of which they do what it takes to ensure that they validate your faith in them.

Be connected to the Purpose* of the organization, and the team

At every moment and in every conversation, are you connected to the 'for the sake of what result am I having this' conversation? You will notice that very often we are operating inside of what is called 'making ourselves right' or sometimes 'making the other wrong'. I invite you to stop and ask, 'Why am I saying or doing what I am saying or doing at this moment?' Or another similar question to ask may be: 'For the sake of what result am I saying or doing what I am saying or doing?' You will start to see the meaninglessness of some of your conversations/actions. The unfortunate part is not that the conversation is meaningless – often, it may actually be counterproductive.

A senior director of a global IT services company was a participant in one of our in-company coaching programmes, meant to develop

---

*   Purpose: to have a commitment inside of your care is to have purpose.

leaders and managers as coaches. He was thrilled with the idea of being a coach to his co-workers. Initially, amongst several faux pas, one of the things that would put off his co-workers was that in every conversation he would talk about how good he was and what all he had to do to get to where he was in life.

This senior director's conversations were not only meaningless, they were counterproductive. With every coaching conversation he had with his co-workers, he corrupted the space between him and his co-workers a little more than the last time. He was blind to the 'for the sake of what result' was he sharing his success stories, which rather than inspiring his team, were becoming a source of annoyance for them. And as we progressed further in the programme, this fact began to get clearer for the senior director. He started to see how he was not connected to 'for the sake of what result' was he having these conversations. He said that he was so blind that his conversations were not inside of the purpose of their organization, or inside the purpose of their team. (He later even admitted that he was blind earlier that these conversations were more inside of the purpose of showing how good he was).

Drop your assessments about the co-worker and about yourself in relation to the co-worker

Assessments about your co-worker

Emotional space is often consumed by our judgements, opinions, assessments and views. So, the first step – amongst the other important steps – is to drop any assessments you have of your co-worker. These assessments could be either positive or negative. Irrespective of that, these can potentially come in between you being an unbiased observer and may hamper your effectiveness to serve your co-worker.

Coaches often write down their assessments, judgements, opinions or views about their co-worker prior to the commencement of the coaching conversation. It is an excellent practice to observe the observer you are about the co-worker and then ask yourself the impact these assessments may have on your coaching.

Some of these coaches then tear up this sheet on which the assessments and opinions have been listed. This is a symbolic way of stating that this is not 'who the co-worker is'; this is 'who I made him or her out to be' and that you are choosing to 'clean up the space' by symbolically tearing this piece of paper.

To hold space is not only about giving up your assessments and judgements prior to the leadership coaching conversation. It is also about dropping them as and when these assessments and judgements crop up during the conversation. Sometimes you may find it frustrating that your co-worker refuses during the conversation your subtle invitation to being a new observer.

In that moment, you pause and observe your assessments that bring forth the feeling of 'frustration'.

To hold space is to drop these feelings as they come up. In my experience, co-workers can sense these feelings that get manifested in leaders, and this can corrupt the space for the co-worker.

Assessments about yourself

Any assessments or judgements that you subtly have about yourself being great, or about your inadequacy, also corrupt the space between you and your co-worker. Like you write down assessments about your co-worker, you may even write down assessments that you have about yourself and about your being great or about your inadequacy to lead.

Connect with your care and 'for the sake of what result' are you having this leadership coaching conversation with your co-worker. This may help you in 'clearing up the space'.

Be present to the Care and Commitment of the co-worker

In the world of Ontological Coaching, we claim that *the world you see is a function of the observer you are*. So, the question here is, 'what observer are you?' and, 'What are you looking for?'

As a leader, keep your attention on what is the care of your co-worker; and, what is the commitment of your co-worker. That will help you take a detached view; and this detached view will enable you to serve your co-worker, and more importantly, your organization.

My experience of interacting with several leaders is that they get so embroiled and bought into their own assessments and often the assessments that their co-workers offer them, that they lose connection with the care and the commitment of the co-worker. Your role as a leader is to first 'listen for the care and commitment' of the co-worker, because most times this is not obvious, and then to hold this as the context.

Often, people are not present to their care and commitment, and their actions may be counterproductive to their own cares and commitments. As a leader, to listen to this care and commitment of the co-worker, that which may even be blind to the co-worker, is an invaluable skill in becoming an extraordinary leader or manager.

Take care of the Emotions in the conversation

Often leaders and managers are blind to the emotions and mood of their team or organization. Think about it, every person, every team and every organization has an underlying mood. When a leader is aware of the mood of their co-workers, teams or their organization, they give themselves the choice to take action.

However, the unfortunate part of the corporate world is that most often leaders and managers are unaware of the underlying moods.

What's worse is that a lot of them claim not to care about emotions or moods of their co-workers; they claim they only care about results; and often they are blind to their role in generating these moods.

It is important for managers and leaders to recognize that emotions shape how people listen and how people respond. With all good intention, even if a manager has the leadership-coaching conversations listed in this book, but if he or she remains blind to the mood in that conversation, he or she may be even blind to what the co-worker is 'listening' to (the interpretation created by the co-worker) in that conversation. The leader may say to the co-worker; 'I believe you have great potential', but the co-worker may interpret it as 'my manager is trying to manipulate me'.

In this case, the leader or the manager may be blind to the co-worker's mood of resignation or resentment.

The mood of the co-worker does not only impact the 'listening'. It also impacts their 'response'. So, if the mood of the co-worker is resignation, chances are the co-worker has an assessment like 'nothing will ever work with this manager'. If that is the case, it does not matter what the co-worker says to the leader – there will be no commitment to action from the side of the co-worker.

The job of the manager or the leader is to first address this 'emotion' of the co-worker. Till this underlying issue is observed first, and then effectively dealt with, any conversation will at best be meaningless, and at worst be counterproductive.

Allow space for Failure

I have quoted Roger Martin's article in the TAP Matrix too. However, here I would like to share, in greater detail, what he has to say about failure.

> Most people agree that the two strongest human urges are survival and procreation, but there is very little consensus on the next most powerful. I believe it's the need to succeed. Humans hate to fail – hate it more than almost anything else.

But what about all the people in the world who apparently have no drive for success, for instance, kids who choose to be drug dealers rather than get an education and 'succeed'? I see a different explanation for such behaviour. If you hate failure, you have a wonderful way of ensuring that you don't experience it: Play the game you know you can win.

Think about it. On one hand, you can tackle a difficult challenge and face the prospect of failing. On the other, you can strive for a manageable goal and pretty much guarantee that you'll achieve it. I would argue that most people systematically choose the second course of action.

So it's not that kids who drop out of high school and become drug dealers lack a desire to succeed. Quite the contrary. Their desire is so great, in fact, that they risk their lives and liberty to fulfil it. But they take care to do something they can succeed at, not something for which they feel set up to fail, namely, the path followed by more-privileged kids.[6]

The interesting point here is that in Martin's opinion, the third strongest human urge, after survival and procreation, is the urge to succeed. The question that I would like you to consider is: Are your co-workers setting up small games, games they know they can win? (Although it's important to note that the team and the organization loses when they set up such small games and win.)

I invite you to transform your relationship with failure, and support your co-workers to transform their relationship with failure too. For that, first, we will need to have a shared understanding of what failure is.

In my assessment, failure is only a conversation that many continue to indulge in. I have seen many people make past failure an excuse for inaction today, perhaps even an excuse for not playing boldly today.

More particularly, failure is an assessment stating that the desired outcome wasn't achieved.

The world we live in, we give way too much importance to failure. However, there is a key distinction between 'I am a failure' and 'this attempt failed'. This is where the big difference lies! Your attempts can fail. However, 'I am a failure' is merely a declaration you make, something that becomes the context of future action (or inaction).

Distinguish between 'what is so' and 'what I make of what is so'; between 'Who am I' and 'What I do'.

You never are a failure – remember – failure is only an assessment! So, if you choose the assessment, I am a failure – then that is *your* choice!

Yes, attempts can fail – and that is fine. The problem happens when you stop making attempts due to failure. The choice is between inaction and failure. For me, it is a no-brainer; I would much rather choose failure. And the more you are in inaction, the more you are in conversation of wanting to avoid failure. A failed attempt is a reminder of something that is missing. Some action, some practice, some conversation, or some coordination. A failed attempt allows you to distinguish what is missing and bring that forth.

As a leader or a manager, when you create room for failure, you create room for new learning, for new practice, for expansion and for growth. It opens up a space of trust between the leader and the co-worker, it breaks barriers, and the co-worker starts to give their wholehearted attempt because for both of you now failure is just an opportunity to learn.

Virat Kohli, on becoming the captain of the Indian cricket team, in his tribute to M.S. Dhoni stated, 'He [Dhoni] will always be the person who guided me initially and gave me opportunities. He gave me ample time and space to grow as a cricketer, saved me from getting dropped from the team many a times.'[7] Virat Kohli has turned out to be quite a cricketer, and had he not been allowed space for failure, history would have been written differently.

Invalidation does not work

Invalidation is the experience of feeling dishonoured and humiliated. Invalidation happens in the experience of the other person. Given the importance of the concept of invalidation, the widespread blindness with regard to it taking place in teams and organizations, and considering its sizeable negative impact, there is an entire section below for this particular topic.

However, two important points have relevance for leaders:

No solutions approach

To hold space is to have trust that your co-worker is smart enough and that when you invite them to be a new observer, they will find actions or solutions to the issues that concern them. As a leader, you do not jump to advise your co-worker. You set up a space for them to discover the answer that works for them. Assuming that you do jump to offer solutions, and even if your co-worker accepts your solution, chances are the co-worker may not 'own' this solution and hence may not act with full commitment on your solution.

Worse, if the co-worker rejects your solution, some leaders and managers immediately become self-justifying and start to defend their solutions. This, often, is a sure way to corrupt the space between you and your co-worker.

Opportune use of silence

Silence is the most underutilized tool in all types of conversations, particularly leadership-coaching conversations. Silence allows the co-worker to think about your question or reflect upon the answer to a previous question.

Your co-worker may have emotional outbursts, which may include tears, exasperation or other emotions that need to be expressed and released. As a leader, you allow this to happen, and let it unfold in a way that works for them.

The real value of leadership coaching conversations for the co-worker is in their reflections. And these can happen in moments of silence, at the right time and in the right amount of time. I understand 'right' is subjective – but as you gain experience in these conversations, you will learn what the right time for silence is, and the right amount of time for silence. Silence needs to be held in a way, such that it does not land on the co-worker as if you are waiting on something. Silence is held in a way that allows the co-worker the space and time they need for reflection.

Read more on invalidation later in this chapter.

The importance of Rigour

Rigour, as described by the Oxford Dictionary, means the quality of being extremely thorough and careful; or harsh and demanding conditions.[8] At the workplace, rigour has a completely different meaning. To have rigour in a working relationship between the line manager and his co-worker, or between the leader and the co-worker, would mean having an environment that is stimulating, engaging, supporting of high standards of achievement, and most importantly, where commitments are kept, and when commitments cannot be kept, they are revoked or renegotiated well in advance.

The head of the engineering services of a US-based farm equipment organization and I were in a conversation after a workshop with his management team. A few months ago, they had received 93 per cent score in an employee engagement survey. In the last five years, ever since these employee engagement surveys began in this organization, the score of this group of about 600 people hovered between 60 and 65 per cent. According to him, the team had started to respectfully hold this entire group accountable for results. He also believed that because the focus had shifted towards outcomes, they generated more trust and credibility with their internal customers, and that resulted in more work and better-quality work coming their way. This is what, in his opinion, resulted in this huge jump in the employee engagement surveys.

There is accountability in a relationship where there is rigour. In such relationships, when there is need for help, requests are made without making disempowering assessments, such as: 'I will be thought of as incompetent if I make this request', or 'in my position, I should already be knowing this'.

When there is rigour, there is an environment where:

- the observer you are is regularly challenged;
- you generate new actions;
- there is continuous learning of new practices to expand capacity;
- there is a mood of ambition and resolution;
- the focus is on the fulfilment of the commitments – those that we make and those that we are; and
- you are a demand on people, and yet, you are respectful.

While rigour would mean achieving at high levels, the leader recognizes that high levels of achievement cannot be arrived at overnight. There is focus on practices, on learning, on small steps that regularly show growth.

Focus on Small wins

Wins create a space of possibilities and confidence like nothing else does. It doesn't matter whether a win is big or small – a win is a win. A win changes the mood of the team, and energizes its members to generate more wins. Many managers trivialize small wins – they only like big wins.

I like big wins too. However, you need to have created a space inside of which you can play a big game. Often, managers and their co-workers don't do adequate grounding to go for the big wins and they lose – this upsets the mood of their conversations. In my experience of coaching senior executives in the corporate world, we do not give small wins adequate credit. What managers and leaders may want to recognize is that a series of small wins can lead to a *huge* win. And that, eventually, is the objective.

In his book *One Small Step Can Change Your Life – The Kaizen Way*, Robert Maurer quotes John Wooden, one of the most successful coaches in the history of college basketball:

When you improve a little each day, eventually big things occur. When you improve conditioning a little each day, eventually you have a big improvement in conditioning. Not tomorrow, not the next day, but eventually, a big gain is made. Don't look for the big, quick improvement. Seek the small improvement one day at a time. That's the only way it happens, and when it happens, it lasts.[9]

In the same book, Maurer goes on to add, 'As you probably know, Japanese businesses – which built themselves on the bedrock of small steps – soon rocketed to unheard of levels of productivity. Small steps were so successful that the Japanese gave them a name of their own: Kaizen.'

Trust is the foundation of holding space

For a relationship between the leader and the co-worker to develop, and thrive, the key element is trust. It is the responsibility of a leader or a manager to build trust.

Trust produces safety. Trust is about having a future you and others can share and rely on. It is the space for action and possibility. As a leader, it is important for you to know that trust is a result of certain actions, of how you show up in the relationship and the space that gets created in that relationship. All of this determines whether your co-worker trusts you.

In Chapter 5, on Commitment, we looked at 'the promise that you are as a coach'. I stated there too that the five conversational domains in the acronym COACH provide a great basis to look at the promise the leader or the manager is – as a coach. As a leader or a manager, you are also a coach in the eyes of your team(s). So, whether you think you are a coach or not, it doesn't matter. To develop a relationship of trust with your team members, you need to fulfil the promise you are as a coach.

If you breach any of the (implicit) promises, you risk creating distrust in your relationship with your co-worker. Look around you

– there are so many co-workers that do not trust their line managers – if you look closely enough, you will see that the genesis of that distrust lies in one of the above broken implicit or explicit promises.

Nothing corrupts space more than distrust in a relationship. This book is about generating extraordinary results. To do so, you need a space of a high degree of trust between you and your co-worker. That's when you unleash possibilities for magic to happen.

Holding space is a skill, and like with all skills, you cannot master it overnight. While I have listed several points above on what it means to hold space, it is about allowing space to the co-worker to be himself or herself.

Holding space is a complex practice that evolves as we practise it, and it is unique to each person and each situation. Holding space conceptually may seem like an easy thing to do. Yet, it is not trivial, and it is not something that comes naturally to many leaders. On the contrary, to be able to hold space, the leader may need to curb his or her natural instinct to speak and 'resolve the problem' of the co-worker.

You cannot experience holding space of conversation intellectually. You hold space somatically, i.e., using the coherence of the body and the mind. For that purpose, in Appendix 3, somatic practices for each of the ten points listed above have been provided. Please engage with these practices and that is how you will build mastery in 'holding space of conversation'. (Remember, by reading the ten points you do not learn – you only 'know about' holding space. You learn through practice.)

HOLDING SPACE IS SEEING THE CO-WORKER AS A POSSIBILITY

The use of the word possibility, in this case, is not about possibilities in the conventional sense – a phenomenon of chance, prospect or likelihood. The possibility I am talking about here is a creation of yours, that empowers you in this moment, shapes the way you think and feel, to take new action. When you create this kind of a possibility, you impact your now, your present.

Every individual is a possibility of generating extraordinary results. Many of us are blind to the possibilities that we are, and hence do not take action inside of the context that we are a possibility to generate a certain result.

Often, several people generate the possibility of impossibility, and they may be blind to that fact that they are generating this possibility of impossibility. For example, at such times, people may state 'this is impossible for me' or 'this action is impossible'. They are blind to that fact that this impossibility is their creation, and not a fact out there in the world.

This section invites the leader to recognize that their every co-worker is indeed a possibility. They may just be blind to this; and one amongst many other roles of the leader or the manager is to invite the co-worker to see that they are a possibility. This is a context-shifting observation.

When I see someone as a possibility, as against someone as a dud, I see completely different things. New actions emerge for me when I see someone as a possibility.

For example, when I started to see myself as a possibility, I thought of setting up the Institute for Generative Leadership in India. I remember it changed the way I felt in that moment about myself. I felt a new surge of energy, a new power to take actions that were hitherto unknown to me.

When you create a new possibility it excites you automatically and puts you in the mood for taking action in that moment. You know you can make this happen as long as you take actions in line with achieving this possibility.

The primary challenge for a manager today is to stand in the abundant possibility that their co-worker *is*; no matter how badly at times they perform; no matter how often it may seem like you want to give up with this co-worker. If you want to continue working with this co-worker, like I stated in the first chapter of this book, there is then no choice.

Either ask them to leave their job, or look for the possibility that they are. Anything in between is a compromise. To stand in the posture that your co-worker is indeed a possibility will inevitably open new avenues for action for you, and for your co-worker. It will give you the necessary impetus required to support your co-worker in generating results.

ARE YOU INVALIDATING YOUR TEAM MEMBERS?

A team is constituted to fulfil a promise an individual cannot fulfil on his or her own. For a team to achieve its promise, the members of the team need to work as a cohesive, single unit. Often, that is not the case. Team members may be ready to work hard; they may have all the intention to achieve the promise. And yet, many times they do not achieve the promise of the team. In my experience of working with teams, one of the key barriers for teams not achieving their promise is 'invalidation'.

Invalidation happens in the experience of the other person

You do not invalidate another as a fact, or as an assertion. Invalidation happens in the experience of the other person. For example, two employees, George and Natasha represented their organization at the annual industry conference. After their return from the conference, they were both in a conversation with Grace, their director, to provide feedback about their visit.

George began to share his thoughts; just then Natasha cut George, and began to offer a different opinion. At that moment when Natasha cut George, George experienced being degraded in front of their director. He experienced his opinion being discredited by Natasha – despite her not having said a word against his opinion. In Natasha's opinion, she did not invalidate George.

However, it is not for Natasha to decide whether or not she invalidated George. Invalidation does not happen as a fact; invalidation happens in the experience of the other. Facts are facts – same for all. But experiences on the same facts can differ from person to person.

For example, if there was a camera in that room, the camera would pick up that while George was speaking, Natasha began to speak. This would be called a fact – it does not matter who sees the recording. Whoever sees the recording will state that this is what happened.

However, the experience of feeling dishonoured and humiliated cannot be picked up by the camera. That is the experience of an individual person. Assuming the other person was not George, let's say it was Peter. If the exact same thing happened with Peter – he may not experience invalidation, like George experienced invalidation in the exact same situation.

People have different histories, different cultural backgrounds and different ways to interpret what is going on, or what happened. The way we experience an incident (for example, Natasha cutting George while George was offering his opinion to Grace) has a great deal to do with the interpretation the individual makes for that particular incident. George may have interpreted what Natasha did as an insult, and hence experienced what he experienced. While Peter may not interpret what Natasha did as an insult, but just something that she needed to say in that moment. And hence he had a different experience of the exact same situation.

If we were to get rigorous in this discussion, I would add that the interpretation an individual makes also has a great deal to do with the emotional state of that individual at that moment. So, continuing with George's example, assuming the same incident between George, Natasha and Grace were to happen on another day, when George was in a different emotional state, chances are George may not experience invalidation.

Invalidation is like 'hitting' someone

When someone gets hit, he or she is hurt physically. Similarly, when someone experiences invalidation, there is that similar feeling of getting hurt. However, this hurt is not physical. This is a hurt to some-one's self-identity. Recently my three-year-old daughter slapped her twin brother because he snatched her toy. My son simply twitched and moved on with his business of playing. For a moment, I thought that slap would spark off a physical fight between the two. However, that was not to be (thank God!). Most people would have slapped back as a way of protecting their self-identity, but for my little son, his self-identity, at that moment, was not threatened and hence he went on with playing.

Blindness around invalidating another

Often, people are blind to invalidating a team member, or another person. To be blind is to be unaware. They don't know that what they said, or what they did provoked something in the other that caused the experience of invalidation in the other person. Invalidation arises in the other person based on their history and triggers. What is missing is connection and 'listening', noticing the reactions of the other, and amending your actions based on what is being provoked. The question to consider here is whether you are provoking in the other what you intend to provoke. Most people are focused on what they are doing, rather than connecting with what is being provoked by what they are saying or doing.

When we consult organizations, often we sit in team meetings where members regularly strike 'hard blows' at their colleagues (by invalidating them). What's worse, they are unaware of what they're doing. Some teammates respond by striking back, while others go into a shell. An important cause of teams not working as one cohesive unit is that there is so much invalidation taking place within teams, and team members are not even aware that they are causing such damage.

When a person feels invalidated, his or her performance significantly reduces. That person may start to question his or her own abilities and begin to doubt himself or herself. This could work the other way around too – the person feeling invalidated may begin to doubt the intentions of the other person who invalidated him or her.

Either way, this person starts to lose focus from the team promise, and from his role in fulfilling the team promise. He or she starts to (again blindly) operate as a victim – and victims do not take responsibility. From thereon, this person may not work any more towards achieving the team promise. Certain times, he or she may be working, subconsciously, at cross-purposes.

All of this is happening at a surface below most human awareness. We are just not taught to be present to these dynamics in our life. But just because we cannot see this, or are not aware of it happening, is not evidence enough that it is not happening at all. In our experience of coaching, this experience of feeling invalidated by team members is greatly damaging to the cause of the team, and puts to risk the fulfilment of the team promise.

How does one deal with this?

There are several ways to deal with this. Here is what you could do:

Develop a practice to observe how you are being listened to

One of the key skills for leaders and managers is to develop the skill of observing how their team members, their customers, their vendors, their collaborators in other teams, and everyone else they are associated with is 'listening' to them. This is a practice of listening and connection. Remember, 'hearing' and 'listening' are two completely different phenomena. People may hear you accurately, however, what they interpret, and what you intend to communicate may be completely different.

I have had leaders and managers say to me that they are only responsible for what they say, and that they are not responsible for what others understand. This is such a huge myth – as leaders and managers, you are accountable for results. If how people understand what you say as invalidation, and if that impacts the results (individual, team or organizational), then it is important that you take responsibility for how they listen to you.

Take responsibility for what you provoke, otherwise, you are not operating as a leader. As mentioned above, this is a key missing skill in the corporate world, and worse, the learning and development teams within many organizations may have not discovered this yet – and hence no one is being trained to build this skill.

Apologize whenever required and let people know of your commitment

Let us presume in a conversation you said something in the best interest of the team, and someone in the team experienced invalidation. You could see that in the way the team member's body responded to what you said (you will notice these small twitches, small body movements, gulping, etc. when you develop the skill to observe how others 'interpret' what you say.)

At that moment you have a choice to let that sign of the body response pass, or use that sign to communicate with that team member. I often hear people say, 'I cannot help someone else feeling invalidated – that's their problem.' That is only one way of looking at it. However, if this invalidation is going to impact your relationship with that person, if it is going to impact your team promise and your individual promise, honestly, it is your problem as much as it is the other person's problem.

You can ask if what you said had, in some way, a negative impact on the team member, let them know that your intention was not that; and apologize, if required, for not having chosen the right words to communicate what you had originally planned. This is a dignified apology, where you are not necessarily admitting you are wrong (although that may also be true) – but stating that what was provoked in the other is not what was intended.

At that moment, it is important to explicitly state that you said what was stated inside of your commitment to the organization, the team and the individual team members. If it is relevant in that moment, remind the other person of your and their commitment towards the team promise.

The above two ways to responding are for people who knowingly or unknowingly cause the experience of invalidation in another person. However, how should you respond, if you experience invalidation?

Respectfully, bring out the experience of being invalidated

The best way to deal with invalidation is to respectfully let the person know that their actions or words made you feel humiliated. Be open to listening to their views too, so that you can arrive at a shared understanding.

Bringing out respectfully ensures that this does not continue as a pattern in your team, and even if there are disagreements in the team, which is healthy, there need not be invalidation, which is unhealthy. The team has to learn the fine art of disagreeing, and yet not be invalidating each other.

Ignore the invalidation, move on and remain committed to the team promise

If you have experienced invalidation, and it is one of those one-off experiences, let's say in the middle of an important meeting, you have a choice to ignore it. If you do so and move on with life, then do indeed move on and let go of that experience.

Do not hold anything against the person who you think caused the invalidation, do not keep this in the back of your head, or bring it up later. Sometimes in the heat of important meetings, invalidation may happen. You have a choice to ignore it and be bigger than every interpretation that you have.

If we refer to the example of the conversation between George, Natasha and Grace – we also looked at if George was not there and there was Peter in that conversation, chances are Peter may have not experienced invalidation. Assuming the same conversation were to happen on another day, then maybe even George may not have experienced invalidation. We discovered that an individual experience has a great deal to do with the interpretation the individual makes for that particular incident. If that is the case, you have a choice to recreate your interpretation of that same incident.

It is one thing to understand about invalidation and another to learn to build 'great' relationships, generate 'great' results and 'great' moods in teams. The next section will introduce you to the 'Great' model, a model designed to support managers and leaders to create and then hold space for conversation with co-workers, customers and other people they work with.

THE 'GREAT' MODEL

In every conversation, in every person-to-person interaction, there are five critical elements that matter to the experience of communication. These five elements are critical not only in coaching conversations, but in conversations of all types. These include questions like:

- How can you share new ideas with people without them feeling that you're infringing on their space?
- How can you find out what others are thinking about?
- How can you handle your teams better?
- How can you assist in resolving people-to-people concerns within your team?

I call the abbreviation of these five elements as 'GREAT'. It is indeed an appropriate acronym, because the experience of interactions when all factors of 'GREAT' are present is indeed great. When these five elements are present, you generate 'great' relationships, 'great' moods in teams and organizations and 'great' results.

The acronym GREAT stands for:

- **G**ood feel
- **R**eality Shared
- **E**ffective Conversations
- **A**greement
- **T**rust

Each of these elements are related and impact the other elements. Whenever one of them goes up, it sets up the others to go up too. Similarly, when one of these elements goes down, it pulls the others down too. It is unlikely, in my experience, that you can have one of these go up, while the others remain unaffected.

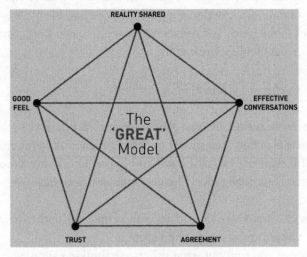

Figure 7.3: The GREAT Model

This also means that each of these elements are access points to taking the other elements up. Let's have a look at what each of these elements mean and the connection between them.

Good Feel

Good feel is the emotional response. In a conversation, we either feel good about being in that conversation or not; we either feel affection or we don't.

If you notice, people draw towards groups and conversations that make them 'feel good'; and they move away from groups and conversations that do not make them feel good. The more 'good feel' there is, the more the person opens up to new ideas and new conversations. The opposite is true too. The lesser the 'good feel' the more the contraction and resistance to new ideas and new conversations.

Intrinsically, 'feeling good' is a human need.

Reality Shared

What does reality mean? When I ask this question in leadership programmes, I get responses such as 'truth', 'fact', etc. I then ask another question: 'Can two people have different realities?' and most times the response I get is in the affirmative.

Yes, two people can indeed have different realities.

Facts, on the other hand, are assertions – they are the same for all in communities. Facts are not dependent on the observers. Realities, however, may differ from observer to observer. So, what does reality mean?

Reality is 'what seems true to the observer'. It further means what shows up for the observer and the observer's experience of it. These are not facts, but interpretations of facts.

For example, the manager asks for a project to be completed by a certain date. The reality of one of the co-workers is that this date is unreasonable and the project cannot possibly be completed within this date. Another co-worker has a different reality – he thinks that the project can be completed within the time frame set by the manager.

The fact in both these cases is the same (which is – 'the manager has asked for a project to be completed within a certain timeframe'); however, what seems true to both these co-workers is different.

The claim this model makes is that the more reality you share, the more the other person 'feels good' in your presence. The more the reality differs, the lesser the 'feel good factor in the conversation'.

Effective Conversations

The third and perhaps the most significant element in this model is effective conversations. As we have discovered, conversations are critical. It is with effective conversations that you make someone 'feel good', and it is with effective conversations that you arrive at a 'shared reality'.

Similarly, it is with conversations that someone does not 'feel good' and it is with conversations that different realities get created.

The more effective the conversations, the more there's 'good feel', and 'shared reality'.

When I use the word 'conversation' here, I just don't mean talking and listening. I mean conversation the way we distinguish it at the Institute for Generative Leadership, which includes not just words, but 'the whole-body reactions that are provoked when we interact in language and when we interact and language is provoked in the other person.'

At IGL, we claim that conversations include not only language, but also moods and emotions of the parties involved in the conversation.

And most importantly, the key part of conversation is not what is said, but what gets listened (the interpretation created by the listener). 'What gets listened determines whether or not there is 'good feel' and 'shared reality'.

Leaders, in their conversations, then need to focus on what gets listened rather than on what they say. They need to put their awareness on the listening of the other to see if 'good feel' is generated and if a 'shared reality' is going to be produced.

Agreement

As a team, as a manager and co-worker, what is critical is agreement on the result that we want to generate; agreement on the assessments based on which we act; agreement on the next steps of action that are required to be taken to generate the result agreed upon.

Agreement is critical.

More importantly, as we saw in Chapter 5, on Commitment, each person is a promise to another in a relationship. To what extent we keep that promise (agreement) determines the extent of 'good feel', and 'shared reality'. Even if we do not keep the promise, are we having conversations around revoking a promise that we cannot keep, or renegotiating a promise?

If agreements are kept, other elements of this model go up; if agreements are not kept, other elements are impacted – to the extent agreements are not kept.

Trust

Trust is such a crucial element in any relationship, and is that underlying hidden element that makes or breaks teams and results of teams. If you see all the other four elements in the GREAT model – each of these have a role to play in the building of trust. And likewise, trust has a role in each of these too.

Let's look closely:

- In a relationship, if there is trust, there is 'good feel'; and, if there is no trust, there is no 'good feel'.
- I share reality with people I trust; with people I don't trust, the very fact that I do not share reality with them is because I do not trust them, and I do not trust their version of reality.
- Effective conversations would mean that the gap between what I am saying and what the other is listening is almost non-existent. You understand the intention of what I say. When trust is missing, there is a gap between what I say and what you listen.
- As we have seen in the Commitment chapter, trust is directly related with the agreements you keep. When you keep agreements, trust goes up. And when you do not keep agreements, trust comes down.

I have used the GREAT model on many occasions in my coaching programmes. What my participants have learnt along the way is the interconnectedness of each of these elements. In my assessment, you cannot have one of these elements go up, while the others come down. If you work on any one of these, you are automatically working on the others.

While we were discussing this model in one of my programmes with senior executives of a large Swedish organization, the marketing head of the India unit stood up and shared an example, and we used that example to clarify this model. He stated that he was furious with one of the team members for not only not achieving his targets, but also for not disclosing his numbers accurately quarter by quarter. I asked him, in that conversation:

- Was there any 'good feel' for any one of you?
- Did you share reality with each other?
- Was the communication effective?
- Was the agreement met? (And while here in this section of the book we are only looking at the explicit agreement of the co-worker of meeting the target, the implicit agreement of manager's support to this co-worker was also not met. We discussed this at length in the programme, and the marketing head fully acknowledged *his role* in the fact that the target was not met. So, in essence, both had not kept their agreements.)
- And finally, was there trust in this conversation?

The marketing head admitted that the answer to all the questions was a loud 'no'!

I cannot stress enough how this model works both ways – when one of the elements goes up, the others go up too. And similarly, when one of the elements goes down, the others go down too. This awareness is critical, and through the understanding of this, I invite you to see that each of these elements are an access to revealing your blindness of how the GREAT model is working, and you may not even be aware of it.

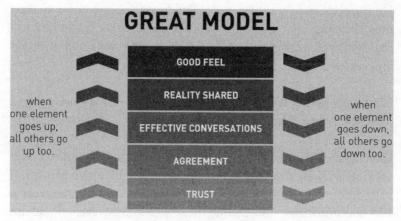

Figure7.4: The interconnectedness of elements in the GREAT model

POWERFUL QUESTIONS ON HOLDING SPACE

In this chapter, I have combined the powerful questions and the generative practices. Please refer to the generative practices in the box starting p. 243.

COMMON MYTHS

Myth: 'I am a resulted oriented person, and I don't have the time for such "soft topics".'

Busting the Myth: This book is about generating extraordinary results, and the claim is that these conversations are critical to generating the desired results. If you are operating in isolation, and generating your desired results, you do not need the distinctions provided in this book. However, if you are working with people, then these distinctions are non-discretionary.

Holding space of conversation is a critical container inside of which you have conversations with your team members. You can risk not understanding what it takes to 'hold space of conversation'. And then the price you pay is that you do not generate the results you could otherwise have generated – had you understood and practised these distinctions.

Myth: 'By giving freedom to my co-worker – I will lose control over him or her. That is not okay with me.'

Busting the Myth: The bigger myth is that you have control over your co-worker. Your co-worker is an independent human being with different cares and commitments. To acknowledge these cares and commitments, and giving them freedom in every moment, ensures that they 'feel good' in your presence. This will ensure that you have a longer relationship, and one that is significantly more successful.

The big question here is: 'Are you committed to control, or are you committed to the results?'

Myth: The leader and the co-worker have an equal role to create the space and then hold the space.

Busting the Myth: Let me state this clearly. It's not necessarily the manager or the leader who has the responsibility for creating 'the space'. Neither is it the co-worker who has this responsibility.

The question then is who has this responsibility of creating 'the space'?

The response is, the responsibility for creating the space is with *you*. People often tell me that they have done their part, and now, it is the others who need to do their part. At the end of the day, it is important to recognize that it is *your* result, in an area of *your* care that is not getting achieved. If that is the case, then it is *your* responsibility to generate the space, hold the space of conversation, and have the necessary conversations to generate the results that matter to you.

Own the future and the actions required to get there with others.

Myth: 'I am the leader and I am good at my job; if the co-worker does not trust me, there is something wrong with the co-worker himself.'

Busting the Myth: My response to this is similar to my response to the above myth. If it is a result that matters to you, then *you* take the necessary action to get others to align with you. To claim that there is something wrong with the other is taking the easy way out. There is a heavy price to be paid in the form of not generating a result that matters to you. The choice is yours – stick with the story that there is something wrong with the other person; or create a new context – the one that this book invites you to – which is, if something is missing, *you* take the necessary action.

TAKING CARE OF WHAT MATTERS, AND YET BEING RIGOROUS
A case study by Umang Bedi

At Adobe Systems India, we had a gentleman called Anand Kumar, who was our senior-most technology consultant in data and analytic solutions. Within Adobe, he was considered the best technology consultant and practitioner around data and analytics in India. However, he was not very popular within the team because of his very abrupt, abrasive and non-people-oriented style of functioning. There had been times when even in front of customers, he had snubbed one of his team members or disregarded or invalidated what they said. Often, he pushed his boundaries with his colleagues and sometimes did the same with the customer as well.

Even though he was extremely well regarded from the standpoint of subject matter, and his technical knowledge was second to none, his acceptability and leadership within the team was questionable because people did not relate to him as a thought leader who was carrying the organization forward. During one of the conversations with Anand, we were talking about his career and how things were going. He said, 'You know Umang, every time I'm in a meeting with a sales professional or someone from industry strategy or someone from value engineering and other different cross-functional teams, I'm the best guy in the room. I have the most technical knowledge, I am number one on technology, I know more than anyone else in the room.'

The moment I heard that, I knew we had a problem. The opportunity here was to figure out what he was striving to achieve. What I learnt when I pressed him a little bit more was that he wanted to be regarded as a thought leader in the industry. He wanted to be regarded as the go-to guy, or the subject matter expert that people would want to talk to. He was wondering why he had not made that progress despite having the best technical knowledge. I think the opportunity there, for me, as a coach in that conversation, was to show him the mirror.

I asked him a couple of questions that created a new observer in Anand, and created a whole new space between us:

If you were so technically good, have you ever shared your knowledge with others?

Have you ever helped others learn and improve their own understanding of the product line or the technology?

Did you huddle together in a team meeting to say, 'Hey guys, why can't we build a strategy deck or a strategy proposal for customer X in a manner that would be so refreshingly different for that client, because it would show a very deep insight into his business?'

And most importantly, assuming you were to do this, what would be the impact on other's perception of you – people within and outside the company?

The reaction to that was pure silence. Anand was completely in shock and in awe, and he said, 'You know what, I completely understand, Umang, why people don't look at me as that thought leader, because I've never gone and had those conversations with them. For me, it was always about being number one technically and demonstrating to others that I'm the best. It was never about carrying the organization forward.'

In that conversation, I understood Anand's commitment to wanting to be a thought leader in his field both internally within the company and externally in the industry. The conversation helped him discover that he had a superiority complex, and when he became aware, he could see the changes he needed to make.

It is amazing to see what that one conversation did. Anand went out of his way after that on every opportunity to share his knowledge. He held what we called 'kickbox situations' within the company to share his insight, talk about different industries, how his knowledge could be applied, how different teams could value from his expertise.

He even started writing blogs, posting stuff on LinkedIn, writing inputs on cmo.com, and is now regarded as a great thought leader within the company. He's made tremendous progress towards achieving his own personal goals, and his relationship with others has transformed too.

GENERATIVE PRACTICES

The next time you feel stuck or come upon some uncertainty try holding space for the issue rather than trying to fix it. Get curious about it – ask more questions – feel free to have a pen and paper handy to get some of those thoughts out. Try practising holding space in your work – with your co-workers and clients – and see what it does for you. Practices for taking a stand for your co-worker's success:

1. Look for the Green
    a. Keep this book aside after you read the first three points of this practice (points a, b and c). Do the short ten-second practice that is recommended and then come back to continue reading the rest of the practice.
    b. I want you to focus in this exercise, and do it with intention, rather than doing it just for the sake of doing it.
    c. So let's start – keep the book aside, and look around where you are sitting now and find all the green that you can find. In

ten seconds, see how many things you can find with the colour green in it.

Do the exercise now.

    d.   Did you find any green that you had not noticed ever since you sat where you are currently sitting?

    e.   Did any other colour stand out for you, other than green?

Most people, when doing this practice at home or office or any other surrounding familiar to them, notice green in places that they hadn't noticed in weeks/months – or ever for that matter. Interestingly, for many people, other than green, no other colour stands out loudly – lots of people completely miss seeing any other colour.

The question I have for you: How is it that you found green?

Simple: because you went looking for green.

It is straightforward – in life, you find what you go looking for.

If you go looking for the greatness of your co-worker, you will find greatness there. The question is not whether there is greatness. The question is – are you looking for the greatness in them – particularly, when they fail.

2.   Have you stood up for someone's success?

    a.   Have you ever been committed to someone else's success?

    b.   If yes, take a moment to reflect on how you showed up in that relationship, and what actions you took to ensure that person succeeded?

    c.   Did that person succeed?

3.   Are you currently standing up for the success of your co-workers?

    a.   In your mind, run through all your co-workers / all people who directly report to you.

    b.   Are you committed to their success?

    c.   Really, are you committed to the success of each one of them?

    d.   If not, what may be missing from your end? (Please do not be dismissive about this – the deeper you go, the greater the benefit you get.)

4. Practices for being connected to the purpose of your organization and your team:
   a. Reflection on your last leadership-coaching conversation
      i. Reflect on your last 'leadership-coaching conversation' with your co-worker.
      ii. Reflect on whether that conversation could have been more impactful.
      iii. If yes, what was missing, that, if present, would have made the conversation more impactful?
      iv. If no, what was present, and because of its presence – the conversation was impactful?
   b. Develop a practice of asking yourself before or while you are in a conversation with any one:
      i. For the sake of what result am I having this conversation?
      ii. Is my conversation inside of that purpose?
      iii. Is this conversation helping my purpose or defeating my purpose?
5. Practices for dropping your assessments about your co-worker, or about yourself in relation to your co-worker:
   a. What are the assessments that you have for each of your co-workers? Are these assessments corrupting the space between the two of you? Be rigorous in your reflection. The deeper the reflection, the greater the benefit you will receive.
   b. Have you ever experienced having a conversation with someone significantly senior to you, and having an automatic assessment, 'Am I good enough?' or, 'How can someone like me add value in a conversation to someone like this person?' or any other similar disempowering thoughts?
      What was the impact on the conversation with these thoughts?
   c. A leader begins and has every conversation with the co-worker inside of the space of nothingness (meaning thereby – the leader holds no assessments about the co-worker or himself/herself) with the objective of supporting the co-worker to generate results that matter to them.
      I invite you to practise having conversations with your co-workers by keeping aside any such assessments that you have while in conversation with them – to help them generate results that matter.

6. Practices around building trust:
    a. Is your conversation expanding or depleting trust?
        i.   For example, John wanted to get his co-worker to take certain actions that his co-worker was not taking. John got upset with him and yelled at him to get the job done. The job got done – however, the price paid by John was that there was a depletion in the relationship with the co-worker. John was asked: Do you think you could have had a different conversation such that your co-worker did the job, and yet, there was an expansion in your relationship with this person.
        ii. Interestingly, because John was so used to being right – his initial response was no – and that he had already tried these 'softer ways'. Next morning, he realized that the same thing could have been achieved without the need to yell.
        iii. While John was connected to the obvious purpose of the organization of generating the immediate result, he was blind to the objective of using every conversation as an opportunity to grow the space between with his team members.
    b. Take a moment to reflect on John's example above, and see how this resonates with you. Observe if your conversations are expanding or depleting trust in the eyes of your co-workers. If you notice that the trust between you and your co-workers is not as high as it should be, identify what could be the missing conversation with that co-worker.

7. Practices around invalidation:
    a. Think about the last time you were in a conversation and you felt invalidated? Distinguish between an event and your interpretation of the event – i.e., distinguish between what actually happened (event or fact) and what you made of what happened (interpretation).
    b. What new interpretation can you create of the same incident? Your ability to do so regularly will greatly enhance your skills for leadership.

    c.   Think of a time when someone else felt invalidated by you:
        i.   Think of their body reactions at that moment;
        ii. What did you say that caused that reaction in them?
        iii. How could you have said what you said differently such that the other person would not have had the experience of invalidation?

    d.   As a regular practice, be present to how you speak with others and observe if others are getting invalidated by your actions.

8.   Practices around the 'Great' model:

    a.   In your day-to-day interactions with people, see the interconnections between the elements of the 'GREAT' model, i.e., good feel, reality shared, effective conversations, agreement and trust.

    b.   The claim this book makes is that, if one of the elements goes up, the others go up too. Look at your relationships in your office, and see the relationships that you consider to be working – notice the interconnectedness between these elements. Also, notice the interconnectedness of these elements present in relationships that you consider not to be working.

    c.   Use the different chapters of this book to build a working relationship that works for you, and for the others.

Part III

Part III

8

WHAT NEXT?

If you have reached this page of the book, something about this book has interested you. All the five coaching conversational domains are critical. See which ones you would like to develop your skills in. Then jump into practice. First do the practices yourself, gain a certain level of competence in these and then invite your co-workers to these practices.

You now 'know about' critical conversational domains and need to practise these (by regularly doing the practices recommended at the end of each chapter).

I cannot overemphasize the importance of these practices, and the impact they will have on your results, your confidence, your public identity and on the authority you receive from others in coaching them.

I want to forewarn you that while you practise these distinctions yourself and then coach your co-workers – failures will happen. As a matter of fact, I would invite these failures. Real skill will get developed when you navigate through these failures. Also, it's important to remember that failures are normal and integral to life. They are bound to happen. Just because you have practised these five conversational domains does not mean failures will not happen. To deal with failures is an art and practice.

The more you practise, the more artful you get. Such is the case with every skill.

Remember, authority is a function of mastery and mastery comes with regular practice. (If you have mastery in an area, people will give you authority in that area.)

The promise of this book was to provide the fundamentals of the critical leadership-coaching conversations to enable you to generate sustainable results. I am hoping I have kept this promise to you. If you have any questions, need clarifications or would like to share feedback, please visit www.sameerdua.com or email me on sameer@sameerdua.com. I would be delighted to respond back to you.

Finally, I take great delight in inviting you to:
- a new way of learning,
- a new world of extraordinary performance,
- new seeing, new awareness and new choices, and,
- a world full of possibilities!

9

RE-IMAGINING AND REINVENTING ADOBE SYSTEMS, INDIA

A Case Study

Here's an incredible success story shared by Umang Bedi when he was the managing director of South Asia region for Adobe Systems. He is currently the managing director of Facebook India and South Asia.

You will notice all conversational domains of COACH used by Umang and their team in Adobe Systems, India's journey from not being present in the top twenty-five global markets to being the fifth largest country-business in the world serving small and medium businesses and amongst the top seven businesses in the world serving the entire enterprise vertical.

This entire case is in first person, in Umang's words. What I have done is added my comments in brackets highlighting the relevant conversational domain used by Umang.

Before I start off on the Adobe journey, I'd like to give you a context of the IT market in India for any large multinational software Internet or hardware technology company. India does not represent more than 1 to 2 per cent of the global business for any software, hardware or Internet technology company which is a multinational operating its business in this region.

That's the harsh reality – even though India is a market with a lot of potential and promise, the business in terms of volume and revenue is no more than 1 to 2 per cent for any company globally. Also, for any of the MNCs in the tech space, India does not figure in their top twenty-five markets of the world. Even when you look at the Asia-Pacific region alone, India does not figure amongst the top three or four markets. The leaders are usually Australia followed by Korea or China, South-East Asia and then India. That's typically the pecking order for the business within the Asia-Pacific region as well.

Coming to Adobe, when I joined in 2011, all the above factors applied to Adobe in India too – in fact we were the smallest business in the Asia-Pacific region, by country.

In my first thirty days on the job, I learnt three interesting aspects about our business. One, Adobe was known for its tools and technologies that helped create the world's most compelling content and applications around the creative and document business – where we were serving a small section of small and medium enterprises only. Two, we had absolutely no enterprise business in the country for our digital media or our creative products, nor did we have any enterprise business with large customers for even our upcoming digital marketing category of products. And three, we had absolutely no direct-to-consumer model where we were serving consumers, students or teachers via our direct dotcom presence. In summary, the business was an extremely small entity that was being driven through a two-tier channel distribution model that was largely being driven and controlled by about twenty registered partners of Adobe in India. I saw a massive, massive growth opportunity in a market that had very high potential.

(Author's note: As I have stated in the 'Observe' chapter, opportunities do not exist out there in the world. Possibilities exist and only exist in the

'way you see'. Umang was a unique observer – he saw a 'massive, massive growth opportunity in a market that had very high potential' and because he observed the way he observed, new domains of actions emerged for him, and for his organization. If the observer was not Umang, and some other managing director, he or she may or may not have seen this as a possibility. They may have observed differently, and hence perhaps taken completely different actions.)

I'm going to break up the journey of re-imagining and reinventing, and it will be in two parts. The first part is going to focus on the 'what', and the second part is going to focus on the 'how'. Let's begin with part one of the journey: the 'what'.

The first step was to bring out or come up with a vision or a strategic intent for the business that was extremely ambitious yet very motivating, powerful and extremely energizing for everyone in the organization. So, we did a two-day off-site. By the time it ended, we came up with a strategic intent that consisted of three significant bullets.

The first one was that we wanted to be a company that was helping drive digital technology and digital transformation for every consumer, small business, and most of the large enterprises in the country. The second bullet was that we wanted India to be amongst the top five to seven markets for Adobe across the world, globally. And the third was that we wanted to be the largest, or the second largest, market (as consolation) in the Asia-Pacific region.

(Author's note: In the chapter titled 'Care', we looked at CARE as an acronym for 'Creating Action and Reconstructing our Existence. You can see how the top leadership team at Adobe Systems, India began by creating their cares, by identifying what matters to them. They came up with three bullet points. Once they came up with these three bullet points of their cares, all 'action' was geared to achieve these three bullet points.)

Once the leadership team arrived at strategic intent, our first step was to help people believe, show them a new future, provide them the lens to say, 'Here's the art of the possible', and imagine India amongst the top five to seven markets in the world, or as the largest market in the Asia-Pacific region. Just to see the impact our contribution would make to the company globally.

We invited them to see what this would do in terms of investments the company would bring into the region; to see the runway this could provide us for our own growth, tap learning opportunities and lateral movements across various cross-functional jobs. It would help people learn, grow and achieve a much larger dream of being significantly important to the larger global family of Adobe.

(Author's note: Once the 'care' of the organization was clear, Umang and his team began to connect this with the care of individuals within the organization. Most professionals care to be relevant to their global organization; care for their personal growth, and care for their learning and development. Umang tied this in and made the organization's care – the shared care of all concerned.)

I remember that being the hardest part of the exercise. Sitting with employees, different cross-functional teams, showing them this vision, showing them the 'what if', showing them the art of the possible, taking them along in that journey and making them believe that these big, alarmingly difficult, audacious goals were achievable if we got our act right. And it was this entire process that took us almost around two or three months of galvanizing the entire organization towards this one strategic intent and vision that we had set up for the business.

This was the journey about the 'what'. And the key ingredients of this journey were broadening the lengths of the team, showing them a new future, showing them the mirror of what today looks like and what tomorrow could be. And it was uplifting for everyone because if we did indeed get to what we had stated in our vision, the outcome would have been remarkable not only for the individuals involved in the business, but for India as a nation, and for our strategic importance within the Adobe corporate family.

(Author's note: In addition to the Care conversation, Umang also invited his team to new commitments, to new actions, and to new practices. The very fact that the team felt uplifted was because Adobe Systems, India now showed up as a new promise; Umang showed up as a promise for his team; and each member could see what promise they were in fulfilling this broader vision.)

I'm now going to focus my attention on the 'how' – how we went about re-imagining and reinventing Adobe in depth. I'm going to further break this up into two parts. The first was the focus on the innovation and the transformation that we drove around our creative and our document technologies, popularly known as the digital media business and the second part was about focusing on starting from scratch in the digital marketing business.

So, let's begin with part one around the digital media business. When we looked at the environment around us, we saw a very compelling change in India's landscape. We were producing more and more content across print, web, television, mobile and online. More and more images were being produced. More and more photography was being done. More movies were being released. Video was exploding and content creation and content consumption was exponentially increasing because of social and mobile technologies. However, our business was largely flat. And it was not growing year on year for several reasons. One of the biggest ones that was impeding our growth was piracy in the market. But deep down, there was a cause for piracy. We found that there were three problems. I like to call them the 'triple As' playing our business.

The first was the problem of 'affordability'. Take for example, Photoshop. If you want to buy Photoshop for your son or daughter to learn in school, it would have cost you around Rs 66,000 to 72,000 depending upon the exchange rate at that time.

The second problem was that of 'awareness'. There is a lack of awareness in the market that Photoshop was in fact a big software. Piracy, while being the ultimate flattery, was known as the most popular way to consume that software.

And the third problem was that of 'access'. There was no place to go and purchase genuine Adobe software. We had only twenty small resellers in the marketplace.

The last two problems, access and awareness, were easy to fix and we went about fixing them by means of what I refer to as 'business hygiene'. In terms of accessibility, we expanded our partner ecosystem from twenty partners to over 500 partners across the country so that small and medium businesses and enterprises could transact with them. We also introduced an Adobe direct enterprise model so that the large enterprises could transact directly with us. In addition, we added Adobe.com, where anybody could go and discover what Adobe products were available – they could try it and then buy it for a fee. So, that was an easy problem to solve because it was all about building distribution channels across, building a direct footprint, and launching Adobe.com.

The awareness challenge was again easy to solve because it was all about marketing, and the right type of marketing which was one on one with our target audience – be it enterprises, consumers or small businesses. And we made significant efforts to drive this one-on-one marketing without any pre-advertising, but with more intimate, personalized, contextual conversations that we had over various events, forums and social media to drive that awareness in the market.

The hardest problem to solve was that of affordability. While looking at solutions for affordability, we identified three other challenges. The first was that our software was updated only once in twelve to eighteen months, which meant we released a new version once in twelve to eighteen months and customers would buy this technology not on every software release but typically after about two releases. They did so because the previous version already served their purpose. The second problem that we were facing was that while we were creating new features that were slowly released in these release cycles, technology was changing very fast. More and more content was being consumed on devices and on mobile, and being created on mobile. We needed to react a lot more quickly.

And the third key problem with affordability was how to price our products appropriately for the Indian market such that it drives exponential growth for the business.

We made a bold decision. Our engineering team and business unit came up with a subscription version for our desktop offerings that we later rechristened as 'creative cloud', an alternative that we brought out into the market, which gave an easier way for businesses, consumers or enterprises to access our software monthly. With this, India became the first market in the world where we shut down our cash cow for perpetual business and moved the entire business to subscriptions. It meant that those interested in using Photoshop in a legitimate manner could pay Rs 499 per month, instead of the purchase price of Rs 70,000 earlier. What's more, consumers had the option of paying for only those months when they wanted access and not pay us for subsequent months when they didn't want to use it.

This was a revolutionary game-changing model for us in the country.

(Author's note: For me, this is a great example of being a new observer. Bringing the price down from Rs 70,000 to Rs 499 per month is a drop to a price of 0.7 per cent of the original price. If you look at the annual fee of, let's say Rs 6,000, even that is only 8.6 per cent of the original price.)

But it had three challenges. The first was convincing our own teams – they were used to selling the same product for Rs 70,000 but now they had to sell it for a paltry Rs 499 per month. This is a mindset shift to tell a sales team, 'Hey, this is actually better for the business because when you bring the price points down that low what you're hoping is to drive an exponential volume of growth of really happy customers that are so satisfied that they use it month after month after month and they keep renewing the business.'

So, let's say, in the first year you added 100,000 subscribers to the business. In the second year, you renewed 90 per cent of those 100,000 and added, let's say, another 200,000. And likewise, you've got this stacking-up effect of the revenue, but in the first year, revenue would significantly dip, and then of course, it would rebuild over time. But it would add massive predictability to the book of business.

It was a hard challenge to convince our own sales team on the model and really broaden the lens to help them expand the market that was anyway pirating our software. However, this was now a legitimate way for them to use our software. Once it was on the cloud, there was no way for them to go out and pirate it. The second challenge – again, an internal one – was transforming the entire business. From recognizing the revenue, we were recognizing analysed reccurring revenue. We had to change the way. It was literally like changing the engines of a plane mid-flight. So the engineers had to work together to now give constant updates to the cloud if not every day, at least once every week, rather than over the eighteen-month frequency earlier.

(Author's note: What a fantastic example of the COACH conversational domains in practice! When I first met Umang and shared these domains with him, he immediately resonated with these ideas and shared this example with me. I think this one example alone successfully puts all the conceptual ideas I have presented above in this book in context.

All conversational domains of 'care', 'observe', 'action', and 'commitment' are present in this example. And more importantly, if the appropriate 'space' was not held well by Umang, no one in his team internally or otherwise would have trusted Umang with the massive transformation of business.

One final comment: If you read the case above carefully, you will see that Umang had these conversations with himself first, and then with his team. He got connected with his and his organization's cares first, and then connected with the cares of his team. He observed things differently himself, committed to the new game and took new actions first before inviting others to new commitments and new actions.

This book is an invitation for you to have these conversations with yourself first, and only after you are satisfied with the results you have generated, you have these conversations with the others.)

APPENDIX 1

THE EIGHT TENETS OF CREATING A 'PLATFORM' FOR 'BECOMING' A LEADER

P: You are a *promise*. Being blind to the promise you are is no excuse for not fulfilling the promise you are.

L: You don't *learn* first and then 'do'. You 'do' and in the process learn. (This is embodied learning, and not academic learning.)

A: To take *action* is to take care. Everything else is meaningless activity.

T: The *trust* that exists in a relationship determines what results can be generated in and by that relationship.

F: Ask yourself ten times a day - '*For the sake of what result* am I doing what I am doing at this moment?'

O: *Observe* how and what you observe. Keep questioning the observer you are.

R: Take *responsibility* for generating results in your cares. They are your cares after all. If not you, who? Stop playing victim in generating results in your cares.

M: If you don't have a result you want, there is a *missing conversation*. Keep looking for what that could possibly be. If a certain conversation fails to generate the desired result, that wasn't the missing conversation. Start looking again!

APPENDIX 2

CENTERING

Being centred is being in a physical, mental and emotional state of choice.

We are centred when our body, mind and emotions are in a state where we can choose our actions.

When we are not in a state to choose our actions, we are 'off-centre'; our reactions and tendencies choose for us.

In centering, we attain complete balance and focus regardless of our situations:

- Our mind is alert, we are connected to what we care about, and we are free of distracting mental chatter.
- Our mood is serene and open to the current situation.
- Our physical state is dynamically relaxed, alert, balanced around our centre of gravity, and ready for action.

Centering is the skill to put yourself in a state of choice rather than be in reaction when a challenging moment demands your leadership. It is a process to bring yourself in the present moment and to be connected to what matters to you.

In our lives, there are often situations that leave us flustered, irritated, angry and generally in a disempowered state (handling an irate customer, receiving negative feedback from our seniors, managing difficult situations with colleagues and seniors). These may be situations where we are at our reactive best. In such situations, our past experiences, habituated ways of thinking and moving in the world come to the foreground and choose our actions. No wonder then we have angry outbursts, make wrong decisions and have disempowering moods.

These are the very situations that *really* require our body and mind to be in a state to choose the next actions.

When centred, you think clearly and act with choice. There are several types of centering practices; we have one below for you (we have an audio version of this and a few more on www.sameerdua. com).

Centering practice: The Five-point Relaxation Technique

This centering practice uses the 'five-point relaxation technique' to help you relax your mind, ease out the tensions in your body and support you to get back in the present moment. First the basics:

- Sit comfortably on a chair with your spine erect and well rested. Place your palms comfortably on your thighs.
- Let your feet rest flat on the ground with a distance of about a foot.
  Or
  If you wish, you may stand, with your feet slightly apart and parallel to each other.
- Let your shoulders be straight and not stooping.
- Let your knees be slightly bent.
- Keep your spine and neck straight.
- Your eyes can be open or closed. (If you are new to centering, closing your eyes can help you concentrate better.)
- Begin by observing your breath.
- Let your attention follow the path of the oxygen entering your nostrils. As you breathe in, imagine your lungs filling up like a balloon as the oxygen enters them. And as you breathe out, imagine your lungs deflating. This will help you to take fuller and deeper breaths.

- Continue this for a couple of minutes.
- Notice every time your mind wanders, gently bring your attention back to your breathing without any judgement.
- With practice, the wandering of the mind will reduce.
- Now take your attention slowly to these five points in your body:

Point 1 – Forehead

Notice if you are holding any tension on your forehead and eyebrows, and ease them out. Furrowing the eyebrows is a way of signalling the brain that there is tension and anxiety, and a person with furrowed eyebrows generally emits negative emotions. Relaxing your forehead will help reducing the feeling of anxiety and stress.

Point 2 – Eyes

Soften your gaze if your eyes are open.

If your eyes are closed just feel them relax.

Since the optic nerve is connected to your brain, relaxing your eyes will help ease the mind and diminish anxiety.

(Don't be in a hurry; give adequate time to each of these five points. As you pass your attention from one point to the other, don't judge or evaluate, only notice the amount of tension, stress in each of these parts and very gently relax them as if you are gently stroking and caressing each cell to ease out.)

Point 3 – Jaws

Part your lips slightly such that your jaws do not touch each other. Let your tongue hang loose in your mouth. The moment you do that you will notice your breath drop. This can enable you to be more open and receptive in moments of stress.

Point 4 – Shoulders

Move your attention to your shoulders and feel each cell relax. We tend to carry stress and tension on our shoulders and often we're not aware but our shoulders are held rigidly. This rigidity further increases the stress.

Point 5 – Belly

With awareness now ease your belly muscles. Let your tummy protrude out. A lot of us tend to bunch our belly muscles together to increase our aesthetic value and this way of carrying our body can become subconscious. You may not even be aware that you are holding up your belly muscles. When you ease your belly muscles it will help ease out the stress you may be carrying around your centre.

Now place your one palm on your centre of gravity (two inches below your navel) and take a deep breath. Let the breath be deep enough to reach your centre and enable your palm to be pushed ahead. Continue this for a couple of minutes. This form of deep breathing increases the blood flow in the body which in turn increases energy and stamina in the body.

Now slowly and gently ease your breath, let it become normal.

Whenever you are ready, gently rub your palms together, place them on your eyes, feel the warmth on your eyes and stay that way as long as you wish before opening your eyes slowly.

Please visit www.sameerdua.com for an audio of this centering practice and a few more.

Contributed by Sheeja Shaju, Somatic Leader and Leadership Coach, Institute for Generative Leadership, India.
Email: sheeja@generativeleadership.in

APPENDIX 3
SOMATIC PRACTICES FOR 'SPACE FIRST'

Here are a few practices for 'SPACE FIRST' to build your skill of being more aware of what is going on in your bodies. By listening to your bodies, you have access to your moods and emotions, have more choice in actions you can take, and hence are faced with more choice in the results you can generate.

S	Be a **STAND** for your co-workers' success
P	Be connected to the **PURPOSE** of the organization, and that of the team
A	Drop your **ASSESSMENT** about the co-worker and about yourself in relation to the co-worker
C	Be present to the **CARE AND COMMITMENT** of the co-worker
E	Allow **EMOTIONS** to emerge
F	Allow space for **FAILURE**
I	**INVALIDATION** does not work
R	**RIGOUR** cannot be compromised on
S	Focus on **SMALL** wins
T	**TRUST** is the foundation of holding space

BEING A STAND FOR YOUR CO-WORKER'S SUCCESS

Why is this somatic practice important?

In the first chapter of this book, we stated that you can either take responsibility for the results of your co-worker, or you can act as a victim. To take responsibility for your co-worker's results is to take a stand for their success.

This practice will remind you of the promise you are to your co-worker. Through this practice, you will help exhibit a solid presence to your co-worker that will build trust in them, and get you connected to the promise that you are to your co-worker.

Somatic practice

Stand with your feet parallel to each other and about a foot's distance from each other; keep your shoulders squared, your neck and head aligned with your shoulders and spine; keep your knees soft; let your vision be focused in front; and your tailbone parallel to the ground.

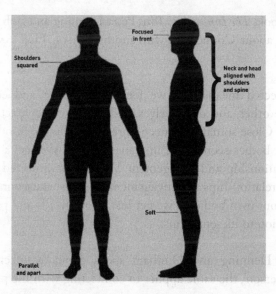

Maintain this stance and imagine your co-worker accomplishing his promises to himself and to the organization. See him as a success. Observe how your body feels and acknowledge the feeling of warmth, pride, or happiness in your heart when you see him achieving his targets in your vision.

If you sense disbelief in your co-worker's ability to fulfil the promise, get connected to why you feel this disbelief.

What may be missing that, if brought forth, will enable your co-worker to succeed?

Share how you feel with your co-worker.

Be fully transparent with him or her, and help them in distinguishing what may be missing in the observer they are, in their commitments, or in their actions.

Seek new commitments from them (if required), and make new commitments of support to them (if required).

BE CONNECTED TO THE PURPOSE OF THE ORGANIZATION AND THE TEAM

Why is this somatic practice important?

In their book, *The Innovator's Way*, Peter Denning and Bob Dunham and speak about 'Connection' with another person. Here is what they state: [1]

> Connected means that we feel the presence and energy of the other, and of ourselves, and we stay in contact with them. Close somatic connection results in limbic resonance, where bodies seem to be in a shared state. We feel a sense of relationship and engagement. We are disconnected if we avoid relationships and engagement. We can be disconnected from our own bodies if we get lost in our heads and pay no attention to its sensations.

While Denning and Dunham speak about 'connection with another person', the same applies to connecting with the purpose of the organization. Connection with the purpose would mean being connected with the care and commitment of the organization, i.e., feeling the 'presence and energy of this purpose, and of ourselves, and to stay in contact with them'. You can deliver an extraordinary result only when you are connected with the purpose.

Somatic Practice

You may sit or stand. If you choose to sit, place your feet firmly on the ground about one foot apart, your spine and neck erect and your back well rested. If you choose to stand, place your feet parallel to each other and about a foot distant from each other, your shoulders squared, your neck and head aligned with your shoulders and spine, and your knees soft.

Now take a deep breath and fill your diaphragm with air, let your tummy protrude out as you breathe in.

Continue this for three breaths.

Continue breathing this way. With every breath orient yourself to the care of your organization.

Get the present to the commitment of your organization, inside each of its care.

With each breath, allow these care and commitments to seep into your body slowly and steadily.

Get the present to your cares and commitments. Now, with each breath allow these to seep into your body slowly and steadily.

With every in-breath, see the connection between the organization's care and commitment and your care and commitment getting stronger.

Continue breathing deep.

Now bring your attention to your team and the promises of your team.

Allow these commitments to seep into your body slowly and steadily.

With every in-breath, see the connection between the organization's care and commitment and your care and commitment getting stronger.

Continue breathing deep.

The entire practice may be followed at the start of your working day for about 3–5 minutes.

DROP YOUR ASSESSMENT ABOUT YOUR CO-WORKER AND ABOUT YOURSELF IN RELATION TO YOUR CO-WORKER

Why is this somatic practice important?

One of the keys reasons the space between the leader and the co-worker may be corrupted is because of the assessments each of them have for the other. Our hidden presumption is that the other person does not know of these assessments. However, there is a certain corruption in the space that takes place if these assessments are not aligned with the team promise.

This somatic practice will help you see how your co-worker lives in your world. You then exercise choice in breaking away from any unwanted or automatic assessments that you may have of the co-worker.

If we must generate results with a co-worker, we need to see the co-worker as a possibility of generating these results. Any other assessment of ours will corrupt the space.

Somatic practice

Sit comfortably on your chair with your spine erect and well rested. You can softly close your eyes to avoid distractions.

Take a deep breath.

Reflect about your co-worker.

Get the present to the stories or assessments you have about them.

Observe if any disempowering assessments show up in your awareness.

Notice how your body feels. For example, do you wrinkle your forehead or does your throat feel a constriction or do your shoulders feel rigid?

Continue breathing.

Remind yourself that these are your assessments and that you have created these assessments about your co-worker.

Get present to your commitment as a leader. Get present that one of your implicit promises is that you are a stand for co-worker's success.

Get present to the possibility your co-worker is.

Now, as you breathe out, imagine the disempowering assessments that are sitting in various parts of your body exit your body, creating space for possibilities to emerge.

Continue this practice till you feel the space has cleared up and that you are ready to begin with a clean slate with your co-worker.

Whenever you feel ready you may slowly open your eyes.

During your leadership-coaching conversations (and any other conversation for that matter) continue to observe your body. Notice the assessments that may show up for you in the conversation. Notice if your body is showing you signs of any disempowering assessments arising.

Acknowledge them and get present to the stand that you are for this co-worker.

This may be practised as often as you like. A good time would be just before a meeting with the co-worker and it could take five minutes or as long as you wish.

BE PRESENT TO THE CARE AND COMMITMENT OF THE CO-WORKER

Why is this somatic practice important?

To listen for the care and commitment of your co-worker is to listen for what matters to the co-worker. As we discovered in the 'Care' chapter, care is critical for generating meaningful results, it is the source of energy and aliveness, it is the 'hidden ground on which we stand'. When we connect to the cares and commitments of the co-worker, we open up a space for magic to happen.

Somatic practice

In conversations with your co-worker, and while seeing your co-worker in action, actively pursue looking for the answer to 'for the sake of what care and commitment would this person be saying or doing this?'

Often, people are blind to their own care and commitment.

As a leader, your role is to first listen for the care and commitment of the co-worker, connect with it (feel its presence and energy).

And if required, invite the co-worker to become aware and connect with their care and commitment.

This is a powerful practice to be done as often as possible, when in conversations with people. You can practise connecting to others' care and commitment while speaking to your family, customers, neighbours, co-workers and just about anyone. People will experience being a lot more connected with you when you do this practice.

TAKE CARE OF THE EMOTIONS IN THE CONVERSATION

Why is this somatic practice important?

Human beings are emotional beings. Our emotions are always present and are very much a part of our make-up. It is critical to take care of emotions in any conversation, primarily because emotions shape how we listen; and emotions also predispose us to action.

If a co-worker is resigned, chances are whatever possibilities you invite them to see, all they will see is 'impossibilities'. So, first, you need to become aware of this emotion of the co-worker.

Further, what you speak will also generate emotions in the co-worker. As a leader, you need to be connected to what emotion is getting generated in your co-worker.

Somatic practice

Start with observing emotions consciously in at least three conversations every day.

Observe yourself and the other person in the conversation.

Notice anything different about the way your or their (the other person's) body moves in response to the conversation.

Observe:

- if the pitch of the voice changes,
- the way the sitting position changes,
- the breathing (moving from shallow to deep or any other way),
- the shift in eye contact or any other twitches.

Observe your internal reactions of contraction and expansion. All this is happening in coherence with the emotions of the conversation.

If you think the conversation is moving towards a result that is not desired by you, open up your body by spreading your arms and taking a few deep breaths.

Consciously, choose to shift the emotions of your conversation.

Shift the conversation in order to take the responsibility for driving the result of the conversation.

Begin with three conversations a day and as you get better at it, your body will automatically get attuned to it. Then it will not have to be an orchestrated practice.

ALLOW SPACE FOR FAILURE

Why is this somatic practice important?

Often, the way to growth is through failure. Failure is likely to happen if we play big games, if we would like to grow, and have others in our team grow. One of our promises as a leader is to ensure the growth of our teams, and for that we need to recognize that failure is part and parcel of that growth.

This somatic practice is important to build trust in our co-workers that, despite failure, we still trust them to generate outcomes that matter to the team and the organization. It is important for building confidence and self-trust in the co-worker.

Somatic practice

Open up your body.
Spread your arms and feet.
Take a deep breath and fill each breath with possibilities (despite an immediate failure).
You can also do this practice by having your co-worker in front of you. If so:
Have a faint smile on your lips.
Look into the eyes of your co-worker – one of our accesses to somatic connection is through your eyes
Somatically, invite your co-worker to new possibilities, to learn from the failures, and move on to newer actions to generate the committed outcomes.

INVALIDATION DOES NOT WORK

Why is this somatic practice important?

Feeling invalidated can make a person lose focus from the promises made to the team. It builds distrust, and a general feeling of being struck by someone from within the team. As Sameer states in the section on Invalidation, 'When a person feels invalidated, his or her performance significantly reduces. That person may start to question their abilities and begin to doubt themselves. This could work the other way around too – the person feeling invalidated may begin to doubt the intentions of the other person who invalidated him or her.'

This somatic practice will help you to get the present to and acknowledge how your body feels while being invalidated; it will help you make space for empowering emotions to concentrate on the promised outcomes.

Somatic practice

a. *Sit in silence and think about an instance when you last felt invalidated.*

Think about details of that conversation and feel the sensations in your body that you may have felt in the moment of the invalidation. (For example, you may feel a constriction in the throat, and an example of a thought that may come into your mind may be, 'She is so arrogant, she always cuts into my conversations.')

Observe the disempowering assessments that caused the discomfort.

Next, take in a deep breath and as you breathe out imagine yourself dropping off these negative assessments from your body (particularly from those parts which felt the uneasiness) thus making space for new empowering assessments that can serve you.

Do this for every assessment that showed up.

Continue this for as long as you want and for as many breaths as you feel comfortable for dropping each assessment.

If you feel the need to have a conversation with that co-worker, please do so, inside of your commitment to clearing the space between the two of you, and not as a complaint. When you have the conversation, have an open body disposition as we practised in the 'Allow space for failure' practice above.

b. *Reflect on the last time you may have invalidated someone. (It could be your peer, friend or even your child.)*

Think of the details of the conversation and focus on the body responses of the other person, that you may have missed at the time of the conversation.

Get present to what possible assessments you made and what you felt in your body when you were saying what you said. Get the present to the assessments the other person may have made at that moment that caused the experience of invalidation in them.

Ask yourself and reflect on:

'Did this serve the purpose of my conversation?'

'Did this serve my relationship?'

Now, get present to what you are sensing in your body right now about the invalidation. Get present to the feelings and body sensations that may be arising.

If you feel the need to have a conversation or make a dignified apology to complete this with your co-worker, please do so.

THE IMPORTANCE OF RIGOUR

Why is this somatic practice important?

Often we confuse rigour with sternness. You can be highly respectful and loving, and yet be rigorous with your co-workers. To build trust and respect, you have to *invite* your co-workers to a higher standard of delivery. And that can happen when you bring rigour in your conversations with your co-worker.

When there is rigour, there is an environment where:

- the observer in you is regularly challenged;
- you generate new actions;
- there is continuous learning of new practices to expand capacity;
- there is a mood of ambition and resolution;
- the focus is on the fulfilment of the commitments – those that we make and those that we are; and
- you are a demand on people, and yet, you are respectful.

In this practice, you learn to face your co-worker with respect and yet hold him or her accountable for the results committed to the team.

Somatic practice

The best way to do this practice would be to do this with a partner.

Sit upright; facing each other, close enough to have your knees almost touch each other (the gap between the knees may be about an inch or less, and yet not touch).

Look each other in the eye.

Keep looking at each other in the eye for as long as it takes to get comfortable doing so.

Your body will automatically manifest twitches, aches or a need to scratch. A lot of our natural tendency is to avert our gaze, turn away, put our attention elsewhere, etc.

Every time either of the two partners notice this, you start over again, till such a time you get past all these twitches and urges to a point when both of you believe you can keep sitting there as long as required.

Facing is an incredible practice to dealing with any challenge, person or situation. When you look in the eye of your co-worker, face him or her, and request for a higher standard, chances are you will see them rising up to meet your expectations.

FOCUS ON SMALL WINS

Why is this somatic practice important?

Expansion happens when we play big games. When we play big games, the focus has to be on small immediate wins, and these small wins give us an abundance of confidence, and together they constitute a big win.

When you direct your attention on the big wins, you may lose focus from the present, and end up not winning at all.

Somatic practice

Ruminate about some result that you have been wanting in your life that matters to you; and yet have been avoiding or procrastinating for some time.

Notice, when you think about it, what is the feeling you get in your body; does your heart feel heavy, do your shoulders droop or do you feel your jaw tense up? Notice your body response to this reflection.

Get present to any assessments that come.

Centre yourself.

Break this up into small, chewable commitments, such that when you act on these commitments, it does not seem like a burden at all (for example, if you want to reduce your weight by 15 kg, start by walking five minutes every day in your house itself).

Gradually increase the intensity, once the earlier practice becomes a habit.

Acknowledge yourself for having achieved every small win.

Celebrate.

Get back to the next small, yet slightly higher challenge.

TRUST IS THE FOUNDATION OF HOLDING SPACE

Why is this somatic practice important?

Trust is the key in helping any relationship thrive. To build trust in the relationship with your co-worker, you have to connect with the promise that you are to your co-worker. If you breach any of the below-mentioned (implicit) promises, you risk creating distrust in your relationship with your co-worker. Look around you – there are so many co-workers that do not trust their line managers – if you look closely enough, you will see that the genesis of that distrust lies in one of the broken implicit promises.

Nothing corrupts space more than distrust in a relationship. This book is about generating extraordinary results, and to do so, you need a space of a very high degree of trust between you and your co-worker. That's when you open up possibilities for magic to happen.

Somatic practice

The five conversational domains in the acronym COACH provide a great basis to look at the promise the leader or the manager is – as a coach. As a leader or a manager, you are also a coach in the eyes of the teams. So, whether you think you are a coach or not, it doesn't matter. To develop a relationship of trust with your team members, you need to fulfil the promise you are as a coach

The promise that you are is that *you:*

Care

- Have distinguished your co-worker's cares and are committed to taking care of these cares;
- Understand that the co-worker has his or her cares too and that the co-worker may have different cares than the ones you have – and you respect these cares of the co-worker;
- Enable the co-worker to see – 'for the sake of what result' they are taking the actions that they are taking; and support them to be connected to 'for the sake of what result' for every action they take.

Observe the Observer

- Support the co-worker to observe the way the co-worker is observing;
- Offer alternative ways of observing, and give the co-worker a choice to observe differently;
- Show up to work with a mood that the results are entirely possible to achieve – and it is upon the team to take the requisite missing actions.

Actions, Practices and Habits

- Co-create actions and practices with the co-worker, so that the co-worker can embody new habits that work for the co-worker;
- Focus on 'what's missing' (action that needs to be taken that will give the desired result) rather than on 'what's wrong' (problem);

- Understand that irrespective of how good individuals are and what they do, breakdowns will happen – you enable the co-worker to navigate through these breakdowns;
- Respectfully support the co-worker to discover whether he or she is operating as 'the safe person', 'the busy person', the 'jerk' or 'the performer'.

Commitment

- Keep and manage your commitments to the co-worker and to the organization, and support the co-worker to keep and manage their commitments;
- Stand totally committed to the co-worker, and to achieving the promise of the organization;
- Work backwards from the promise, and support the co-worker to work backwards from the promise, rather than from the history of the group/ individual (past).

Holding Space

- Create and hold a space of mutual trust and respect;
- Stand in people's greatness, particularly when they cannot see their own greatness;
- Speak from a stand to achieving the promise, rather than from reactions;
- Be open to receiving and giving honest feedback.

Contributed by Sheeja Shaju, Somatic Leader and Leadership Coach, Institute for Generative Leadership, India.
Email: sheeja@generativeleadership.in

APPENDIX 4
DISTINCTIONS/ GLOSSARY OF TERMS[1]

Action
a. Action = generative acts in language that shape subsequent physical action (behaviours, activities, physical acts) for the sake of an agreed-upon outcome that takes care of our cares.
b. In the world of generative leadership, we interpret action not as some disembodied activity that we have to organize 'out there', but rather as generated by acts of commitments by people who care about some concern.
c. Action is *taking care* of what you care about. If you are not doing so, you are only doing tasks, not taking action.
d. To act is to take care. Taking care is the fundamental aspect of action that brings meaning, value and satisfaction.

Assertion
An assertion is a claim of fact, which is either true or false, to a standard established by the community. Assertions can be substantiated or refuted through observation and evidence.

Assessment
An assessment is a statement of evaluation, opinion or judgement. Assessments are neither true nor false. Instead they can be grounded (supported by evidence) or ungrounded. Other words for assessments are stories, opinions, judgements, assumptions and so forth.

(Hidden) assessment

Hidden assessment is an assessment that you have made, and yet, you are unaware that you have made this assessment; this assessment lands to you as an assertion, i.e., fact.

Authority

a. To have authority, in the context of leadership would mean to have 'permission from another'. This permission is not generally explicit, and most often implicit.

b. Authority is not a function of seniority. To have authority over someone means to have a certain degree of power over that person. And in this case, power would mean that that person grants you the right to present choices to him or her to make a decision or in certain cases even exercise choice on their behalf.

Awareness

a. Awareness means that something has been distinguished in our perceptual field, giving us the potential of paying attention to it and putting it into language. Awareness creates choice. Without awareness, nothing exists for us. When we are aware, we shape what we see, we can make choices about it.

b. Awareness is the foundation of our power to act and interact with another. To be unaware is to be blind. By becoming aware, you are taking out the blindness that existed the moment before you became aware.

c. When we are unaware we have no choice. The moment you become aware, you are presented with choice. The realization that awareness is the foundation of all action is behind the principle that 'awareness creates choice'. We are literally aware only of what our bodies are trained to be aware of.

Capacity

Capacity is the ability to make and fulfil promises.

Care

a. Care is the part of our internal way of being that shapes how we see the world, what we find worth committing to, how we take action, and is the foundation of meaning and value.

   As leaders, we are looking to take care of what we and others care about together.

   Care is an assessment and an emotion that is fundamental to our experience of life. We care because we have a future, and we have reactions to futures we want, and futures we don't want. In every moment we face our future, and in every moment we care, whether we know how to stay connected to our care or have habits to disconnect from it.

   Care is more than just another emotion. It is an emotion, yet it is a curious one that is related to all other emotions. For example, let's take anger or sadness. We aren't angry or sad unless we care about something, something that has been damaged or lost to us. So, care is fundamental to most, if not all, emotions. We care because we have a future, and we have assessments of futures we want and futures we don't want. This generates our embodied coherence of care, with its assessments, opening and closing of our body to action, and the emotional energy of care.

   Care is a fundamental dimension of all action. It can be present or absent, but in either case it has a fundamental shaping of how the action is carried out, and the meaning and value of the outcomes to be produced.[2]

b. What matters.

Centering
Being centred is being in a physical, mental and emotional state of choice.

We are centred when our body, mind and emotions are in a state where we can choose our actions. When we are not in a state to choose our actions, we are 'off-centre'; our reactions and tendencies choose for us. We cannot blend when we are off-centre. In centering, we attain complete balance and focus regardless of our situations:

✓ Our mind is alert, we are connected to what we care about, and we are free of distracting mental chatter.
✓ Our mood is serene and open to the current situation.
✓ Our physical state is dynamically relaxed, alert, balanced around our centre of gravity, and ready for action.

Centering is the skill to put yourself in a state of choice rather than be in reaction when a challenging moment demands your leadership.

Please refer to one such centering practice in Appendix 2.

Coach

a. A coach is someone who can see things that the person being coached has not yet seen or experienced; he or she has embodied the distinctions of generative leadership and has the competence to share this with the person being coached. This doesn't mean they are superior in any way, and may not even have the skill in a particular domain that the person being coached has, but their competence and depth can add immeasurable value for the them.

b. A coach is someone who begins and has every conversation with the person being coached inside of the space of nothingness (there are no assessments) with the objective of supporting them to see what they cannot see on their own.

c. A coach is a leader who enables the person being coached to generate a new future, invite them to commit to that new future of their choice and then take action to achieve that future.

d. Tracy Goss, in her book *The Last Word on Power* states, 'Your role as a coach is to create an opening for action that allows people to get untangled from their structure of interpretation, and focus on the future to which they are committed.'[3]

(Missing) Commitment

A missing commitment is a commitment that is (often) blind to the observer. It is this missing commitment when made that will lead to actions, those that will generate the desired results.

Connection

'Connected means that we feel the presence and energy of the other, and of ourselves, and we stay in contact with them. Close somatic connection results in limbic resonance, where bodies seem to be in a shared state. We feel a sense of relationship and engagement. We are disconnected if we avoid relationships and engagement. We can be disconnected from our own bodies if we get lost in our heads and pay no attention to its sensations.'[4]

Conditions of Satisfaction

Conditions of satisfaction are a clear description of the standards of the outcome that will satisfy the customer, when the request is completed. The objective of describing the conditions of satisfaction is to arrive at a shared understanding between the customer and the performer of the future outcome.

Conversation

a. Conversation is the interaction of human beings that creates action, meaning, listening, moods and emotions, and the future.

  Conversations are not just words, but the whole body reactions that are provoked when we interact in language and when we interact and language is provoked. Conversations include language, moods and emotions, body reactions and experiences, and the listening that is based on the history of the people in the conversation. Conversations are shaped in linguistic and cultural practices.[5]

b. We are now learning, through neurological and cognitive research, that a 'conversation' goes deeper and is more robust than simple information sharing. Conversations are dynamic, interactive and inclusive. They evolve and impact the way we connect, engage, interact, and influence others, enabling us to shape reality, mindsets, events, and outcomes in a collaborative way. Conversations have the power to move us from 'power over' others to 'power with' others, giving us the exquisite ability to get on the same page with our fellow humans and experience the same reality by bridging the reality gaps between 'how you see things and how I see things'.[6]

c. Words are not things – they are the representations and symbols we use to view, think about, and process our perceptions of reality, and they are the means of sharing these perceptions with others. Yet few leaders understand how vital conversation is to health and productivity of their company.[7]

(Missing) Conversation

The model 'Anatomy of Action' makes a claim that that all 'results come from conversations'. So, if there is a certain result you would like to generate but have not generated, there is a 'missing conversation' to be had – with yourself and/or with another.

Even if an element of the conversation is missing (please refer to the generative meaning of conversation above), it means there is a missing conversation.

The path from where we are to where we want to be is a path of conversations – and we may be missing the key conversations for this path to be effective for us. We may be blind to these missing conversations. However, in generative leadership, we take a perspective and a posture to continuously look for these (missing) conversations that will generate results that matter to us.

Customer

Customer is the person to whom a promise is made.

Dignified apology

A dignified apology is an apology where you are not necessarily admitting you are wrong (although that may also be true) – but stating that what was provoked in the other is not what was intended.

Emotions and Moods
Emotions are our reactions triggered by events; and, moods are emotional states that precede events and are prevalent without triggering.

Freedom
Freedom comes from two words - 'free' and 'dom'. To be 'free' means 'to not be affected or restricted by a given condition or circumstance' and, 'dom' denotes a 'state' or 'condition'.

So, if we take the literal meaning of freedom, it means, 'being in a state that is not affected or restricted by a given condition or circumstance.'

'Freedom is a felt experience of being unrestricted in a particular moment.' You may experience freedom in one moment, and not experience freedom in another. And it could be the other way around too. You could experience restriction in one moment and then the next moment you could experience freedom too.

Generative Practice
A generative practice is a conscious choice to embody a behaviour that can be used in whatever situation we find ourselves in. It's a commitment to a way of being in the world. It is life-affirming, creative, and it produces a reality by how we orient to our life situation.

Learning to type, on the other hand, is a specific practice; it's specific to a certain context and it takes care of a specific concern. But typing is useful only when we are typing. A generative practice we can use any time, any place, even when we're learning to type.[8]

'GREAT' Model
The 'GREAT' model is a model designed to support managers and leaders to create and then hold space for conversation with co-workers, customers and other people they work with.

This model includes five elements coming together forming the acronym 'GREAT'. When these five elements are present, you generate 'great' relationships, 'great' moods in teams and organizations and 'great' results.

The five elements of the 'GREAT' model are:
   Good Feel
   Reality shared
   Effective conversations
   Agreement
   Trust

The claim of this model is that when one element goes up, all others go up; and when one element goes down, all others go down too.

Grounding of Assessments

Grounding is a practice to make assessments about assessments. If an assessment is *'grounded'*, it has evidence to an acceptable standard, and is more likely to be effective in producing a desired outcome than an assessment that is *'ungrounded'* – lacking clear standards, evidence, or specification of the domain of concern. Grounding does not make an assessment true; it only provides evidence and argument that it is a good assessment for our purpose. And ungrounded assessments only mean the assessments lack relevant evidence to trust the assessment. In grounding, we recommend that you ask certain questions.

To ground assessments, we find answers to the following questions:
- For the sake of what future action?
- In which domain of action?
- According to what standard?
- What true assertions support the assessment?
- What true assertions are against the assessment?

So, in general, grounding is a way to produce more trust in an assessment.[9]

Hidden assessment

Hidden assessment is an assessment that you have made, and yet, you are unaware that you have made this assessment; this assessment lands to you as an assertion, i.e., fact.

Holding space of conversation

Holding space of conversation is a domain of conversations that is like a 'container' inside of which leadership conversations take place. If this container didn't exist, these leadership conversations would not be effective.

Invalidation

Invalidation is the experience of feeling dishonoured and humiliated. Invalidation happens in the experience of the other.

Leadership-Coaching Conversations

This book has distinguished five key leadership-coaching conversations using the acronym COACH.

The word COACH is used for leaders and managers because in my assessment, a good leader and a good manager is most importantly a good coach. It is through these leadership-coaching conversations that leaders and managers enable their co-workers to take 'new' actions and hence generate 'new' results. The idea of coaching is not to just get the co-worker to do more actions, or just take more competent actions, but to generate 'new' actions for the sake of generating 'new' results, those that may not have been available to the co-worker prior to the leadership-coaching conversation.

These five leadership coaching conversation domains are:

Care: Care is fundamental to being human. When you take care of the care of the other, you create value and open up a space for magical results.

Observe: When you observe 'the way you observe', you become aware that there exists a whole world outside of the way you observe; and when you become aware you give yourself new choices for what you pay attention to.

Action: Action is central to generating results that matter to you. Only when you take action, do you get the desired results. Actions taken on a regular basis lead to practices, and practices lead to embodiment.

Commitment: Look around you and you see that the world operates on promises (or commitments). For example, there is a promise of the elevator; of my car, of the chair you may be sitting on while reading this book, of the security guard at the gate; of my colleagues, and so forth.

Results are a function of actions, and actions come from your (sometimes hidden) commitments. To generate new results, you have to make new trustworthy commitments. Commitments are generated in conversations.

Holding Space of Conversation: For effective and authentic conversations, a particular safe space needs to be created and then held by the leader.

Managing a Promise

We are looking to highlight a specific set of actions with this word 'manage'. When we say 'manage', we mean to be in agreement with the customer for a promise. This is to keep the customer informed and satisfied that the promise is still trustworthy for their future. But it also means to alert a customer to risks and potential breakdowns with the promise, so that they can take prudent action about the promise. When the promise is no longer fulfillable, for whatever reason, to manage it means to let the customer know, to give them the options you or they can take to deal with the consequences, and to offer to negotiate a new promise.

By managing, we mean to keep the promise alive, fresh, trustworthy and current in your conversations with and in relationship to the customer.

Managing promises also means declaring the completion of a promise and checking the customer's satisfaction after declaration of completion.

Missing Commitment

A missing commitment is a commitment that is most of the time 'hidden' from the observer. It is missing because the observer is generally blind that it is this missing commitment which when made will lead to actions, especially those that will generate results.

Missing Explicit Promise

The promise exists in the eyes of the customer, except the explicitness of that promise and the agreement to it is missing for the performer. In other words, the promiser is blind to the existence of the promise. And yet, often, he is not released from the consequences of not keeping the promise.

Organization

An organization can be understood as a network of *commitments* generated and maintained in a network of conversations to fulfil bigger *commitments*. 'Bigger commitments' in this context means commitments that individuals do not have the capacity to fulfil on their own, and hence group(s) of people come together to fulfil these commitments.[10]

Performer

Performer is the person who makes the promise.

Possibility

The common sense understanding of possibility, as per the Oxford Dictionaries, is 'a thing that may happen'. I am not talking about this as possibility that may happen someday in the future. The possibility that I am talking about in this book is a creation of yours, that empowers you at this moment, shapes the way you think and feel at this moment, to take new action. When you create this kind of a possibility, you impact your 'now'. You impact your present.[11]

Potential

When you operate at your full capacity, such that your capacity expands – it would mean that you are operating at your potential. In the TAP Matrix, there is a quadrant called the 'safe person'. Even the safe person makes and fulfils promises. The safe person is operating within his or her capacity. But the safe person is not operating at his or her potential, because he or she can make more promises and still fulfil those promises.

So, while your capacity is your ability to make and fulfil promises, your potential is operating at your full capacity. And when you operate at your full capacity, you keep increasing your capacity, and hence your potential and the value you create for others and for yourself.

(Generative) Practice

A generative practice is a conscious choice to embody a behaviour that can be used in whatever situation we find ourselves in. It's a commitment to a way of being in the world. It is life-affirming, creative, and it produces a reality by how we orient to our life situation.

Learning to type, on the other hand, is a specific practice; it's specific to a certain context and it takes care of a specific concern. But typing is useful only when we are, well, typing. A generative practice is something we can use anytime, anywhere, even when we're learning to type.[12]

Promise

Promise is one kind of a declarative act that we make that internally organizes us to be in action for the sake of producing a specific outcome. It is also an act that we make externally and socially that produces an interpretation in others of what we will produce as outcomes of our actions.

Promises are acts of coordination between people.

A promise is akin to taking a stand, that you are responsible for the outcome. That is, you take the posture that you will be at the cause of the outcome, and that you are at the cause of the outcome of the promise, both in its fulfilment, and in its non-fulfilment. This means we do not act to 'do the best we can' (unless this is what we promised), or to, 'do what is appropriate and see what happens', or 'do what you thought should do the trick', and or use breakdowns as excuses for non-fulfilment.[13]

Promises exist in the listening of the customer, and hence, I present a perspective that *implicit expectations of the customers are the performer's promise*.

Purpose
To have a commitment inside of your care is to have a purpose.

Rigour
To have rigour in a working relationship between the line manager and his co-worker, or between the leader and the co-worker, would mean having an environment that is stimulating, engaging, supporting of high standards of achievement, and most importantly, an environment where commitments are kept, and when commitments cannot be kept, they are revoked or renegotiated well in advance.

While rigour would mean achieving at high levels, the leader recognizes that high levels of achievement do not happen immediately. There is focus on practices, on learning, on small steps that regularly show growth.

Somatics
The term somatics derives from the Greek *somatikos*, which signifies the living, aware, bodily person. It posits that neither mind nor body is separate from the other; both being a part of a living process called the soma. The soma is often referred to as the living body in its wholeness; somatics, then is the art and science of the soma.[14]

TAP Matrix
TAP Matrix is The Actions–Promises Matrix, which enables the reader to make an assessment whether they are performers. The Matrix has four quadrants the 'safe' person, the 'busy' person, the 'jerk' and the 'performer'.

The 'safe' person
The safe person makes few promises, but takes action to fulfil them. They can be trusted to fulfil the promises they make, but cannot be trusted to play a big game or make big promises. They respect status quo, and operate inside of the boundaries of the status quo. They may claim to being satisfied here, but on deeper questioning,

it emerges that they are keen to emerge, and make big promises.

The safe person is also the complacent person. They are always thinking small, making small commitments, and taking small action. They are also averse to learning and growing – they find it threatening or too much work.

The 'busy' person

The 'busy person' is very busy. They actually enjoy being busy. For businessmen, this is 'busyness', and not business. One of the biggest problems people have in tapping their full potential is that their calendars are full of tasks or actions that are not inside of promises. The busy person is trapped in a small world. The busy person has no problem with taking action, or doing hard work. They consider themselves good performers, or they even do a lot, yet they are limiting their potential.

When you question them, 'for the sake of what are you taking this action?' they are dumbfounded. While, they are good at taking actions, they are still in the 'drift', and not in 'design', because they are busy with what shows up as a to-do in the moment.[15]

The 'jerk'

'The jerk' makes a lot of promises, but does not fulfil most of them. They want to think big, but do not back up promises with action. There are different levels of 'jerks', and at the highest level, 'the jerk' is even blind to the promises they are making.

The jerk has a low self-esteem, because they cannot trust themselves. Others also cannot trust the jerk, because historically, the promises made to others were not fulfilled. This lack of keeping promises, to themselves and to others, impacts the success the jerk can achieve.

This person can also be the yes-man who wants to please everyone by saying yes to every request, and they end up not keeping most of their promises. They are dreamers thinking big possibilities, and do not take actions to make these dreams come true. They are also victims, who blame others and the world around for not fulfilling their promises.

The 'performer'

The performer makes promises, and backs their promises with action. The performer may not always know what action needs to be taken, and yet makes promises, and does whatever it takes to fulfil those promises. When the performer is not able to fulfil their promise, they take the 'action' of informing and keeping the customer posted on the status of the fulfillment of the promise.

The performer is successful (or will eventually be successful), has high self-esteem (because they make promises they can fulfil and fulfil them), others trust them, and they have good public identity. The 4R impact is positive and all 4 Rs are rising.

In learning to making bigger promises, and backing these promises with action, the performer is expanding their capacity.

Target

Targets are requests, not promises. If a leader or a manager gives a target to their co-worker, it in effect means that the manager has made a request for a certain outcome to be achieved. If this is accepted, it becomes a promise.

Task

A task is that which consumes human time and energy, but which is articulated by a description of what is being done. In other words, the distinction between task and action is that actions are inside of cares and commitments, while tasks are activities that take up time, and yet do not move forward a certain fulfilment of a promise.

Team

A team is a group of people with a *shared promise*. A team exists to make a *bigger promise* that one person alone can fulfil. [16]

Trust

Trust is an assessment of whether someone will fulfil the promises and the future actions they commit to. It amounts to choosing to risk something you value vulnerable to another person's actions.

When you trust someone, what you make vulnerable can range from concrete things such as money, a job, a promotion, or a particular goal, to less tangible things like a belief you hold, a cherished way of doing things, your 'good name', or even your sense of happiness and well-being. Whatever you choose to make vulnerable to the other's actions, you do so because you believe their actions will support it or, at the very least, will not harm it. [17]

Distrust

It is an assessment that what is important to me is not safe with this person in this situation (or in any situation). [18]

Victim

To be a victim means that a certain result that matters to you is not caused, and that is because someone else is not doing their job correctly.

Wonder

Wonder is an emotion, when you create a story that states, 'I don't know what is going to show up next – irrespective of what shows up, I will enjoy myself.'

NOTES

Chapter One: Getting Started

1. Sameer Dua, *Declaring Breakdowns: Powerfully Creating A Future That Matters, Through 6 Simple Steps*, Sage Publications, New Delhi, 2016.
2. This distinction of 'Conversation' has been created for the Institute for Generative Leadership by Bob Dunham.
3. Judith E. Glaser, *Conversational Intelligence: How Great Leaders Build Trust and Get Extraordinary Results*, Brookline, 2014.
4. https://en.oxforddictionaries.com/definition/become
5. George Leonard, *Mastery: The Keys to Success and Long-Term Fulfillment*, Plume, 1992.

Chapter Two: One Key Role of a Leader Is to Coach

1. This has been taken from the Online Etymology Dictionary, http://www.etymonline.com/index.php?term=coach
2. http://jackcanfield.com/when-we-grow-others-we-grow-ourselves/
3. Robert Hargrove, *Masterful Coaching*, 3rd ed., Jossey-Bass, a Wiley Imprint, 2008.
4. Ibid.
5. Tracy Goss, *The Last Word on Power: Executive Re-invention for Leaders Who Must Make the Impossible Happen*, Currency, 1996
6. Anatomy of Action is a creation of Bob Dunham. He has referred to the Anatomy of Action in several of his papers, some unpublished. He has also referred to this in his paper 'The Generative Foundations of Action in Organisations: Speaking and Listening' published in the International Journal of Coaching in Organisations, 2009.

7. Stephen Lundin and Bob Nelson, *Ubuntu: An Inspiring Story About an African Tradition of Teamwork and Collaboration*, Broadway Books, New York, 2010.

8. Rob Asghar, *What Millennials Want in The Workplace (And Why You Should Start Giving It to Them)*, http://www.forbes.com/sites/robasghar/2014/01/13/what-millennials-want-in-the-workplace-and-why-you-should-start-giving-it-to-them/#13d5dc372fdf

9. I heard these points from Bob Dunham in the Coaching Excellence in Organizations programme organized by the Institute for Generative Leadership, USA.

10. http://www.kenburnett.com/BlogTheBataShoesStory.html

11. This is a powerful distinction created by Bob Dunham.

12. Richard Strozzi-Heckler, *The Leadership Dojo: Build Your Foundation as an Exemplary Leader*, Frog Books, Berkeley, California, 2007.

Chapter Three: Care

1. I heard this from Bob Dunham in the Coaching Excellence in Organizations programme organized by the Institute for Generative Leadership, USA.

2. I heard these points from Bob Dunham in the Coaching Excellence in Organizations programme organized by the Institute for Generative Leadership, USA.

3. http://www.gallup.com/poll/188144/employee-engagement-stagnant-2015.aspx

4. http://www.inc.com/paul-spiegelman/why-a-caring-workplace-matters-as-much-as-your-annual-budget.html

5. https://www.linkedin.com/pulse/creating-history-one-person-time-ashish-ambasta. This extract has been used with permission from Ashish Ambasta.

6. Judith E. Glaser, *Conversational Intelligence: How Great Leaders Build Trust and Get Extraordinary Results*, Brookline, 2014.

7. I learnt this from Bob Dunham in the Coaching Excellence in Organizations programme of the Institute for Generative Leadership, USA.

8. http://www.generativeleadership.in/professor-begs-in-local-train-to-educate-the-poor/

9. Sameer Dua, *Declaring Breakdowns: Powerfully Creating A Future That Matters, Through 6 Simple Steps*, Sage Publications, New Delhi, 2016.

10. Matthew Budd and Larry Rothstein, *You Are What You Say*, Three Rivers Press, New York, 2000.

11. In my book, *Declaring Breakdowns: Powerfully Creating A Future That Matters, Through 6 Simple Steps*, Sage Publications, New Delhi, 2016, I have quoted Bob Dunham. Here I am quoting from my book, in full acknowledgment of the work of Bob Dunham.

12. Teresa Amabile and Steven Kramer, 'How Leaders Kill Meaning at Work', McKinsey Quarterly, January 2012, http://www.mckinsey.com/insights/leading_in_the_21st_century/how_leaders_kill_meaning_at_work

Chapter Four: Observe

1. Brother David Steindl-Rast, *Gratefulness, the Heart of Prayer: An Approach to Life in Fullness*, Paulist Press, New York, Mahwah, New Jersey, 1984.

2. I have used this phrase several times in this book. I learnt this from Bob Dunham in the Coaching Excellence in Organizations Programme at the Institute for Generative Leadership, USA. Bob attributes this to Richard Strozzi-Heckler of the Strozzi Institute.

3. I learnt this also from Bob Dunham in the Coaching Excellence in Organizations Programme at the Institute for Generative Leadership, USA. Bob attributes this to Richard Strozzi-Heckler of the Strozzi Institute.

4. This model was initially developed by Chris Argyris and Robert Putnam. It has appeared in articles and books by both and is an influential model. I learnt this model in The Art and Practice of Ontological Coaching (TAPOC) programme at Newfield Network, USA. I believe others have used this model as well.

5. I learnt this also in the 'The Art and Practice of Ontological Coaching (TAPOC)' programme at Newfield Network.

6. I have been a student of Newfield Network, and there they speak about an observer being the coherence of B-E-L, which is Body, Emotion and Language. Bob Dunham, the founder of the Institute for Generative Leadership expanded the BEL model to BELPH, where in 'P' stood for Practice, and 'H' stood for History. He then reframed this from BELPH to SELPH.

7. Richard Strozzi-Heckler, *The Art of Somatic Coaching: Embodying Skillful Action, Wisdom, and Compassion*, North Atlantic Books, 2014.

8. Charles Duhigg, *The Power of Habit: Why We Do What We Do in Life and Business*, Random House, 2012.

9. I learnt the connection between body, emotions and language from Julio Olalla, of the Newfield Network in the Art and Practice of Ontological Coaching programme.

10. For more information on emotions and its connection to language and body, please refer to Dan Newby and Lucy Núñezs book, *The Unopened Gift: A Premier on Emotional Literacy.*

Chapter Five: Commitment

1. I was introduced to all these generative interpretations by Bob Dunham in the Coaching Excellence in Organizations programme of the Institute for Generative Leadership.
2. I learnt this distinction of the word 'Promise' in the Coaching Excellence in Organisations program at the Institute for Generative Leadership, USA.
3. The distinction of designers rather than drifters comes from Josephina Santiago, one of my master teachers in somatics and generative skills.
4. In the IJCO article, Bob credits part of this meaning to Flores and Ludlow (1980).
5. I am a student of the Coaching Excellence in Organizations (CEO) programme at the Institute for Generative Leadership, USA. In that programme, Bob Dunham has a paper titled Generative Foundations of Leadership.
6. I am a student of the Coaching Excellence in Organisations (CEO) program at the Institute for Generative Leadership, USA. In that program, Bob Dunham has a paper titled 'Generative Foundations of Leadership'.
7. This is a distinction created by Bob Dunham and I learnt this in the Coaching Excellence in Organization program at the Institute for Generative Leadership, USA.
8. The distinction of designers rather than drifters comes from Josephina Santiago, one of my master teachers in somatics and generative skills.
9. The forty-second amendment of the Constitution of India in 1976 added duties of Indian citizens (*originally, the Constitution of India did not contain any list of fundamental duties*). There are two interesting points that I want to highlight:
    • Unlike in the erstwhile Soviet Union, which made the enjoyment of fundamental rights conditional on the fulfilment of duties – India does not have any such provision in the Constitution.
    • The fundamental duties are non-justiciable (subject to trial in a court of law) in character. This means that no citizen can be punished by a court for violation of a fundamental duty.
10. If you are interested in seeing your duties as an Indian, please click here   http://india.gov.in/sites/upload_files/npi/files/coi_part_full.pdf and refer to Part IVA

Chapter Six: Action

1. I have referred to the work of Fernando Flores on this topic. He has a book titled *Conversations for Action and Collected Essays: Instilling a Culture of Commitment in Working Relationships,* ed. Maria Flores Letelier, CreateSpace, 2013.
2. Roger Martin, *Harvard Business Review,* 2 May 2014.
3. I first heard the phrase 'being in drift and not in design' from Josephina Santiago, master coach and Somatic Programme Leader for the Institute for Generative Leadership.

Chapter Seven: Holding Space of Conversation

1. http://www.oxforddictionaries.com/definition/english/space?q=Space
2. Richard Strozzi-Heckler, *The Art of Somatic Coaching: Embodying Skillful Action, Wisdom, and Compassion,* North Atlantic Books, 2014.
3. Judith E. Glaser, *Conversational Intelligence: How Great Leaders Build Trust and Get Extraordinary Results,* Brookline, 2014.
4. Robert Hargrove, *Masterful Coaching,* 3rd ed., Jossey-Bass, a Wiley Imprint, 2008.
5. Rosamund Stone Zander and Benjamin Zander, *The Art of Possibility: Transforming Professional and Personal Life,* Harvard Business School Press, 2000; Penguin Books, 2012
6. Roger Martin, *Harvard Business Review,* 2 May 2014.
7. BCCI TV: www.bcci.tv/c8930d5a-fdb4-41da-93a3-209285ee70bf
8. http://www.oxforddictionaries.com/definition/english/rigour?q=Rigour
9. Robert Maurer, *One Small Step Can Change Your Life – The Kaizen Way,* Workman Publishing, New York, 2004.

APPENDIX 3: Somatic Practices for Space First

1. Peter J. Denning and Robert (Bob) Dunham, *The Innovators' Way: Essential Practices for Successful Innovation, MIT Press,* Cambridge, MA, 2010

APPENDIX 4: Glossary of Terms

1. All of these distinctions of actions have been provided by Bob Dunham, in the Coaching Excellence in Organization Programme organized by the Institute for Generative Leadership.

2. Care is one of the key distinctions of leadership, and I have learnt the primacy of care, and this powerful meaning of care from my coach Bob Dunham in the Coaching Excellence in Organizations programme of the Institute for Generative Leadership, USA.

3. Tracy Goss, *The Last Word on Power: Executive Re-invention for Leaders Who Must Make the Impossible Happen*, Currency, 1996.

4. Peter J. Denning and Robert (Bob) Dunham, *The Innovators' Way: Essential Practices for Successful Innovation, MIT Press*, Cambridge, MA, 2010.

5. This distinction of 'Conversation' has been created for the Institute for Generative Leadership by Bob Dunham.

6. Judith E. Glaser, *Conversational Intelligence: How Great Leaders Build Trust and Get Extraordinary Results*, Brookline, 2014.

7. Ibid.

8. Richard Strozzi-Heckler, *The Leadership Dojo: Build Your Foundation as an Exemplary Leader*, Frog Books, Berkeley, California, 2007.

9. Learnt in the Coaching Excellence in Organizations programme at the Institute for Generative Leadership, USA.

10. In the IJCO article, Bob credits part of this meaning to Flores and Ludlow (1980).

11. http://www.oxforddictionaries.com/definition/english/possibility?q=Possibility&searchDictCode=all

12. Richard Strozzi-Heckler, *The Leadership Dojo: Build Your Foundation as an Exemplary Leader*, Frog Books, Berkeley, California, 2007.

13. Learnt in the Coaching Excellence in Organizations programme at the Institute for Generative Leadership, USA.

14. Richard Strozzi-Heckler, *The Art of Somatic Coaching: Embodying Skillful Action, Wisdom, and Compassion*, North Atlantic Books, 2014.

15. I first heard the phrase 'being in drift and not in design' from Josephina Santiago, master coach and Somatic Program Leader for the Institute for Generative Leadership.

16. This is a distinction created by Bob Dunham and I learnt this in the Coaching Excellence in Organisations program at the Institute for Generative Leadership, USA.

17. Charles Feltman, *The Thin Book of Trust: An Essential Primer for Building Trust at Work*, Thin Book Pub Co., 2008.

18. Ibid.

ACKNOWLEDGEMENTS

This book would not have been possible without the support of Bob Dunham and the Institute for Generative Leadership, USA. I have learnt about Generative Leadership through the papers and practices of Bob Dunham, and used a lot of his work as references in this book.

Bob has been extraordinarily supportive throughout the process of writing this book. He has reviewed its contents patiently, had extensive discussions with me, helping me ground my claims, and contributed thought-provoking quotes for the start of each chapter. This collaboration with him has significantly enriched my learning.

In addition, I'm grateful to three key people who have added great value to this book and I'd like to acknowledge their contributions:

1. Marshall Goldsmith. For graciously contributing the foreword for this book. His message is simple, yet immensely powerful.
2. Umang Bedi. The two of us were to initially co-author this book. However, he went on to become the managing director (India and South Asia) for Facebook and therefore requested to be relieved from this project. Nonetheless, he has contributed some delightful and practical case studies for most of the key chapters of this book. In addition to these, he has shared an outstanding case study, 'Re-imagining and Reinventing Adobe Systems, India'. Umang has added immense value and this book is certainly richer and more meaningful, thanks to him.

3. Sheeja Shaju. My colleague at the Institute for Generative
    Leadership, an acknowledged somatic leader and a leadership
    coach, Sheeja has generously contributed two appendices. The
    first one (Appendix 2) is a key leadership practice of Centering
    (in addition to audio versions for the website). This is a key
    somatic practice of leadership and the foundational practice of
    several other practices. The second one (Appendix 3) contains
    the somatic practices for the chapter on 'Holding Space of
    Conversation'.

Moving on, I must admit how privileged I am for studying at
Newfield Network and learning directly from Julio Olalla, the
pioneer of ontological coaching, and one of the gentlest men I have
ever met.

In his remarkable book *The Consolations of Philosophy*, Alain de
Botton asked, 'Where should people get their ideas from?', and
went on to answer the question himself: 'From people even cleverer
than they are. They should spend their time quoting and producing
commentaries about great authorities who occupy the upper rungs
of the tree of knowledge.'

This is exactly what I have done in this book. I stand on the broad
shoulders of several masters of this subject. In addition to Bob and
Julio, I have learnt from Martin Heidegger, John Austin, Fernando
Flores, Richard Strozzi-Heckler, Humberto Maturana and many
others whom I have quoted in this book and many of whom I
have not had the privilege of meeting. However, I have immensely
benefitted from their published work.

I am thankful to Captain Dheeraj Sareen, Sumit Gupta, Jagdish
Chawla, Pam Fox Rollin, and Julie Davies for supporting me in
this work by being forthright, suggesting meaningful changes,
recommending deletions and for asking hard questions. I understand
this is a time-consuming process and remain deeply appreciative of
their big-hearted support.

I am also grateful to Judith Glaser, Robert Hargrove, Ashok
Soota, Klaus Trescher, Charles Feltman, Pam Fox Rollin, Dr Julie

Davies, Professor Andrew St George, Terrie Upsher Lupberger, Dilip Kukreja and Jagannath Vasudevan for reviewing this initial work and endorsing it.

My colleagues Anuradha and Madhurya have had unending conversations on the title of the book with me, and have created outstanding designs for covers. They must have created over fifty different cover options, using a variety of titles and typefaces, and yet, continued to remain patient with me. Thank you, guys!

Geeta, Safoora, Joe, and Lipika are my other colleagues who take our work out to the world and they are incredible at their job.

Prashant, my older brother, for being a friend, confidant, business partner, my go-to person for anything that I need. I can never thank Prashant enough for all his contributions in my life.

Above all, I am blessed with a large and a loving family – I remain indebted to all of them for their enduring love and I am particularly grateful to my wife Tina and my children Ashna, Anaaya and Ayaan for their unflagging support.

25 🏛 HarperCollins India Pvt. Ltd

Celebrating 25 Years of Great Publishing

HarperCollins India celebrates its twenty-fifth anniversary in 2017. Twenty-five years of publishing India's finest writers and some of its most memorable books – those you cannot put down; ones you want to finish reading yet don't want to end; works you can read over and over again only to fall deeper in love with.

Through the years, we have published writers from the Indian subcontinent, and across the globe, including Aravind Adiga, Kiran Nagarkar, Amitav Ghosh, Jhumpa Lahiri, Manu Joseph, Anuja Chauhan, Upamanyu Chatterjee, A.P.J. Abdul Kalam, Shekhar Gupta, M.J. Akbar, Tavleen Singh, Satyajit Ray, Gulzar, Surender Mohan Pathak and Anita Nair, amongst others, with approximately 200 new books every year and an active print and digital catalogue of more than 1,000 titles, across ten imprints. Publishing works of various genres including literary fiction, poetry, mind body spirit, commercial fiction, journalism, business, self-help, cinema, biographies – all with attention to quality, of the manuscript and the finished product – it comes as no surprise that we have won every major literary award including the Man Booker Prize, the Sahitya Akademi Award, the DSC Prize, the Hindu Literary Prize, the MAMI Award for Best Writing on Cinema, the National Award for Best Book on Cinema, the Crossword Book Award, and the Publisher of the Year, twice, at Publishing Next in Goa and, in 2016, at Tata Literature Live, Mumbai.

We credit our success to the people who make us who we are, and will be celebrating this anniversary with: our authors, retailers, partners, readers and colleagues at HarperCollins India. Over the years, a firm belief in our promise and our passion to deliver only the very best of the printed word has helped us become one of India's finest in publishing. Every day we endeavour to deliver bigger and better – for you.

Thank you for your continued support and patronage.

■ HarperCollins*Publishers*India

Subscribe to Harper Broadcast

Harper Broadcast is an award-winning publisher-hosted news and views platform curated by the editors at HarperCollins India. Watch interviews with celebrated authors, read book reviews and exclusive extracts, unlock plot trailers and discover new book recommendations on www.harperbroadcast.com.

Sign up for Harper Broadcast's monthly e-newsletter for free and follow us on our social media channels listed below.

Visit this link to subscribe: https://harpercollins.co.in/newsletter/

Follow us on

YouTube ■ Harper Broadcast

Twitter 🐦 @harperbroadcast

www.harperbroadcast.com

Follow HarperCollins Publishers India on

Twitter 🐦 @HarperCollinsIN

Instagram 📷 @HarperCollinsIN

Facebook 📘 @HarperCollinsIN

LinkedIN 🔲 HarperCollins Publishers India

www.harpercollins.co.in

Address

HarperCollins Publishers India Pvt. Ltd
A-75, Sector 57, Noida, UP 201301, India

Phone: +91-120-4044800